Eurafrica

THEORY FOR A GLOBAL AGE

Globalization is widely viewed as the current condition of the world, only recently come into being. There is little engagement with its long histories and how these histories continue to have an impact on current social, political and economic configurations and understandings. Theory for a Global Age takes 'the global' as the already-always existing condition of the world and one that should have informed analysis in the past as well as informing analysis for the present and future. The series is not about globalization as such, but, rather, it addresses the impact a properly critical reflection on 'the global' might have on disciplines and different fields within the social sciences and humanities. It asks how we might understand our present and future differently if we start from a critical examination of the idea of the global as a political and interpretive device; and what consequences this would have for reconstructing our understandings of the past, including our disciplinary pasts.

Each book in the series focuses on a particular theoretical issue or topic of empirical controversy and debate, addressing theory in a more comprehensive and interconnected manner in the process. With books commissioned from scholars from across the globe, the series explores understandings of the global – and global understandings – from diverse viewpoints. The series will be available in print, in eBook format and free online, through a Creative Commons licence, aiming to encourage academic engagement on a broad geographical scale and to further the reach of the debates and dialogues that the series develops.

Eurafrica

The Untold History of European Integration and Colonialism

Peo Hansen and Stefan Jonsson

Bloomsbury Academic
An imprint of Bloomsbury Publishing Inc

B L O O M S B U R Y
LONDON · OXFORD · NEW YORK · NEW DELHI · SYDNEY

Bloomsbury Academic

An imprint of Bloomsbury Publishing Plc

50 Bedford Square	1385 Broadway
London	New York
WC1B 3DP	NY 10018
UK	USA

www.bloomsbury.com

BLOOMSBURY and the Diana logo are trademarks of Bloomsbury Publishing Plc

First published 2014
First published in paperback 2015

© Peo Hansen and Stefan Jonsson, 2014, 2015

British Library Cataloguing-in-Publication Data
A catalogue record for this book is available from the British Library.

ISBN:	HB:	9781780930008
	PB:	9781474256803
	ePub	9781780930176
	ePDF:	9781780930015

Library of Congress Cataloging-in-Publication Data
A catalog record for this book is available from the Library of Congress.

Typeset by Fakenham Prepress Solutions, Fakenham, Norfolk NR21 8NN
Printed and bound in Great Britain

Yes, the European spirit is built on strange foundations.
Frantz Fanon

Contents

Illustrations

Series Editor's Foreword

One of the aims of the Theory for a Global Age series is to address the impact a properly critical reflection on 'the global' might have on disciplines and different fields within the social sciences and humanities. In this compelling book, *Eurafrica: The Untold History of European Integration and Colonialism*, Peo Hansen and Stefan Jonsson criticize the standard, continental, histories informing most accounts of the emergence and development of the European Union and argue, instead, for a different frame – Eurafrica – within which to locate its development. This is a meticulously researched and forcefully argued book that challenges standard historical narratives and produces new conceptual insights.

Eurafrica, as Hansen and Jonsson set out, was a particular intellectual and political project, conceived and articulated in the interwar period. It saw Europe's very survival as dependent upon its ability to appropriate land and extract labour and resources from the African continent. This project, they argue, was to go on to shape the process of European integration in the second half of the century, but is rarely addressed by scholars seeking to understand the European Union today. As a consequence, they suggest, the long entanglement of Europe with Africa, that is of European colonialism and imperialism within Africa, is also sidelined. Their focus on the common *European* project of colonialism – not just the colonial projects of the different European states – and the centrality of this to Europe's eventual integration is truly ground-breaking.

Beyond bringing to the fore the long-standing histories that unite Africa and Europe and examining the import of those histories for understandings of the European Union, Hansen and Jonsson also develop 'Eurafrica' as a conceptual tool. For too long, they suggest, the histories of Africa and Europe have been understood solely in national or continental terms. In contrast, 'Eurafrica' focuses on the *common* and *connected* histories that have created a broader political space. As such, their book also contests the methodologically nationalist or civilizational approach of much social scientific research. It points, instead, to the importance of acknowledging the broader global entanglements of coloniality as necessarily constitutive of any understanding of the contemporary age. Their telling of these untold histories deserves to transform contemporary debates.

Gurminder K. Bhambra

Preface

This book retrieves a history of the European Union (EU) long neglected or ignored in scholarship. By providing a more accurate view of the EU's past, especially of the colonial and geopolitical concerns that played central roles in its establishment in 1957, our book can perhaps also offer a better understanding of the present predicaments of the European integration process. As we put the finishing touches to the book in December 2013, crisis and division continue to permeate the EU's internal scene. As many member states' staggering unemployment and poverty go in tandem with a resurgent fascism and gains for racist parties, a similar relationship is establishing itself between growing national antagonisms within the Union and a widening disparity between its core and peripheral members.

In contrast to the internal difficulties, however, the global aspirations of the EU remain vigorous. This is starkly illustrated by the clash with Russia over the Ukrainian geopolitical pivot. When the EU 'offered' Ukraine to sign an association and free trade agreement with the EU this was not framed in terms of geopolitics. From Brussels' perspective, the offer is rather an act of solidarity with a popular struggle for freedom and dignity against corrupt, authoritarian leaders. Said Manuel Barroso; then President of the European Commission: 'They want freedom, they want prosperity, they want stability.'[1]

This is a common message from the EU. As we shall see in the following pages, it dates back to the very founding of the current EU in the 1950s.

Even in those cases when the EU is calling for the application of

---

[1] European Commission, 'President Barroso at the European Council: 2013 A breakthrough year for EU economy', 20 December 2103, http://ec.europa.eu/news/employment/131220_en.htm

military force (as in Chad, Libya, Mali, Somalia or the Central African Republic), such engagements are almost always pitched at a safe distance from crass interest and power politics. Instead they are coded in terms of promoting human rights, democracy, women's rights, the rule of law, and European and universal norms and values.

Some of this is certainly not unique for the European Union. Yet, the EU seems uniquely adept at promoting – some would say masquerading – its geopolitical ambitions and economic interests as democracy, freedom and the dissemination of universal norms and values. Whereas Russia, China and the US continue to play the old game of power politics, the EU travels the world on soft power; it does not make adversaries, it negotiates, it creates partners, it associates, it facilitates trade and it cultivates its neighbourhood. It also receives the Nobel Peace Prize.

When the EU received the Nobel Peace Prize in 2012, Manuel Barroso emphasized not only the EU's benevolent global role in general. In his Nobel Lecture he also made sure to mark out the uniqueness of the EU on the world stage. The EU 'is a new legal order, which is not based on balance of power between nations but on the free consent of states'; it 'attests to the quest for a cosmopolitan order, in which one person's gain does not need to be another person's pain'. Most of all, perhaps, the EU's unique conduct in global affairs builds on an equally unique historical experience:

> The concrete engagement of the European Union in the world is deeply marked by our continent's tragic experience of extreme nationalism, wars and the absolute evil of the Shoah. It is inspired by our desire to avoid the same mistakes being made again. That is the foundation of our multilateral approach for a globalisation based on the twin principles of global solidarity and global responsibility; that is what inspires our engagement with our neighbouring countries and international partners, from the Middle East to Asia, from Africa to the Americas.

'As a community of nations that has overcome war and fought totalitarianism', Barroso continued, 'we will always stand by those who are

Preface

in pursuit of peace and human dignity. [...] the European Union will help the world come together.'[2]

As we show in this book, assertions of the EU's exceptional status as a benevolent global actor have a long history, harking back to the very beginnings of the European integration project in the early 1920s. More importantly, we also explain that the political valence and credibility of such assertions have always presupposed that history is continually and permanently evaded. Put differently, Barroso's words do not testify primarily to the EU's ability to learn from historical experience but to its ability to bend history to fit its own purposes. Historians of Europe and the EU have often contributed to this distortion, as they have held European integration at arm's length from the dirty business of geopolitics. Scholars have often failed in the historical examination of the global ramifications of European integration and therefore they have also failed to interrogate the role of European integration in global affairs. In part, this can be explained as the outcome of an original and erroneous conception of European integration that we take to task in this book.

Eurafrica is a co-authored book. It is the result of a scholarly and intellectual collaboration that confirms the advantages of a transdisciplinary approach to European history, the history of European integration in particular. It is only by combining our competences, our respective fields of knowledge and methodological skills – one originating in political science and EU studies, the other in cultural theory and the intellectual history of European modernity – that we have been able to resolve the problem that we pose in this book: the relation of European integration to colonialism, and the almost complete exclusion of this relation from both EU studies and histories of colonialism.

A first exploration of this relation indicated that the history of colonialism and decolonization has been formative of the

---

[2] José Manuel Durão Barroso, 'From War to Peace: A European tale', Nobel Peace Prize Lecture on behalf of the European Union, Oslo, 10 December 2012, http://europa.eu/rapid/press-release_SPEECH-12-930_en.htm?locale=EN

contemporary EU's endeavour to foster a collective sense of European identity among its citizens, but that this influence is either unrecognized or denied.[3] To this point of departure a historical examination of Pan-European ideas was then added, which brought to the fore the seemingly peculiar fact that in most programmes for European unification of the interwar period, Africa stood at the centre.[4] As we sought to integrate these early approaches – one observing the disavowed centrality of the colonial legacy in contemporary EU identity politics, the other one noting the centrality of Africa in early blueprints for European integration – we realized that they staked out a new and largely unexplored research area, which concerned the geopolitical and colonial foundation of the European integration project and the EU as such.

In exploring this domain, we have relied heavily on the Historical Archives of the European Union in Florence. We are grateful for the generosity and assistance we have received at this excellent institution, and we owe special thanks to its former director Jean-Marie Palayret, himself a pioneering expert in the area, for having pointed us towards relevant collections. This project got off to a good start thanks to a generous fellowship awarded by the Remarque Institute, New York University, and its late director Tony Judt; at Remarque we would also like to thank Katherine E. Fleming and Jair Kessler.

For acquisition of materials we have also benefitted from the services of the Bibliothèque nationale de France, Paris; the National Library of Sweden, the Riksdag Library and the Labour Movement Archives and Library, all in Stockholm; the Kenya National Archives, Nairobi; and the Humboldt University Library, Berlin. Above all, we are indebted to the Linköping University Library and the outstanding

---

[3] Peo Hansen, 'European integration, European identity and the colonial connection', *European Journal of Social Theory*, Vol. 5, No. 4, 2002, pp. 489–98.

[4] Stefan Jonsson, 'Why we live together: Notes on European Utopias and the Utopia of Europe'; paper presented at the conference 'The Future of Utopia: Is Innovation Still Possible in Politics, Culture, Theory? An Interdisciplinary Conference in Honor of Fredric Jameson', Duke University, 24–27 April 2003.

staff at its interlibrary-loan services who have facilitated our research on countless occasions.

We have presented drafts and sections of this book at numerous academic and public events where we have received valuable feedback. Here we are particularly grateful to Mai Palmberg at the Nordic Africa Institute; Catherine Perret and Fredrik Tygstrup who invited us to present at a symposium at the University of Paris 8 Vincennes-Saint-Denis; Marilyn Young at the International Center for Advanced Studies, New York University; Gurminder Bhambra at the Institute of Advanced Study, University of Warwick; Håkan Thörn at the Department of Sociology, University of Gothenburg; Carl Tham at Arbetarnas Bildningsförbund (the Workers' Educational Association) in Stockholm; Åsa Wall at the Swedish National Heritage Board; and Patrik Tornéus at the literary festival Littfest, Umeå.

Gurminder Bhambra at the University of Warwick deserves special mention not only in her role as series editor of Theory for a Global Age, but most of all for her continuous contribution of ideas and inspiration to this project. Special thanks also go to Anders Stephanson who read the completed manuscript and provided invaluable feedback. In addition, a number of colleagues have discussed or read parts of the manuscript. For such help, we are grateful to Per Axelson, Nicholas Bancel, Erik Berggren, Herrick Chapman, Matthew Connelly, Ipek Démir, Giuliano Garavini, Mattias Gardell, Ragnar Haake, Jan Ifversen, Christoffer Kølvraa, Nicola Labanca, Victoria Margree, Walter Mignolo, Kalypso Nicolaidis, Magnus Nordenman, Agneta Persson, Oliver Rathkolb, Pierre Rosanvallon, Joan W. Scott, Robbie Shilliam, Robert Young and Mattias Åkeson. Our colleagues and friends at the Institute for Research on Migration, Ethnicity and Society (REMESO), Linköping University, have encouraged this project throughout; our work has benefitted in many ways from the Institute's inspiring intellectual atmosphere.

We also acknowledge our publisher's support; we are particularly indebted to the expertise and patience of Caroline Wintersgill, Mark Richardson, Jyoti Basuita and Sandra Stafford.

Finally, we thank our immediate colleagues, Anna Bredström and Patricia Lorenzoni. Their intellectual generosity and warm encouragement have sustained each of us over the years.

Funding for our research has been provided by the Swedish Research Council through two generous project grants. We acknowledge this support with gratitude.

Earlier versions of some pieces of this book have appeared in *European Journal of Social Theory* 5: 4 (2002); *Race & Class* 45: 3 (2004); *Journal of Historical Sociology* 26: 3 (2014); *Mediterranean Quarterly*, 24: 4 (2013); *Journal of Common Market Studies* 50: 6 (2012); *Globalizations* 8: 3 (2011); *Interventions: International Journal of Postcolonial Studies* 13: 3 (2011); *Dagens Nyheter*, 9 December 2012; *Echoes of Empire: Memory, Identity and Colonial Legacies*, eds Kalypso Nicolaidis, Berny Sèbe and Gabrielle Maas (London: I. B. Tauris, 2015); and *What's Culture Got to Do with it?* ed. Mai Palmberg (Uppsala: Nordic Africa Institute, 2009). All translations in the book are our own, unless otherwise noted.

In this paperback edition of *Eurafrica* we have corrected a handful of minor factual mistakes and stylistic shortcomings. We thank Karis Muller for having drawn our attention to some of these. The text is otherwise unchanged. Responsibility for remaining errors is of course ours alone.

Norrköping, May 2015

Introduction: The Past that Europe Forgot

Looking at an official map of the European Union one may be struck by the little dots that lay scattered around the globe and which all indicate territories that form integral parts of today's EU. Grouped under the official heading 'Outermost regions of the EU', they make up France's Guadeloupe, French Guiana, Réunion, Martinique, Mayotte and the overseas Collectivity of St Martin; Portugal's Azores and Madeira; and Spain's Canary Islands. While not showing under the label 'outermost regions', Spain's contested enclaves (or colonies) in Moroccan North Africa, Ceuta and Melilla, should also be mentioned since they too are fully incorporated into the EU. In addition, 26 non-sovereign 'Overseas countries and territories' (OCTs) share the status of being associated with the EU through their constitutional ties with certain EU member states (Denmark, France, the Netherlands and the UK). Although the OCTs are not part of the EU, most of the inhabitants of these still not decolonized territories are nonetheless EU citizens and as such able to, for instance, vote in EU Parliament elections.

The territories in question are rarely dealt with in the vast literature on European integration.[1] Considering their ostensible insignificance this may come as no surprise. Scratching the surface though, it becomes apparent that many of these small territories carry big economic and geopolitical stakes, both for individual member states and for the EU

---

[1] For some notable exceptions, see e.g. Peter Gold, *Europe or Africa: A Contemporary Study of the Spanish North African Enclaves of Ceuta and Melilla* (Liverpool: Liverpool University Press, 2000); Karis Muller, '"Concentric circles" at the periphery of the European Union', *Australian Journal of Politics and History*, Vol. 46, No. 3, 2000, pp. 322–35; Nic Maclellan and Jean Chesneaux, *After Moruroa: France in the South Pacific* (Melbourne: Ocean Press, 1998); and the contributions in Rebecca Adler-Nissen and Ulrik Pram Gad (eds), *European Integration and Postcolonial Sovereignty Games: The EU Overseas Countries and Territories* (London: Routledge, 2012).

as a whole. Besides their obvious utility as sites for naval bases and other military installations, the many island possessions in the oceans also provide sea borders and territorial waters that afford rights and access to current and future maritime resources (such as fish, oil and minerals).[2] Moreover, whereas Spain's North African possessions of Ceuta and Melilla serve as hubs in the EU's militarized quest to control migration from Africa, French Guiana has for decades offered the European Space Agency, which is closely affiliated with the EU, an ideal launching site for its rockets. 'Europe's Spaceport' is thus located in Kourou, French Guiana.

Given, too, that the sheer existence of these territories is so fundamentally at odds with the EU's dominant self-understanding, one must also ask how such a strong and contradictory symbolism has managed to escape the attention of EU research. Indeed, since the founding of the current EU in 1957, the EU's treaties have always had a paragraph stipulating that only a 'European state' can acquire membership of the EU; and, to our knowledge, this paragraph has only been applied once, in the rejection of Morocco's bid for EU membership in 1986.[3] In order to 'join Europe', therefore, the country in question first has to be European. But if this is so, what are we to make of those member states that continue to divide their location between continents – that is, those member states that are both European and African, both European and South American and so on?

In some sense this book sets out from this curiosity. We suspect that this negligence or disinclination of EU scholarship and the EU organization itself to acknowledge its overseas outposts can also be seen as synonymous with a disinclination to deal with the history and legacy of colonialism. For scholars and policy-makers to truly

---

[2] See Johan Galtung, *The European Community: A Superpower in the Making* (Oslo: Universitetsforlaget and London: George Allen & Unwin, 1973), p. 64.

[3] As Iver B. Neumann notes, when Morocco applied for membership in 1986, '[t]his application was dealt with in no uncertain terms; Rabat was simply told that the organization was open only to Europeans, and that was that. There was no room for ambiguity here, only unequivocal exclusion and marking of Morocco as clearly "non-European."' 'European identity, EU expansion, and the integration/exclusion nexus', *Alternatives*, Vol. 23, No. 3, 1998, p. 400.

recognize these 'non-European' domains, this would presuppose a European Union ready to explain, debate and come to terms with the historical as well as current relationship between European colonialism and European integration. In other words, an inquiry into the whereabouts of today's forgotten outposts of EU-Europe inevitably takes us to an equally forgotten history of European integration. To date, this history has not been examined in any rigorous fashion.[4]

This book addresses this lack of historical inquiry. However, it does not just set out to address a lacuna in studies of Europe and of European integration. The purpose of our study is to place the history of European integration on a new and solid foundation by recovering its colonial and geopolitical dimension. In so doing, we take issue with

---

[4] So far there is no account that traces the bond between European integration and colonial Africa in its full historical extent. The works that come closest are the contributions in Marie-Thérèse Bitsch and Gérard Bossuat, *L'Europe unie et l'Afrique: De l'idée d'Eurafrique à la convention de Lomé I* (Brussels: Bruylant, 2005), as well as Thomas Moser, *Europäische Integration, Dekolonisation, Eurafrika: Eine historische Analyse über die Entstehungsbedingungen der Eurafrikanischen Gemeinschaft von der Weltwirtschaftskrise bis zum Jaunde-Vertrag, 1929–1963* (Baden-Baden: Nomos Verlagsgesellschaft, 2000). A recent German dissertation covers the economic aspects of the association to the EEC of African states in the 1960s; see Urban Vahsen, *Eurafrikanische Entwicklungskooperation: Die Assoziierungspolitik der EWG gegenüber dem subsaharischen Afrika in den 1960er Jahren* (Stuttgart: Franz Steiner Verlag, 2010); and a recent French one covers the French context of the 1950s, see Yves Montarsolo, *L'Eurafrique – contrepoint de l'idée d'Europe: Le cas français de la fin de la deuxième guerre mondiale aux négociations des Traités de Rome* (Aix-en-Provence: Publications de l'Université de Provence, 2010). However, several scattered scholarly accounts cover specific parts, aspects and time frames of this history; see e.g. Gérard Bossuat, *L'Europe des Français, 1943–1959: La IVe République aux sources de l'Europe communautaire* (Paris: Publications de la Sorbonne, 1996); Matthew Connelly, *A Diplomatic Revolution: Algeria's Fight for Independence and the Origins of the Post-Cold War Era* (New York: Oxford University Press, 2002); Anne Deighton, 'Entente Neo-Coloniale? Ernest Bevin and the Proposals for an Anglo–French Third World Power', *Diplomacy and Statecraft*, Vol. 17, 2006, pp. 835–52; Pierre Guillen, 'Europe as a cure of French impotence? The Guy Mollet government and the negotiation of the Treaties of Rome', in Ennio Di Nolfo (ed.), *Power in Europe? II: Great Britain, France, Germany and Italy and the Origins of the EEC 1952–1957* (Berlin: Walter de Gruyter, 1992); John Kent, *The Internationalization of Colonialism: Britain, France, and Black Africa, 1939–1956* (Oxford: Clarendon Press, 1992); Guia Migani, *La France et l'Afrique sub-saharienne, 1957–1963: Histoire d'une décolonisation entre idéaux eurafricains et politique de puissance* (Brussels: Peter Lang, 2008). The first survey of writings about Eurafrica was published in Cameroon; see Max Liniger-Goumaz, *Eurafrique: Utopie our réalité?* (Yaoundé: Editions CLE, 1972) and *Eurafrique* (Geneva: Les Éditions du temps, 1970). See also Ch. 5, note 16.

the dominant narrative of EU history, which has often been officially endorsed.

It is certainly not surprising that Brussels disseminates an image of EU history as grounded in a popular approbation of the organization's founding period after World War II as a time when European leaders, thanks to European integration, chose peace and cooperation over nationalist rivalry and imperial aspirations. We recognize this in the European Commission's promotion of various narratives concerning historical landmarks, founding fathers and an assortment of other historical tropes, all intended to conjure up an image of the EU's allegedly noble cause and benevolent historical purpose before today's EU citizenry.[5] During the 2007 celebration of the 50th anniversary of the EU, this strategy was manifested with utmost clarity. The 2012 award of the Nobel Peace Prize to the EU of course only served to consolidate this image.

What is surprising, however, is the tacit correspondence between this official story and the assumptions that often guide EU scholarship. Research on the historical trajectory of European integration thus often fails to uphold a critical distance towards the type of 'Europeanism' underpinning Brussels' affirmative account of the origins of the EU, a distance that historians and social scientists have long since learnt to employ when scrutinizing the various nation-building and nationalist projects of late-nineteenth-century Europe. Such a critical attitude is called for also in the case of the EU, not because the EU is a nation state or can easily be compared to a nation state in the making, but because the EU in its quest for popular legitimacy makes use of similar methods and strategies as once did nation-building states. Historiography being one of the most powerful of these strategies, it becomes particularly important to examine the complicity of historians and EU researchers in establishing a selective and one-sided interpretation of the EU's past. In this context, we note a general tendency through which the

---

[5]   See e.g. Peo Hansen, *Europeans Only? Essays on Identity Politics and the European Union* (Umeå: Umeå University, 2000); Cris Shore, *Building Europe: The Cultural Politics of European Integration* (London: Routledge, 2000).

historical process of European integration is told as rather dissociated from processes of colonialism and decolonization, and designated as a non-colonial, a-colonial or sometimes even as an anti-colonial project.

We contend that this selective interpretation fulfils its foremost function as a myth, a foundational tale of pure origins, of an Immaculate Conception, which sets in place the main elements of a wishful and idealized European identity. Although not referring to the issue of colonialism per se, Mark Gilbert's point that EU studies has yet to cast off its dominant 'whiggish' approach to its subject matter is well taken.[6] Too often, then, EU studies posits European integration as imbued with a progressive spirit and teleology, much like nationalist intellectuals' refusal in earlier periods to critically scrutinize the historical origins of national projects. There is a danger involved in this replacement of history by myth. We will then be educating students and the general public to think of the European project in the least European way thinkable – namely, as unrelated to one of Europe's major histories: the imperialist project.

European integration as a Eurafrican project

The aim of this study, in short, is to establish and analyse the relation of European integration and colonialism. More specifically, we seek to retrieve a political project and geopolitical constellation, long forgotten or suppressed, that in our view is indispensable for a proper under-standing of the history of European integration and the interconnected histories of Africa and Europe in the twentieth century. The name of this constellation was *Eurafrica*, the story of which we recount in this book.

Many books have analysed Europe, the European Union and Africa as political, cultural and economic formations. Important works of more recent date have also charted the historical relations between

---

[6] Mark Gilbert, 'Narrating the process: Questioning the progressive story of European integration', *Journal of Common Market Studies*, Vol. 46, No. 3, 2008, pp. 641–62.

Africa and Europe and demonstrated how they, having been inseparable parts of a single Mediterranean culture in antiquity, separated and
settled as seemingly autonomous continental units with contrasting or
even antithetical features, and all this through the slow and violent
processes of crusading, exploration, conquest, slavery and colonization
that made the peoples to the north appear as authors of progress,
civilization and universal values, and those to the south as incarnations
of ignorance, darkness and savagery. How Africa and Europe were
discursively, politically and economically fashioned in this pattern is
by now a fairly well researched topic.[7]

Few if any of these books, however, take notice of the Eurafrican
project that consolidated colonial inequality in the mid-twentieth
century and perpetuated it into the contemporary world order. This
is where we make a contribution. We examine a complex twentieth-
century history in which efforts to unify Europe systematically
coincide with efforts to stabilize, reform and reinvent the colonial
system in Africa. What to make of this strong correlation? As we show,
Eurafrica, even as it was transformed from a geopolitical representation with utopian overtones in the 1920s into a political reality in the

---

[7] A number of important works have contributed to the clarification of this issue, perhaps
above all the works of Ali A. Mazrui and V. Y. Mudimbe – for Mazrui, see for instance
The African Condition: A Political Diagnosis (London: Heinemann, 1980) and *Africa
and Other Civilizations: Conquest and Counter-Conquest*, The Collected Essays of Ali
A. Mazrui (Trenton: World Africa Press, 2002); and for Mudimbe, see *The Invention of
Africa: Gnosis, Philosophy, and the Order of Knowledge* (Bloomington: Indiana University
Press, 1988) and *The Idea of Africa* (Bloomington: Indiana University Press, 1994). For
other seminal contributions, see: Samir Amin, *L'eurocentrisme: Critique d'une idéologie*
(Paris: Anthropos, 1988); Martin Bernal, *Black Athena: The Afroasiatic Roots of Classical
Civilization*, Vol. 1: The Fabrication of Ancient Greece, 1785–1985 (New Brunswick:
Rutgers University Press, 1987); James M. Blaut, *The Colonizer's Model of the World*,
Vol. 1: Geographical Diffusionism and Eurocentric History; Vol. 2: Eight Eurocentric
Historians (New York: Guilford Press, 1993 and 2000); Basil Davidson, *Africa in History:
Themes and Outlines* (London: Phoenix, 1991); Christopher Miller, *Theories of Africans:
Francophone Literature and Anthropology in Africa* (Chicago: The University of Chicago
Press, 1990); Walter Rodney, *How Europe Underdeveloped Africa*, rev. edn (Cape Town:
Pambazuka Press, 2012); Kwasi Wiredu, *Philosophy and an African Culture* (Cambridge:
Cambridge University Press, 1980); Robert C. Young, *White Mythologies: Writing
History and the West* (New York and London: Routledge, 1990); and Paul Tiyambe
Zeleza, *Rethinking Africa's Globalization*, Vol. 1: The Intellectual Challenges (Trenton:
World Africa Press, 2003).

1950s, always marked the site where interests in European integration overlapped with colonial ambitions. According to the Eurafrican idea, European integration would come about only through a coordinated exploitation of Africa, and Africa could be efficiently exploited only if European states cooperated and combined their economic and political capacities.

Our study presents the origins and development of Eurafrica as a geopolitical conception in the interwar period, when it was strongly promoted by the Pan-European organization among many others. It goes on to demonstrate how Eurafrica was politically realized with the establishment in 1957 of the European Economic Community (EEC), today's EU. At the time of its foundation, the EEC comprised not just Belgium, France, Italy, Luxembourg, the Netherlands and West Germany, but also all major colonial possessions of the member states. In official language they were called 'overseas countries and territories' or OCTs and they included, most importantly, Belgian Congo and French West and Equatorial Africa, whereas Algeria, which in this time was an integral part of metropolitan France, was formally integrated into the EEC yet excluded from certain provisions of the Treaty.

For the promoters of European integration, their community thus extended far beyond the European continent and constituted a new geopolitical sphere of influence. Colloquially as well as officially, the EEC negotiations referred to this sphere as Eurafrica, and one of the main intentions of the advocates of European integration was precisely to bring this entity into being. This would resolve primarily France's, but also Belgium's, increasingly untenable colonial problem. At the same time this aimed to consolidate European interests in a world order where its range of opportunities rapidly dwindled. 'Toward Eurafrica' ran the front-page headline of French daily *Le Monde* on 21 February 1957, the morning after the six European leaders had successfully concluded their negotiations in preparation of the Treaty of Rome.[8] A couple of days later, French premier Guy Mollet climbed out of his

---

[8]   'Première étape vers l'Eurafrique', *Le Monde*, 21 February 1957.

aeroplane in Washington to pay an official visit to President Eisenhower, bringing with him the news that not only had Europeans decided to unite but also 'an even greater unity was being born, Eurafrica'.[9]

As we shall demonstrate, the Eurafrican project was reducible neither to Europe nor to Africa, nor to any simple effort to bridge the gap between them. Rather, Eurafrica should be seen as the wider formation within which the relation of Europe and Africa was reconceived during the greater part of the twentieth century. Put differently, our study reasserts the importance of a forgotten historical causality that was constitutive both of the European integration project or the EU itself and of the foundation of postcolonial Africa. We say *re*-assert, because in its own present – from the 1920s to the 1950s – Eurafrica was loudly and repeatedly asserted. 'When today rereading the articles and speeches of the principal political leaders in France', states the leading historian of French colonialism René Girault, 'one is struck by the pervasiveness and intensity of the Eurafrican theme'.[10]

Depending on the context, Eurafrica was asserted now as a necessity, now as a possibility, now as a common European task, now as a utopian future, now as a strategic interest, now as an economic imperative, now as a peace project, now as the white man's burden, now as Europe's last chance, now as Africa's only hope. Commentators, politicians and other moulders of public opinion who advocated the project tended to stress its epochal significance; Eurafrica was, quite simply, indispensable for Europe's geopolitical and economic survival. Of course, not everyone agreed with this view. There was strong opposition from many sides and, needless to say, the Africans scarcely had a say. 'At that time no one asked their opinion on the matter for they had no voice of their own', wrote Schofield Coryell in a 1962 issue of *Africa Today*.[11] But the

[9] HAEU (Historical Archives of the European Union), EN 2735, 'Statement given by Premier Guy Mollet on his arrival at the Washington Airport'.

[10] René Girault, 'Les indépendances des pays d'Afrique noire dans les relations internationales', in Charles-Robert Ageron and Marc Michel (eds), *L'Afrique noire française: L'heure des indépendances* (Paris: CNRS Éditions, 2010), p. 549.

[11] Schofield Coryell, 'French Africa and the Common Market', *Africa Today*, Vol. 9, November 1962, p. 12.

European majority prevailed, marshalled by convinced Eurafricanists like France's prime minister Guy Mollet, Belgium's foreign minister Paul-Henri Spaak and West Germany's chancellor Konrad Adenauer, and the EEC was politically instituted as what *Business Week* in its report after the signing ceremonies in Rome described as a 'New deal for the dark continent'.[12]

In retrieving this once salient entity, we shift the terrain upon which scholarly analyses of the political, economic and ideological developments on the two continents have taken place up until now. Eurafrica delineates a geopolitical context that, once reconstructed, allows us to elucidate or answer a set of crucial historical and political questions, including, for instance, why the momentum for European integration accelerated during the 1950s, why Pan-Africanism never got off the ground in Africa after independence and why the agreements and treaties between the European Union and the African Union have been designed in their current forms. Of course, the history of Eurafrica does not furnish the only answers to these questions. But all answers remain incomplete until the history of Eurafrica is put back into the picture.

Europe as a global power

A short book cannot account for all the initiatives, organizations and controversies that surrounded the Eurafrican project. This will be the task of a forthcoming work, which will also contain a comprehensive assessment of how Eurafrica in its various conceptions conditioned European integration and African post-independence history. In the present book, we present the main lines of our historical argument substantiated by the documentation necessary to support it.

---

[12] 'New deal for the dark continent?', *Business Week*, 20 April 1957; quoted in Karis Muller, 'Iconographie de l'Eurafrique', in Marie-Thérèse Bitsch and Gérard Bossuat (eds), *L'Europe unie et l'Afrique: De l'idée d'Eurafrique à la convention de Lomé I*, (Brussels: Bruylant, 2005), p. 29.

On a theoretical level, we argue that the history of Eurafrica indicates the necessity of perceiving Europe and Africa from the perspective of a theory of globality and international relations unconstrained by national, continental and Eurocentric categories. A couple of decades ago, Africa was written off as a stagnant and uneventful periphery, a black hole in the world wide web of the network society.[13] Today, Africa is extolled as a booming 'continent of the future', to which states, international organizations and transnational companies rush to make profits or secure resources. The history of Eurafrica is essential in any effort to understand this 'new scramble for Africa' – how it can happen, which stakes are involved and which role the EU plays in it.

Indeed, since the folding of the Soviet Union and even more so since we have entered the twenty-first century, numerous calls and concrete attempts have been launched in order to have the EU assume a common foreign and security policy, a global mission and responsibility. The assumption is that this will be the first time in the history of the EU that the organization positions itself globally, as a major actor in foreign policy and international relations. According to this assumption, the EU was until recently a regionally anchored organization in the Cold War context, its role and function determined by the truly global superpowers, and it is only today, after the Cold War and end of the bipolar world order that the EU can ascend to a global level and speak with global authority. But if we move beyond the cold-war framework, we realize that the EU had a global and geopolitical rationale from the very start, and this rationale was coded as 'association', 'interdependence' and 'Eurafrica'. To understand what it might mean, then, for the EU to become a global power, we should look at how this worked out the last time European integration aspired to do the same. Similarly, an understanding of the current upheavals in North Africa and beyond, what started out as the so-called Arab

---

[13] Manuel Castells, *End of Millenium*, Vol. 3 of *The Information Age: Economy, Society and Culture* (Oxford: Blackwell, 1998), p. 73.

Spring, and a correct assessment of the EU's attitude and involvement in relation to such processes, presuppose an awareness about the fact that the EU, ever since its foundation, has been heavily invested in this region.

Eurafrica as method

The history of Eurafrica is important also because it undercuts one of the most pernicious features of the geographical and historiographic paradigms that originated in the West. No serious analyst has failed to register that there is a specific historiographical category that imposes itself apriori, as it were, on any description of Africa in the modern world order. This category presents Africa and Europe as poles in a binary constellation. No matter what content we inscribe in this dichotomy – an anti-colonial uprising, a film about a mixed-race love story, a wrecked vessel overcrowded by West African migrants – the binary form itself remains constant, preventing us from conceiving of Africa as anything else but, in Paul Zeleza's expression, 'a basket case of absences' that calls for European presence.[14] A racist and colonial epistemology deeply ingrained in global ideology here forecloses any possibility for Africa to escape its fate as the weaker part of the dyad, while it also forbids Europeans to relinquish their civilizing mission. It compels Africans and Europeans alike to repeat a predictable script where Africans perform as victims or villains while European aid workers, diplomats, oilers, bankers and military personnel are waiting in the wings, ready to correct or eradicate anyone who seriously challenges the pattern of unequal complementarity in which the Afro-European relation is frozen.

Disclosing how this colonial binary at once enabled and corrupted the process of European integration and African decolonization may

---

[14] Paul Zeleza, 'Africa: the changing meanings of "African" culture and identity', in Elisabeth Abiri and Håkan Thörn (eds), *Horizons: Perspectives on a Global Africa* (Gothenburg: Museion, Gothenburg University, 2005), p. 43.

in this context produce something of an estrangement effect. The usual way of critically historicizing the relation of Africa and Europe is to uncover the discursive operations at work in the ongoing fabrication of Africa and Europe as antithetical phenomena. While fully compatible with such anti-colonial, postcolonial or decolonial deconstructions of European colonial epistemologies, our own method is different. We rely on an analysis of sources that bespeak a history of European integration and Euro-African relations that empirically disproves the dominant historical narratives and accounts of Europe's and Africa's paths towards modernity and integration. Put simply, a refutation of the EU's image of itself and of its historical relation to Africa here emerges through the explicit and eloquent wealth of the historical archive itself, in which we can discern a history in which the European subject – anxious about its future geopolitical and economic viability – turns to its African object as a source of rejuvenation. As one analyst put it in 1957, the same year as the EEC was established: 'It is in Africa that Europe will be made.'[15]

But this is also why we must be careful not to misinterpret the archive. Our argument depends on a careful assessment of the prevalent political dispositions in the late 1950s when the Eurafrican project was realized. This also explains the organization of our book. In Chapter 2 we canvass the origins of Eurafrica in interwar debates on 'the crisis of Europe'. Europe's instability and perceived overpopulation in the immediate aftermath of World War I was seen here as a consequence of its lack of 'Lebensraum' and its contracted position between emerging imperial power blocs to the east and west. In this context, leading European politicians, scientists and intellectuals saw Africa as a remedy, the crux being that its possibilities in terms of territories and resources could be realized only by a 'union of all the colonising nations' merging their colonial possessions 'for the greater moral and material profit of all', as French colonialist Hubert Lyautey put it in 1931.[16]

---

[15] Jean-Michel de Lattre, 'Les grands ensembles africains', *Politique étrangère*, Vol. 20, No. 5, 1955, p. 543.
[16] Quoted in Patricia Morton, *Hybrid Modernities: Architecture and Representation at the 1931 Colonial Exposition, Paris* (Cambridge: The MIT Press, 2000), p. 314.

In Chapter 3 we continue to show how these perceptions and plans were revived and gradually operationalized after World War II and became a central concern in all efforts to integrate and promote close cooperation between the war-ravaged states in Western Europe, now even more starkly reminded of their declining standing in global geopolitics. Chapter 3 follows this development until the aborted European Defence Community in 1954.

Chapter 4 then takes its point of departure in the relaunch of European integration that began with the Messina Conference in 1955, which two years later led to the establishment of the European Economic Community (EEC) and the realization of Eurafrica through the association to the Common Market of the member states' colonial territories. While we end our analysis with the successful realization of the Eurafrican association regime in the 1957 Treaty of Rome, we devote our concluding chapter to a broader discussion of the historical explanation and future implications of the Eurafrican enterprise.

In this way we combine a diachronic account or survey of the Eurafrican debates from the 1920s up to the 1950s (Chapters 2 and 3) with a synchronic analysis of the decisive years, 1955–1957 (Chapter 4), when Eurafrica emerged as a necessary condition for the founding of the EEC. As this is a controversial matter in EU scholarship, we closely scrutinize the negotiations leading to the signing of the Treaty of Rome. This is where the Eurafrican idea was orchestrated and became politically operative. With verified plausibility, we can thus argue that Eurafrica enabled the process of European integration and hence constitutes an occluded past of today's European Union. Or to be straight, the EU would not have come into existence at this point in time had it not been conceived as a Eurafrican enterprise in which colonialism was Europeanized.

We have already given some hints as to why this history has been consigned to oblivion and, in what follows, we will delve further into this crucial explanatory undertaking. But as a starting point we should highlight some dominant perspectives that have served to perpetuate Eurafrica's seeming insignificance. First of all we note that in existing scholarship the history of the EU is usually bent to fit Eurocentric presuppositions, and that European and African history are mostly conceived as insular continental narratives. We also note that, in a different body of scholarship, the history of colonialism is typically told as a history of the colonial systems of various separate imperial or nation states. If world history and global processes are cut up and edited by such devices, Eurafrica drops out of the picture, as it belonged to a geopolitical constellation that cannot be mapped by way of continental or national categories. But the historical erasure or misrecognition of Eurafrica also has to do with the fact that the Eurafrican project does not fit a couple of dominant historiographical paradigms, in which the postwar relation between Europe and Africa is either refracted through what Matthew Connelly has called 'the Cold War lens' or told as a narrative structured around a presumed historical rupture of 'decolonization'.[17]

In relation to these perspectives our book proposes a new theoretical departure in the area of European integration as well as in the area of the history of colonialism. As such, our pursuit dispenses with, first, the notion that European colonialism and the EU–African relationship can be construed as the sum total of Europe's national colonial histories. Second, it dispenses with the notion that Europe and Africa can be studied as separate continental units. Rather, we propose a third option, in which the Eurafrican unit serves as our primary frame of analysis – that is, the mindset and institutional energy that developed from the interwar period and onward perceived of Europe as inseparable from a Eurafrican totality. Again, there was no Europe to begin with, unless it was also Eurafrica. By retrieving the history of Eurafrica, we can also extract a new critical concept for the humanities and social sciences in a global age. Eurafrica is of vital importance in the areas of European studies, African studies, EU studies, Globalization studies, Mediterranean studies, studies of colonialism and postcolonial studies

---

[17] See Matthew Connelly, 'Taking off the Cold War Lens: Visions of North-South conflict during the Algerian War for Independence', *American Historical Review*, Vol. 105, No. 3, 2000, pp. 739–69.

precisely because it evinces a forgotten reality lying at their mutual juncture.

As we shall argue in our concluding chapter, the effort to realize Eurafrica comes across as a transition phase or mediatory formation, through which the European states adapted themselves and rescaled their imperial ambitions so as to fit the postwar geopolitical situation. For the European states that entered into the EEC in 1957, Eurafrica was in this sense an arrangement that allowed them to posit their presence and interests in Africa as a new relationship of mutual association, formally accommodating the demands of the anti-colonial movements, while at the same time never really stepping out of their roles as patrons and tutors. For the African states that in the same year of 1957 began liberating themselves, Eurafrica allowed the political elites of the emerging sovereign states to enter a compromise with their former colonial masters, and this through arrangements from which both partners would profit at the cost of the majority of Africans for whom decolonization did not seem to happen or turned out to be 'a non-event', as Achille Mbembe puts it.[18]

If the history of Eurafrica is put back into the picture, we understand why decolonization did not signify the rupture with the past that it is usually described as. In the larger part of Africa, the postcolonial state moved into structures already set up by the colonial government, modelled itself on the routines of the colonial administration, and continued to conduct economic activities and trade according to old patterns. In this context, the Eurafrican programme also turned out to be an efficient antidote to Pan-Africanism and all the other independently organized African integration and regionalization schemes. This may even be said to have been the true historical function of the EEC's association agreement: to adjust international relations, economic extraction and means of production to a world order with nominally independent African states, while retaining control of the continent's

---

[18] Achille Mbembe, *Sortir de la grande nuit: Essai sur l'Afrique décolonisée* (Paris: Éditions La Découverte, 2010), p. 58.

resources. Having fulfilled this task, Eurafrica disappeared from the political agenda by the mid-1960s, as the EEC and various other international organizations by then provided more efficient and less costly means through which European interventions in African affairs could continue, but now in the guise of development, aid and diplomatic counselling.

Thus, if Eurafrica's life in international politics was a short one, and if this should be taken as a sign that the politics of colonial association devised by the EEC proved to be a failure when all countries previously under European sovereignty embraced decolonization, it must be added that this failure was a truly successful one, the consequences of which are still with us today.

2

A Holy Alliance of Colonizing Powers: The Interwar Period

In what place and time did Eurafrica emerge? Let us begin our account at the end of World War I and in the border area along the Western front where millions died in the worst armed conflict in human history to that point. Thousands of acres of graveyards along the old frontline today testify to this near-total collapse of European civilization. Most of the buried were British, French and German. But hundreds of thousands of conscripted soldiers and servicemen from the empires of France and Britain, men of all colours and from all continents, were also recruited to the trenches that diagonally divided European soil from Oostende to Strasbourg. World War I is usually interpreted as a European conflict that expanded into global war. But it was also an event that brought the conflicts of global imperialism back to Europe.

Encapsulated in this situation were some of the key issues that, over the next few decades, would blend into the creation of Eurafrica as a historical entity and political project. Before exploring how these issues developed in their historical and political circumstances, it is useful to lift them out of context and identify them, since they will appear frequently in the following pages.

A first theme to extract is Europe's sense of racial superiority over Africans. Roughly one million soldiers born in the colonies fought on the French and British sides in World War I.[1] European politicians and diplomats of the time negotiated on how to minimize the visibility of black and Arab troops, both during the war itself and in the French

---

[1] Keith L. Nelson, 'The "Black Horror on the Rhine": Race as a factor in post-World War I diplomacy', *The Journal of Modern History*, Vol. 42, No. 4, 1970, pp. 609–12.

postwar occupation of the Rhineland and the Ruhr region. Even if no formal agreement was reached, a gentlemen's understanding prevailed to the extent that all involved found the idea of African presence in Europe repulsive.[2]

A second theme consists of the concrete plans for European integration that emerged in the war's aftermath. The political errors committed by all sides, in addition to the horrendous human sacrifices that ensued, apparently spelled 'the decline of the West', as Oswald Spengler put it. This sense of impotency, destruction and doom, or the uneasy sense that Europe, as Robert Musil quipped in 1922, was 'helpless', gave rise to a utopian wish of unification as a way of rejuvenating the European 'spirit' and regaining its economic and cultural vitality.[3] One of the staunchest defenders of unification was Richard Coudenhove-Kalergi, founder of the Pan-European movement. 'Out of the terrifying crisis in which Germany and France are locked today, they will either emerge as united Europeans – or they will, biting at each others' throats, bleed to death from their mutually inflicted wounds', he stated in 1923.[4] For the initiator of *Paneuropa* – which was at once a book, a journal, a movement and an idea – the need to overcome the French–German conflict and peacefully share the benefits of the resource-rich border area was the first of two key reasons that would make the continent's leaders realize the necessity of European integration, the second one being, as we shall see, the benefits of a joint exploitation of Africa.

Indeed, the war's end also provoked renewed interest in geopolitical scale. Whereas the overhaul of the international system after the war propelled the United States and, soon too, the Soviet Union to global might, the Treaty of Versailles divested Germany of its colonial

---

[2]   Christian Koller, '*Von Wilden aller Rassen niedergemetzelt*': *Die Diskussion um die Verwendung von Kolonialtruppen in Europa zwischen Rassismus, Kolonial- und Militärpolitik, 1914–1930* (Stuttgart: Franz Steiner Verlag, 2001), pp. 53–63, 82–3.

[3]   Robert Musil, 'Helpless Europe: A digressive journey', in Musil, *Precision and Soul: Essays and Addresses*, in Burton Pike and David S. Luft (eds and trans.) (Chicago: The University of Chicago Press, 1990), pp. 116–33.

[4]   Richard Coudenhove-Kalergi, *Paneuropa* (1923, 2nd edn, Vienna and Leipzig: Paneuropa-Verlag, 1926), pp. 107–22.

possessions, which by international mandate were now placed under French, British, South African and Belgian administration. These mutations of the global order fuelled a geopolitical discourse about the political and economic sustainability of Germany and Europe in the new global competition, and many of the continent's politicians and thinkers issued demands for returning to Germany its colonial hinterland. Not surprisingly, geopolitics flourished especially in Germany, as it came to address the predicament of a nation deprived of its imperial scale, or *Lebensraum*. To make things worse, the homeland itself had been amputated from some of its regions and was partly occupied. The outrage against black and Arab troops on German soil attains an additional dimension against this background. From having been a nation that colonized Africa, Germany perceived itself as being colonized by Africans.[5]

As a fourth major theme, the postwar situation exposed the contradiction between the ideals of national autonomy and the realities of colonial dominance. In fulfilment of Woodrow Wilson's fourteen-point plan, a number of European peoples and nations formerly under the imperial rule of Wilhelmine Germany and Habsburg Austria were rewarded with independence by the victors. The peace treaty also safeguarded Belgium and France's territorial sovereignty. Independence stopped short outside Europe, however. Wilson's principles of national autonomy remained unrealized in Europe's overseas colonies. As the colonial troops of the British and French empires returned, they could not understand and much less accept why they should be denied the very freedoms they had struggled to secure for Belgians, French, Serbs, Poles and other European nations. These seeds of anti-colonialism were soon to sprout and grow.

Thus, the aftermath of World War I saw Europeans making more anxious assertions of racial superiority against Africans and other non-Europeans, a number of European plans for economic integration

---

[5] Dirk van Laak, *Über alles in der Welt: Deutscher Imperialismus im 19. und 20. Jahrhundert* (Munich: Verlag C. H. Beck, 2005), p. 118.

and political unification, a geopolitical discourse that sought to redress the lack of territorial scale felt by many European nations (Germany in particular), and a deepening contradiction between national autonomy and colonial dominance. These four themes were preconditions of the Eurafrican idea, which promised to resolve in one stroke many of the problems facing Europe in its prolonged period of imperial decline. From the peak of colonial imperialism around 1914 to the demise of the system around 1960, references to Eurafrica multiplied in European politics and culture. In the final years of colonialism Eurafrica was politically realized precisely because it provided an advantageous rearrangement not only of Europe's struggling economy but also of its relation to colonized Africa and of its geopolitical situation in an emerging Cold War context. At the same time Eurafrica provided an apparent and attractive resolution of the contradiction between national autonomy and colonial dominance: Eurafrica was presented as a way of moving beyond both colonialism and national independence in Africa while at the same time securing Europe's grip on the continent's assets and resources.

The black horror

Let us now turn to discussing how these issues were played out in the historical and political process and how they have been virtually erased from scholarship on European integration and European colonialism. In standard histories of European integration, Eurafrica is scarcely mentioned, in spite of the fact that the European integration that came into being in the 1950s was purveyed and perceived as an integration of Europe and its colonies into a Eurafrican entity. This disregard of historical facticity justifies, in our view, comparing much of canonical EU history to mythology.

Here is one myth to start out with. Scholarship on the history of European integration often points to the experience of and fight against the 'Nazi horror' as key catalysts for amplifying a sense of European solidarity and identity that in turn helped to pave the way for the movement towards European integration. 'The more plainly the totalitarian character, contempt for legality, and racial arrogance of Nazism were shown in action', the late Nestor of European integration history Walter Lipgens writes, 'the more people came to their senses and returned to the true European tradition.'[6] What has gone unnoticed in this extensive scholarship, though, is the fact that a few decades prior to the Nazi collapse another 'true European tradition', namely 'racial arrogance' itself, helped to galvanize European solidarity in the fight against another 'horror'.

The perceived horror consisted of the colonial troops, between 20,000 and 45,000 soldiers from Madagascar, West Africa, Morocco and Algeria, which were deployed by France for the occupation of the German Rhineland following Germany's defeat in World War I.[7] The presence of non-white soldiers in the occupying forces bred strong emotions among the Germans as well as a wider European and American public and intelligentsia. African soldiers were generally perceived as unreliable savages who posed great danger especially for the German female and juvenile population. Talk about 'the black horror', 'the black disgrace', 'the black shame' and 'the black peril' was in everybody's mouth.[8] In *Mein Kampf*, published in 1925, Hitler spoke of the colonial troops in terms of 'the contamination by Negro blood on the Rhine in the heart of Europe [...] bastardizing the European continent at its core'.[9]

---

[6] Walter Lipgens, *A History of European Integration*, Vol. 1: 1945–7: The Formation of the European Unity Movement (Oxford: Clarendon Press, 1982), p. 46.

[7] For the numbers, see Clarence Lusane, *Hitler's Black Victims* (New York: Routledge, 2003), p. 72; Koller, '*Von Wilden aller Rassen niedergemetzelt*', pp. 87–102, 202.

[8] See Lusane, *Hitler's Black Victims*; Koller, '*Von Wilden aller Rassen*'; Iris Wigger, '"Black Shame" – The campaign against "racial degeneration" and female degradation in interwar Europe', *Race & Class*, Vol. 51, No. 3, 2010, pp. 33–46; Jean-Yves Le Naour, *La honte noire: L'Allemagne et les troupes coloniales françaises, 1914–1945* (Paris: Hachette, 2003); and Wolfgang Schmale, 'Before self-reflexivity: Imperialism and colonialism in the early discourses of European integration', in Menno Spiering and Michael Wintle (eds), *European Identity and the Second World War* (Houndmills: Palgrave Macmillan, 2011), pp. 188–9.

[9] Quoted in Lusane, *Hitler's Black Victims*, p. 80.

Hitler was certainly in good company, similar opinions reaching well into Western Europe's liberal and social democratic establishments, as well as into prominent women's organizations, most notably the Women's International League for Peace and Freedom (WILPF). As Elisabeth Röhl ('Frau Röhl') of the Social Democrats pleaded in the German Parliament in May 1920: 'We appeal to all the women of the world that they support us in protesting against the use, completely contrary to nature, of coloureds in the German Rhine districts.'[10] Such calls were answered by women's organization across Europe; the condemnation issued by the Swedish national branch of the WILPF, for instance, managed to collect some 50,000 signatures.[11] When Germany's Social Democratic chancellor Hermann Müller addressed the Parliament in April 1920 he reported that 'French militarism has marched across the Main as into enemy country', and he went on to add: 'Senegal negroes are camping in the Frankfurt University, guarding the Goethe House.'[12] This was the scandal: Goethe, the very monument of the European spirit and proof of German superiority, was now soiled and disgraced by black hands. In a parliamentary address a month later, Müller received strong backing from his foreign minister, Adolf Köster, who fulminated that 'the introduction of nearly 50,000 coloured troops in the centre of white Europe is a crime against the whole of Europe'. As Köster stated:

> [T]hese troops are a terrible danger hygienically not only for Germany, but for all of Europe. The ceaseless brutalities, the murder of harmless citizens, the violation of women, girls and boys, the gigantic increase in prostitution, the opening of numerous brothels, as well as the rapid spread of sexual disease, all this represents a policy which can only be continuation of war with the most ruthless weapons.[13]

[10] Nationalversammlung, Stenographische Berichte, 177 Sitzung, 20 May 1920, p. 5692. Verhandlungen des deutschen Reichstags, www.reichstagsprotokolle.de/Blatt2_wv_bsb00000017_00656.html

[11] E. D. Morel, *The Horror on the Rhine*, Pamphlet No. 44a, 7th edn, February 1921 (London: Union of Democratic Control), p. 7; Nelson, 'The "Black Horror on the Rhine"', p. 616.

[12] Quoted in Koller, '*Von Wilden aller Rassen*', p. 213.

[13] Quoted in Morel, *The Horror on the Rhine*, p. 17.

In the words of Germany's president Friedrich Ebert, also a social democrat, 'the deployment of coloured troops of the most inferior culture as overseers of a population of such high spiritual and economic importance as the Rhinelanders [was] an intolerable violation of the law of European civilization.'[14]

Visual images illustrate that Germany regarded the presence of black and coloured troops as a humiliation so shameful that it rocked the very foundation of national identity. One poster from 1920 shows a happy-looking black man, completely naked except for the helmet usually worn by French troops, standing like a huge colossus with his legs spread wide and his giant feet crushing the cross-framed houses of a German town, at the same time rubbing against his waist and sexual organ ivory-white female bodies that he has caught in his hands.[15] Yet another illustration is a commemorative coin, minted and sold to promote resistance against the French occupation. On one side of the coin is the facial profile of a black soldier, caricatured to look like a monkey, next to which are stamped the words 'Liberté, Egalité, Fraternité' and 'Die Wacht am Rhein' (Guard on the Rhine). On the other side of the coin we see a woman tied to a tree, the trunk of which, on closer scrutiny, turns out to be an enormous erect penis.

The alleged threat that the coloured troops posed to German women was also a preferred theme in the extensive propaganda disseminated by the leader of the British Union of Democratic Control, E. D. Morel, who operated as one of the foremost champions of the cause to have the colonial troops eliminated from Germany. In his voluminous and widely endorsed newsletter, or pamphlet, Morel – subsequently a Labour MP, in 1922, and nearly appointed foreign secretary before his sudden death in 1924[16] – did his utmost

---

[14] Ebert (1926), quoted in Koller, '*Von Wilden aller Rassen*', p. 324. Ebert's opinion was indeed shared by all political parties in Germany of the period, with the exception of the communist party (KPD) and the Independent Social Democrats (USPD).

[15] Klaus Theweleit, *Männerphantasien*, Vol. 1: Frauen, Fluten, Körper, Geschichte, 2nd edn (Munich and Zürich: Piper Verlag, 2000), p. 101.

[16] A contradictory character indeed, Morel also made a name for himself as a relentless critic of European colonial policy in Africa, most notably being instrumental in bringing Belgium's atrocities in Congo to public attention in Europe.

to persuade politicians and militaries alike about the urgency of a
swift removal of *The Horror on the Rhine* (also the title of Morel's
newsletter), often citing as a chief reason the purported rape epidemic
that the coloured troops had inflicted on Germany. The latter was
namely the 'supreme' horror, the one that would soon be forever
irreversible. Putting himself in the shoes of German fathers speaking
to German boys, Morel summarized the injustices dealt to Germany
since the war's end:

> They stole our territory. They seized our colonies. They filched our
> coal and iron. They laid hands upon the property of our citizens
> abroad. They piled humiliation upon humiliation on us. All this
> they did. These things we can forget, though hardly. But that was not
> enough. They inflicted upon us the supreme outrage. From the plains
> and forests, from the valleys and the swamps of Africa they brought
> tens of thousands of savage men, and thrust them upon us. Boys, *these
> men raped your mothers and sisters!* This, neither you, nor we, nor
> they, must ever be allowed to forget.[17]

Such was the image of Africa and of the African at a time when
they were transported into Europe's fatigued and war-torn heart. In
one sense, these statements and images are just a continuation of a
long history of Europe's racial stereotyping of non-European peoples.
Our reason for returning to them now, however, is that they are also
repressed parts of the origin and beginning of a new history: the
history of European integration. For it is in this area and in this period
that the story of what is today known as the European Union (EU) can
be said to have begun.

This is for many reasons. The first of these is that Konrad Adenauer,
the West German chancellor who was instrumental for European
integration after World War II, resided as vice-mayor and mayor
in Cologne during the whole Weimar period from 1919 to 1933.
Adenauer's political worldview was largely shaped by the conflicts in the
Rhineland during and after World War I and by Coudenhove-Kalergi's

---

[17] Morel, *The Horror on the Rhine*, p. 22, emphasis in original.

Paneuropeanism, as well as by what Adenauer took to be the very regrettable loss of Germany's African empire.[18]

A second reason is that the emergence of the European integration project, as we shall see, is far more intimately connected to Africa and to the question of Europe's dominance over Africa than we have been led to believe by standard works on the history of modern Europe. Third, for those who first asserted the necessity of a European Union, it was precisely this geographic area, the Rhineland and the Ruhr region – or the border zone between France and Germany and between Germany and the Benelux countries – that showed both the crux and the proof of their argument. It was the attempts to resolve the centuries-long strife and conflict over this region, blessed by stunning natural resources and a highly developed industrial infrastructure, that in 1951 led to the establishment of the European Coal and Steel Community, the precursor of the EEC and the EU.

Europe's plantation: Pan-European beginnings

We have already mentioned that France's decision to march across the Ruhr and the Rhine with colonial troops turned Germany's political emotions to boiling. However, smaller and soon larger groups of intellectuals reached the opposite conclusion. In their view, France's occupation of the Ruhr only demonstrated that the age-old animosity between France and Germany had led both states into a dead end. 'Europe's Beginnings' ('Anfänge Europas') was the title of an article published in May 1923 by German writer Heinrich Mann. He wrote: 'Will Europe ever become one: then the two of us first. We form the root. Starting with us, the united continent – the others could not but follow us. We carry the responsibility for ourselves and for the rest.

---

[18] Hans-Peter Schwartz, *Konrad Adenauer: A German Politician and Statesman in a Period of War, Revolution and Reconstruction*, Vol. 1: From the German Empire to the Federal Republic, 1876–1952 (Oxford: Berghahn Books, 1995), pp. 95–6.

Through us there will be a state above states and that state will last. Or else, no future will be valid for us, nor for Europe.'[19]

In the same year, Richard Coudenhove-Kalergi published his pamphlet *Paneuropa*, which launched his Pan-European Union movement that was to gather both sizeable and influential intellectual and political support from the best and the brightest of his generation, Heinrich Mann being one of them, and also including Nobel laureates Albert Einstein, Gerhart Hauptmann, Selma Lagerlöf, Thomas Mann, Nathan Söderblom, as well as statesmen such as Winston Churchill, Konrad Adenauer, Ignaz Seipel, Karl Renner, Joseph Caillaux and Aristide Briand – the latter serving as chairman of the Pan-European Union. According to Walter Lipgens, *Paneuropa* was by far the most important among the many proposals for European collaboration of the 1920s, and largely mirrored the worldview of internationalists and liberal progressives of the era.[20]

According to the Pan-European movement, a united Europe was paramount for political reasons, or simply to prevent a repetition of World War I. This was the argument for peace. Or, as Coudenhove-Kalergi proclaimed: 'The alternatives today are clear: Pan-Europe or war!'[21] A united Europe was desirable also for cultural reasons, as history seemed to indicate that Europe made up some sort of civilizational unity. 'Pan-Europe should be the political expression of the European cultural community', Coudenhove-Kalergi explained. All the 'linguistic nations' of Europe would be gathered into 'one single racial nation', just as the Pan-Hellenic movement in ancient times brought together the city-based polities of Greece 'into one great nation for

---

[19] Heinrich Mann, 'Anfänge Europas', in Peter-Paul Schneider (ed.), *Sieben Jahre Chronik der Gedanken und Vorgänge: Essays* (Frankfurt am Main: Fischer Taschenbuch Verlag, 1994), p. 114.

[20] 'After 1923 whole staffs of periodicals, associated pressure groups in many countries, and at least two dozen books published every year pursued this aim.' According to Lipgens, five works were more influential than others: those by Demangeon, Delaisi (both French), Alfred Weber (Germany), Ortega y Gasset (Spain) and Coudenhove-Kalergi (Austria), the last one being most important of all. Lipgens, *A History of European Integration*, Vol. 1, p. 38.

[21] Richard Coudenhove-Kalergi, 'Alarm', *Paneuropa*, Vol. 3, No. 4, 1927, p. 1.

all Hellenics'. Pan-Europe's self-proclaimed 'cultural aim' was thus 'the self-knowledge of the European race as an occidental nation'.[22]

Perhaps most important, the Pan-European movement launched a third, economic, argument for continental integration. The organization's economic programme, authored by economist Otto Deutsch, listed three imminent threats to the European economy: 'the danger of a collapse of all industries' without close access to raw materials; 'the danger of a complete impoverishment of the European population because of increasing unemployment, decreasing production, capital export and indebtedness'; and 'the danger that the European economy in general will become completely dependent on North-American capital'.[23] As a remedy, Deutsch outlined an economic programme that would abolish trade barriers and economic imbalances such as those caused by the retribution payments forced on Germany by the Versailles Treaty. The programme also proposed a planned economy as well as a thorough 'Taylorization of the European industrial totality'. However, this would not suffice to catch up with the rapidly growing economies of the United States and the Soviet Union. They enjoyed the advantage of being able to organize their economies on a continental scale, making them self-sufficient for most raw materials and providing greater markets for the sale of their products. Accordingly, the Pan-European economic zone suggested by Deutsch also presupposed, as 'an indispensable supplement', 'the communal exploitation of the Pan-European colonies from an economic viewpoint'.[24]

Gradually, then, the economic perspective expanded into a geopolitical one, which touched the sensitive issue as to whether Europe would ever again attain its global influence. In this context we encounter the African continent, seen as a necessary condition for economic recovery and also as a sufficient reason for European

[22] Richard Coudenhove-Kalergi, 'Die europäische Nationalbewegung', *Paneuropa*, Vol. 4, No. 1, 1928, p. 8.
[23] Otto Deutsch, 'Paneuropäisches Wirtschaftsprogram', *Paneuropa*, Vol. 3, No. 1, 1927, p. 7.
[24] Ibid., pp. 13–14.

unification. Coudenhove-Kalergi and Deutsch argued for European unity by way of a united colonial effort in Africa. In their view, Africa was seen as a natural and necessary part of Europe's geopolitical sphere, a part that needed to be more strongly connected to Europe, and to be exploited by united European forces in order to turn its resources to full advantage. Indeed, just as African soldiers stationed on European territory were perceived as a shared nuisance that made Europeans close ranks, Africa returned as a common concern in the early plans for European unification, but in this case as a promise and possibility.

The Pan-European strategy designated Africa as 'Europe's plantation', a reservoir of agricultural produce, subsoil mineral resources and hydroelectric power. Moreover, it was promoted as the solution to Europe's demographic problems. It was widely agreed that Europe was overpopulated, an imbalance that could be resolved by the emigration and resettlement of surplus population in the 'empty' territory south of the Mediterranean. Coudenhove-Kalergi certainly spoke for the majority of Europe's political and intellectual elite as, in 1929, he pushed for a Pan-European colonial management of Africa and recounted what Africa offered: 'Africa could provide Europe with raw materials for its industry, nutrition for its population, land for its overpopulation, labour for its unemployed, and markets for its products'[25] (see Figures 2.1 and 2.2). A few months later, *Paneuropa* published an essay by Alfred Zintgraf investigating the possibilities for white settlement in Africa and arguing for a first transfer to suitable areas of 650,000 European colonizers skilled in farming and forestry.[26]

Coudenhove-Kalergi's arguments for assimilating Africa converged into one big argument for the unification of Europe. The common or synergetic exploitation of Africa was so unquestionably attractive and

---

[25] Richard Coudenhove-Kalergi, 'Afrika', *Paneuropa*, Vol. 5, No. 2, 1929, p. 3.

[26] Alfred Zintgraf, 'Die Besiedlungsfähigkeit Afrikas', *Paneuropa*, Vol. 5, No. 10, 1929, pp. 24–36. In subsequent issues, *Paneuropa* also maintained that parts of Africa should be turned into an asylum territory for Europe's unwanted Jewish population; see Spero [pseudonym], 'Notland für Juden in Afrika', *Paneuropa*, Vol. 11, No. 3, 1935, pp. 78–80.

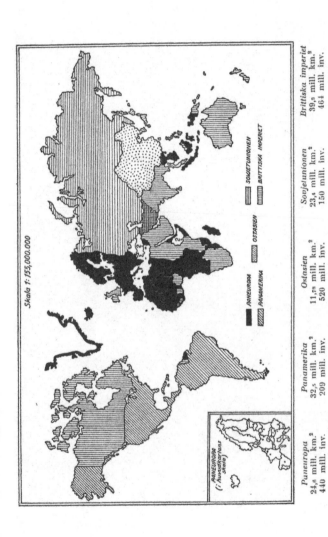

Figure 2.1 Official world map of the Pan-European movement, with Pan-Europe (black) consisting of continental Europe and its colonial possessions. Source: Richard Coudenhove-Kalergi, *Paneuropa*, Swedish edition (Stockholm: Bonniers, 1930). National Library of Sweden.

Figure 2.2 Cover of *Paneuropa*, February 1929, featuring Richard
Coudenhove-Kalergi's essay on Africa. Source: *Paneuropa*, Vol. 5, No. 2,
1929.

beneficial that it constituted in itself a reason for European states to make common cause. A geopolitical calculation based on two symbiotic benefits emerged: the new geopolitical sphere of a united Europe would be sustainable and prosperous thanks to its incorporation of Africa; and correspondingly, the bonds between once-antagonistic European states would be consolidated by the shared goal of developing Africa. The unification of Europe and a unified European effort to colonize Africa were two processes that presupposed one another. Africa could be developed only by Europe, and Europe could develop its fullest potential only through Africa. As Coudenhove-Kalergi proclaimed: 'The African problem thus brings us back to Europe. Africa cannot be made available, if Europe does not unite.'[27] In short, Europe's unification would start in Africa.

Contrary to a common understanding of the roots of today's European Union – in which Coudenhove-Kalergi sometimes is seen as a father figure of the founding fathers – Pan-Europe was a project not limited to Europe alone but included Africa except for its British possessions, although there were competing plans that included that region as well. The African possibility was repeatedly discussed in Coudenhove-Kalergi's journal and data about Africa's population and resources were included in the statistical overviews published in each issue. The joint European colonization of Africa was also highlighted in Article 13 of the draft for a Pan-European Pact of 1930, as one of the organization's defining priorities: 'All European citizens shall enjoy equal economic rights in the tropical colonies of Africa.'[28]

---

[27] Coudenhove-Kalergi, 'Afrika', p. 18.
[28] Richard Coudenhove-Kalergi, 'Entwurf für einen Paneuropäischen Pakt', *Paneuropa*, Vol. 6, No. 5, 1930, p. 152. In comments to this paragraph, Coudenhove-Kalergi repeats an argument put forth also in his essay 'Krieg oder Frieden?', *Paneuropa*, Vol. 3, No. 1, 1927, p. 3.

Empty space in the dark continent: Racial arguments

The strength of the Pan-European movement and idea was due to its resonance with dominant ideological and political tenets of interwar Europe, which also lay behind many related proposals for European integration and rejuvenation through a common colonial project. As we shall see, the general idea of an internationalization and supranationalization of colonialism in Africa was one of the least controversial and most popular foreign policy ideas of the interwar period, and proposals for its practical execution were developed by a wide range of European writers, academics, social planners, politicians and institutions.[29] What allows us to identify them as parts of a single discourse is, first, the fact that most stakeholders involved seemed to agree that *Eurafrica* was the proper name and concept that would put the European star back in the ascendant.[30]

Second, all these initiatives regarded Eurafrica as a project of both inter-continental and intra-continental integration, and it was the latter by virtue of being the former, building bonds of collaboration between European states precisely by fusing Europe and Africa into

---

[29] A full inventory of these writings has not yet been made and will have to wait for another occasion. Important steps were taken by Charles-Robert Ageron, 'L'Idée d'Eurafrique et le débat colonial franco-allemand de l'entre-deux-guerres', *Revue d'histoire moderne et contemporaine*, Vol. 22, July–September 1975, pp. 446–75; and Étienne Deschamps, 'Quelle Afrique pour une Europe unie? L'Idée d'Eurafrique à l'aube des années trentes', in *Penser l'Europe à l'aube des années trentes: Quelques contributions belges*, Michel Dumoulin (ed.), Université de Louvain, Recueil de travaux d'histoire et philologie, (Brussels: Éditions Nauwelaerts, 1995), pp. 95–150.

[30] The notion of Eurafrica was so prevalent at the time that it is difficult to find out who first introduced it in discourses on politics and international relations. According to Charles-Robert Ageron's seminal essay on the topic, Coudenhove-Kalergi was 'the incontestable inventor of the idea of Eurafrica' (Ageron, 'L'Idée d'Eurafrique et le débat colonial franco-allemand de l'entre-deux-guerres', p. 450). However, the concept was derived from anthropology and ethnology, especially the works of Italian anthropologist Giuseppe Sergi. Basing his theory on physical anthropology, Sergi rejected the idea that the peoples of Europe were of Aryan or Caucasian descent, but argued that Europe's population originated in Africa. There was thus one single 'Eurafrican species' with similar cranial features, which was then subdivided into three 'races': the Nordic, the Mediterranean and the African, all of them part of a Eurafrican totality. See Giuseppe Sergi, *The Mediterranean Race: A Study of the Origin of European Peoples* (London: Walter Scott, 1901), pp. 247–65.

a single and cohesive geopolitical entity, to the presumed benefit of both. This is also to say that the Eurafrican project was promoted as a new and higher form of colonialism. All adherents agreed that this would be a colonialism not governed by nationalistic greed, but by the true ideals of European civilization. One of Eurafrica's main advocates in France, Eugène Guernier, asserted in his book *L'Afrique: Champ d'expansion de l'Europe* (1933; Africa: Area of European Expansion), that '[t]oday's colonization is the synthesis of a moral and highly civilizing endeavour: the gradual elevation of the standing of life of the non-developed races, and the no less human endeavour to continuously maintain, or even improve the conditions of life of an industrious Europe.'[31]

In this view, old imperialism had been characterized by nationalist competition for overseas possessions. In Africa, this had been set off in the late 1870s by the attempt of King Leopold of Belgium to lay hold of the waterways into the Congo region. Leopold's quest for the riches of Africa's interior, which he rather successfully secured by relying on the ruthless methods of Henry Morton Stanley, started a European race for African riches that, at the beginning of the 1880s, became a major threat to international peace and stability. It was at this point that German chancellor Otto von Bismarck organized the so-called Congo Conference, at the urgent call of Portugal, which saw many of its long-established trading posts along Africa's coastline threatened by the scramble. What has gone down in history as the Berlin Conference of 1884–5 established the principles for European activities in Africa. As Obadiah Mailafia puts it, the conference in Bismarck's Berlin palace, attended by envoys of fourteen signatory European states, was 'the first true act of European cooperation in Africa.'[32]

The Berlin Conference did not actually carve up the African

---

[31] Eugène L. Guernier, *L'Afrique: Champ d'expansion de l'Europe* (Paris: Armand Colin, 1933), p. vii. Guernier observed that this new Eurafrican colonialism was already in the making, for instance, in the International Colonial Exposition in Paris in 1931 and the development of North Africa by French colonial administrator Hubert Lyautey.

[32] Obadiah Mailafia, *Europe and Economic Reform in Africa: Structural Adjustment and Economic Diplomacy* (London and New York: Routledge, 1997), p. 37.

continent into a number of European colonies, as is commonly believed.[33] Apart from granting the Congo Free State to Leopold, and ascertaining the right of free trade on the Congo and Niger Rivers and in territory stretching from the Congo State to Lake Nyasa and south of the 5th latitude, the Berlin Conference's most crucial result was the so-called 'Principle of Effective Occupation'. As stipulated by this principle, colonies could be claimed only by those who effectively possessed them, meaning there had to be in place treaties with local chieftains, active administrative presence and economic activities. The principle of effective occupation only worked to accelerate the scramble, however, as European powers now rushed to occupy land and subdue native populations, forcing their leaders to accept treaties that delegated power and control to the Europeans. Within a few years, the whole of Africa – with the exception of Ethiopia, South Africa and Liberia – was in colonial European hands.

The scramble was carried out under the pretext of abolishing slavery and introducing civilization in Africa – what in France was called 'the civilizing mission' (*la mission civilisatrice*) and in Britain, after Rudyard Kipling's famous poem, 'The White Man's Burden'. In this context, Africa was, on the one hand, construed as an empty continent, a *terra nullius*, or as the still-white areas on the map that so irresistibly attracts the main character in Joseph Conrad's canonical novel about the scramble, *Heart of Darkness*. Already in 1879, French writer Victor Hugo, in a famous address, exhorted his compatriots to capture the empty spaces. 'To remake a new Africa, to make the old Africa accessible to civilization, that is the problem. Europe will solve it. Go, you peoples! Grab for yourselves that land! Take it! To whom? To nobody. God gives land to men, God offers Africa to Europe. Take it!'[34]

However, on the other hand, Europeans described Africa not as empty but as submerged in pre-historical darkness. It was construed as

---

[33] See further Wm. Roger Louis, *Ends of British Imperialism: The Scramble for Empire, Suez and Decolonization* (London: I. B. Tauris, 2006), pp. 75–126.

[34] Victor Hugo, 'Discours sur l'Afrique du 18 mai 1879', *Actes et paroles. Depuis l'exil*, Vol. 2 (Paris: Nelson, without date), p. 133.

'the dark continent' – a figure of speech and a mode of thinking that remained pervasive throughout the following decades, as European nations would seek a new compact to cooperate with one another in developing, civilizing, or, in one word, *enlightening* the African continent and the African soul. A commonplace idea, so obviously true that it merited neither reflection nor scrutiny, the myth of the dark continent has been one of the most robust components of what may be called the *colonial archive* – that is, a set of ideas, narratives and regimes of truth that, for a long time, have sustained Europe's hegemonic position in the world and over Africa in particular.[35]

The myth of the dark continent was thus a basic precondition of the discourse that was evoked as soon as Eurafrican integration was at stake. Based on scientific racism and social Darwinism, it situated Africa and Europe at the opposite ends of an evolutionary axis from primitivism to modernity in a way that made it self-evident to everybody that one part was superior to the other. Hence also the unquestioned idea that the inferior part was helped, if placed under the superior's colonial tutelage. Although the Eurafrican project presented itself as a 'new' form of colonialism, its mode of political dominance and doctrine of evolutionism were thus unreformed. According to Guernier, Coudenhove-Kalergi and other Eurafricanists, Europe offered to Africa morality, culture and civilization. Africa offered Europe raw materials, territory, resources and opportunities for geopolitical expansion. Precisely because of this complementarity, both continents stood to gain from a thorough unification. However, while Guernier asserted that Europe and Africa are two halves, helpless on their own but in combination forming a viable whole, he was also careful to point out that there was no symmetry between them, much less any equality. 'Africa is the only continent without history', he stated,

---

[35] On the origins and transformations of this myth, see Patrick Brantlinger, 'Victorians and Africans: The genealogy of the myth of the dark continent', in Henry Louis Gates, Jr. (ed.), *'Race,' Writing, and Difference* (Chicago: The University of Chicago Press, 1985), pp. 185–222; on the colonial archive and its relation to evolutionist thinking in Western culture and scholarship, see V. Y. Mudimbe, *The Idea of Africa* (Bloomington: Indiana University Press, 1994), pp. 1–37.

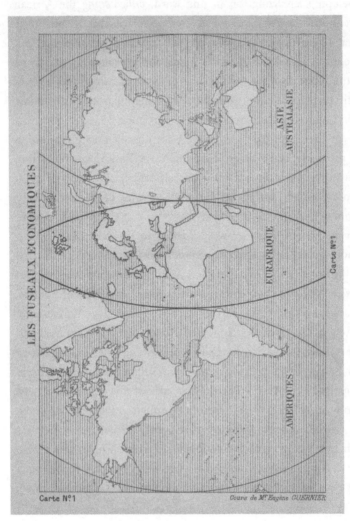

Figure 2.3 Cartographic representation of the three main geopolitical spheres, with Eurafrica at the centre. Source: Eugène Guernier, *L'Afrique et l'Europe: Atlas* (Paris: Centre de documentation universitaire, 1942).

after which he went on to suggest how Europeans could bring Africa out of its primitive and desolate state and help it enter the circle of human culture[36] (see Figure 2.3).

Italy's foremost Eurafricanist, Paolo Orsini di Camerota, presented an interesting variant of the same argument: 'Eurafrica is a figurative synthesis of the two fraternal continents, whose geographical umbilical cord are the Pillars of Hercules; it is a transfusion of blood from a sick continent to a healthy one'[37] (see Figure 2.4). It is an odd sentence, not just because of the strange metaphor that turns the Gibraltar Straits into an umbilical cord or the nonsensical logic (why a blood transfusion from a sick body to a healthy one?), but mainly because it describes Africa as young and strong while Europe is fatigued or even dying and in need of fresh blood. Apparently, the passage goes against the racial logic that underpins all other aspects of di Camerota's book. On the rhetorical level, then, Eurafrica could appear as a synthesis and even be presented as a blood relationship. In reality, however, a mixing of blood was out of the question. In his chapter on migration, di Camerota stressed that African immigration and habitation in Europe would be deleterious to Europe's 'hygiene and morality' (taking the alleged actions of black French troops in Europe as an example).[38] Africa, on the other hand, was described as depopulated and in need of new settlers. Orsini di Camerota was not a fascist but part of Italy's nationalist elite and, as such, a fellow traveller of Benito Mussolini's movement. He became a mouthpiece for what Italy's fascist leaders promoted as 'demographic imperialism': the resettlement of large numbers of unemployed lower-class Italians to Libya and other parts of North Africa, as well as Ethiopia and Eritrea[39] (see Figure 2.5). From 1939 to 1942 the programme was promoted and developed in the scholarly review *Geopolitica*, which counted Orsini di Camerota among its contributors.[40] Many of the same arguments were also expressed

---

[36] Guernier, *L'Afrique*, p. 55.
[37] Paolo d'Agostini Orsini di Camerota, *Eurafrica: L'Africa per l'Europa, l'Europa per l'Africa* (Rome: Paolo Cremonese, 1934), p. 4.
[38] Ibid., p. 106.
[39] Ibid., pp. 87–132, esp. p. 94.
[40] See Marco Antonsich, '*Geopolitica*: The "Geographical and Imperial Consciousness" of

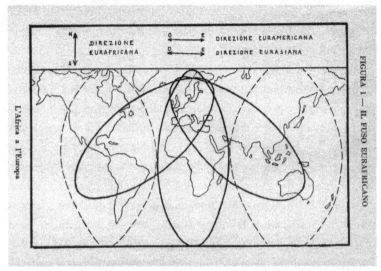

Figure 2.4 Cartographic representation of the three main geopolitical axes,
with the Eurafrican axis at the centre. Source: Paolo d'Agostini Orsini di
Camerota, *Eurafrica: L'Africa per l'Europa, l'Europa per l'Africa* (Rome:
Paolo Cremonese, 1934).

by Coudenhove-Kalergi, justifiably known as pacifist, internationalist
and anti-Nazi in European matters. However, on the topic of Africa he
comes across as a fully fledged biological racist, firmly believing in the
inherent difference between the black and white races: 'Europe's mission
in Africa is to bring light to this the darkest of continents. As long as
the black race is unable to develop and civilize its part of the earth, the
white race must do it.' Coudenhove-Kalergi added: 'Europe is Eurafrica's
head, Africa its body.'[41]

Interestingly, while Coudenhove-Kalergi urged Europeans to settle
in Africa and develop its resources, he also warned, like di Camerota,
that Europe must at all costs prevent 'that great numbers of black
workers and soldiers immigrate to Europe.'[42] Speaking of soldiers,
he was plausibly referring to France's disputed use of black troops

Fascist Italy', *Geopolitics*, Vol. 14, No. 2, 2009, pp. 256–77.
[41] Richard Coudenhove-Kalergi, 'Afrika', *Paneuropa* Vol. 5, No. 2, 1929, pp. 3, 5.
[42] Ibid., p. 5.

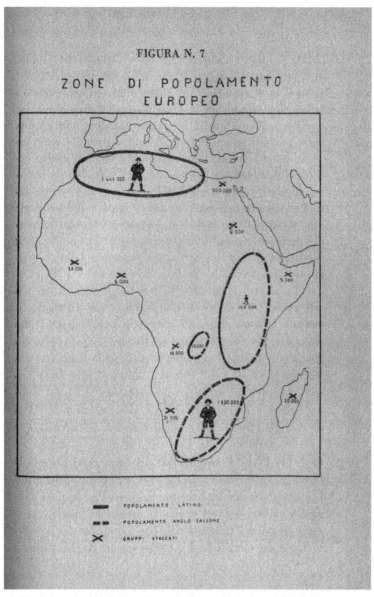

Figure 2.5 Map of Africa with marked areas designated for European settlers. Source: Paolo d'Agostini Orsini di Camerota, *Eurafrica: L'Africa per l'Europa, l'Europa per l'Africa* (Rome: Paolo Cremonese, 1934).

in its occupations of the Rhineland and the Ruhr region. For just as unthinkable as it was to have black soldiers operate as law-keepers in German towns ('Senegal Negroes' in the Goethe House), so it was self-evident to have European physicians and engineers developing Africa. And just as natural as it was to fear these African troops for introducing disease, criminality and vice, and for raping women and children, so it was natural to thank Europeans for bringing health and reason to Africa. What would become of Africa if Europe pulled out from it? Coudenhove-Kalergi asked. 'The answer is: chaos, anarchy, misery, war of all tribes against one another.'[43]

This is where we may locate the deep structure of the interwar discourse on Eurafrica. Illustrating the idea of colonial modernity in pure form, this discourse placed Europe and Africa at opposite ends of an evolutionary axis. Eurafrica then became the epitome of modernization, demonstrating the superiority of European culture by civilizing the dark races, and through this process also establishing at once the unity of Europe and the inferiority of Africa. Like the myth of the dark continent or racism itself, the idea of Eurafrica thus remained locked into the modern and colonial paradigm constituted by all the cases, accumulated in the colonial archive, of Europe's way of establishing its identity through its encounters with otherness. This explains why European politicians and writers could reject African presence in Europe as an absurdity with the same ease as they could affirm European presence in Africa as a necessity, without having to consider the possibility that their position might have been self-contradictory.

Africa as a necessity: Geopolitical arguments

What, then, was *new* in the Eurafrican project? Not the ideas of African inferiority and European superiority, and not the schemes of dominance and salvation evolving from this hierarchy. But what was

[43] Ibid., p. 6.

new, and what we discuss in this book, was the fact that colonialism after World War I emerged as an argument for European integration and, indeed, as a way of rescuing – not Africa, but Europe. Put differently, the colonial idea now attained geopolitical urgency as a path toward the unification of Europe and the establishment of a third geopolitical sphere able to balance a global system that had lost its centre and equilibrium. European expansion in Africa was no longer a matter of political and military dominance, economic wealth and missionary activities alone, but a way of reenergizing Europe and safeguarding its future existence as a social, economic, geopolitical, historical and racial formation.

Paolo Orsini di Camerota was thus onto something when asserting that Europe had become old and in desperate need of injections of fresh energy and blood. Apparently, Eurafrica could be conceived only after the spiritual shock, economic collapse and political destruction inflicted by the Great War, which is also to say that Eurafrica, like the connected idea of European integration itself, first emerged in a post-catastrophic atmosphere of anxiety and pessimism, when nationalist hubris was defeated and Europe was perceived as being in decline. 'Europe no longer rules in the world', wrote Spanish philosopher José Ortega y Gasset in 1929.[44] As demographer Lothrop Stoddard stated in an influential work of 1922, and again in 1935, World War I and the ensuing reorganization of world politics amounted to a collapse of the political universe, which 'in one cataclysmic event' had lost the sun around which the planets moved in cosmic harmony. That sun was the 'European comity of nations', which was now being replaced by terrifying geopolitical processes that Stoddard in the title of his book summed up as *The Rising Tide of Colour against White World-Supremacy*.[45] Similar views were expounded by a range of European thinkers of the interwar

---

[44] José Ortega y Gasset, *The Revolt of the Masses* (1930; New York: W. W. Norton, 1957), p. 129. Published in original as *La rebelión de las masas*, 1929.

[45] Lothrop Stoddard, *The Rising Tide of Colour against White World-Supremacy* (1922, reprint, Honolulu: University Press of the Pacific, 2003), pp. 198–221; and Stoddard, *The Clashing Tides of Colour* (New York and London: Charles Scribner's Sons, 1935), pp. 31–174.

period – from Oswald Spengler and Martin Heidegger to Edmund Husserl and Paul Valéry – and they were reflected in policy proposals and political initiatives that aimed to save the position of Europe and the white race by reigniting its dynamism and bolstering its growth through a more thorough integration of the resources under its control. If this did not happen, there would be disintegration and destruction.

In this vein, Swedish political scientist Rudolf Kjellén had, as early as 1914, anticipated the situation that would be loudly professed after World War I:

> The European federation has not yet been fully appreciated on the agenda, but it carries an old legacy; and what used to be a vague idea is now emerging as a necessity in the interest of Europe's self-preservation. Only through union [or amalgamation] can the present European states preserve their stamina towards rapidly growing adversaries, which already count their territories in double and their populations in triple digit million ranges while they at the same time are self-sufficient in food production. We can already witness the shadows of the American, Russian and Yellow perils being cast over our continent. Thus has Europe come under a pressure which in due time will win out over the mighty facts and traditions which still split Europe into several sovereign small parts.[46]

Kjellén was one of the founders of geopolitical analysis and the inventor of geopolitics as a concept. Early twentieth-century geopolitics under-pinned the discourse on European integration in the interwar period, and it constituted, along with the evolutionist paradigm, one of the conditions of possibility for the Eurafrican idea. Reflecting both the aggressive lust for imperial expansion and the nervous obsession with Europe's uncertain fate in a new global situation, geopolitics was a theory that envisioned the world order as a struggle between various polities.[47] It saw states as dynamic and transmutable, owning specific

[46] Rudolf Kjellén, *Samtidens stormakter* (Contemporary Great Powers), Vol. 1 of *Politiska handböcker*, p. 194. Translated into German as *Die Großmächte der Gegenwart* (Leipzig: Teubner, 1914).

[47] On the ambiguities of European geopolitics, see Michael Heffernan, 'Fin de siècle, fin du

quantities of energy and vitality that were often counted in population and production figures, which were subsequently translated into territorial reach. The 'vital force' of a certain polity would thus also determine what 'space' or 'scale' it needed in order to adequately develop its capacities. Political boundaries were unfixed and turned into elastic demarcations, shrinking or expanding depending on the force of a certain state and on the counter-force exerted by its neighbours and enemies. Unsurprisingly, the outcome of World War I, with the imperial expansion of Europe's nation states stumped by the emergence of what Kjellén called 'the American, Russian and Yellow perils', made European debate and politics ripe for geopolitical speculations and calculations as to the future of the comparatively small European states, which now had to look for new ways of ensuring the development and progress of their populations and economies. In this perspective, integration of Europe's productive capacities was an obvious alternative, as was a concerted effort to exploit the latent wealth of Africa. Indeed, this exploitation was in itself a reason for European states to coordinate and integrate their military, economic and administrative capacities.

Eurafrica was a full-blooded breed of this geopolitical paradigm. Precisely because Africa had been construed as a dark continent locked in prehistory – primitive, static and in geopolitical terms devoid of inherent expansive energies – it could now also be construed as Europe's future, as the means by which Europe would assert itself geopolitically in the form of Eurafrica, the term itself designating the far greater scale through which a set of tiny and fragmented polities would mutate into a viable imperial bloc.

This vision was embraced with particular warmth in Germany. As early as 1901, Friedrich Ratzel, Rudolf Kjellén's teacher, had invented the term *Lebensraum* (living space) to capture the spatial aspect through which the vital force of a particular people or nation manifested itself.

monde': On the origins of European geopolitics', in Klaus Dodds and David Atkinson (eds), *Geopolitical Traditions: A Century of Geopolitical Thought* (London and New York: Routledge, 2009), pp. 27–51.

Mediated mainly by the writings of Karl Ernst Haushofer, for whom Eurafrica formed a constitutive part of his blueprint for a new global geopolitics, the notions of living space and panregions became factors in German foreign policy in the 1920s, and, after the Nazi takeover in 1933, part and parcel of its main motivations.[48] Interestingly, Haushofer figured in Pan-European circles and his theory drew much inspiration from Coudenhove-Kalergi's ideas of panregions.[49] Although in this German discourse there was always a conflict between *Ostpolitik* and *Kolonialpolitik*, between taking space in Eastern Europe and regaining African colonies, all agreed that new 'space' must be obtained in order to ensure the survival of the German race. The reasons behind this perception are obvious enough, given Germany's considerable losses in territory and resources after World War I. The Versailles Treaty stripped it of 13 per cent of its territory, one-tenth of its population, 25 per cent of its coal deposits, 75 per cent of its iron and all of its colonies. This created among many Germans a sense that they had become what Hans Grimm, in a bestselling novel of 1926, called a 'people without space' (*Volk ohne Raum*); their needs, then, could be fulfilled only by a 'space without people' – that is, by Africa, as portrayed in Grimm's novel.[50]

For greater moral and material profit: Eurafrica in foreign policy

Bismarck had initiated the Berlin Conference that set out the principles for European action in Africa. What Germany had won in that contest, it had lost in World War I. Civil administrators and military contingents now lowered the German flag and evacuated their African

---

[48] For an outline of Haushofer's conception of Eurafrica, see Holger H. Herwig, 'Geopolitik: Haushofer, Hitler and Lebensraum', in Colin S. Gray and Geoffrey Sloan (eds), *Geopolitics, Geography and Strategy* (London: Frank Cass, 1999).

[49] John O'Loughlin and Herman van der Wusten, 'Political geography of panregions', *The Geographical Review*, Vol. 80, No. 1, 1990, p. 5.

[50] Hans Grimm, *Volk ohne Raum*, 2 vols (Munich: Langen-Müller, 1926).

dominions. However, this did not entail that German interests in Africa would diminish. On the contrary, in March 1919 the democratically elected parliament of the new Weimar republic demanded, 414 votes against 7, 'the restitution of Germany's colonial rights'. In the same year, Germany transformed its colonial administration into a fully fledged colonial ministry charged with the dual task of dismantling German sovereignty in its former colonies while also securing continuing German presence through other means.[51]

Throughout the 1920s, colonial lobbyists and interest groups multiplied, the most important being the German Colonial Society (Deutsche Kolonialgesellschaft), chaired by former colonial governors Theodor Seitz and Heinrich Schnee, with Konrad Adenauer as one of its vice-presidents. These influential circles regarded the arrangement that had deprived Germany of its overseas outlets and resources as a historical parenthesis during which 'our people's love of colonial possessions must be kept alive', as stated in the preface to *Das deutsche Kolonialbuch* (1926; The German Colonial Book), a luxurious album that celebrated Germany's colonial achievements and requested a continuation of its imperial story.[52] Economist Arthur Dix, for his part, turned to geopolitical analysis and propaganda to advocate a similar message, arguing that Germany's – and Europe's – future depended entirely on Africa: 'Germany needs, for vital reasons, a part of Africa – Africa needs Germany to take part in its world-economic and demographic construction and expansion'[53] (see Figures 2.6 and 2.7).

---

[51] This was not without success. Had there been 15,000 Germans living in German South-West Africa in 1914, they had grown to 30,000 by the 1930s, although the colony had passed into South African hands; and if there had been 73 companies entertaining business in Germany's African colonies in 1914, they were 85 by 1933, when Germany had lost them. See van Laak, *Über alles in der Welt*, p. 112.

[52] Hans Zache (ed.), *Das deutsche Kolonialbuch* (Berlin and Leipzig: Verlags Wilhelm Andermann, 1926), reprinted as *Die deutschen Kolonien in Wort und Bild* (Wiesbaden: Marix Verlag, 2004), pp. 5, 7.

[53] Arthur Dix, *Was geht uns Afrika an? Das heutige Afrika in Weltwirtschaft, Weltverkehr, Weltpolitik* (Berlin: Stilke, 1931), p. 107. See also Dix's *Weltkrise und Kolonialpolitik: Die Zukunft zweier Erdteile* (Berlin: Neff, 1932). On Dix's work and geopolitical arguments for colonialism in interwar Germany in general, see David Thomas Murphy, *The Heroic Earth: Geopolitical Thought in Weimar Germany, 1918–1933* (Kent: The Kent State University Press, 1997), pp. 91–8, 191–214.

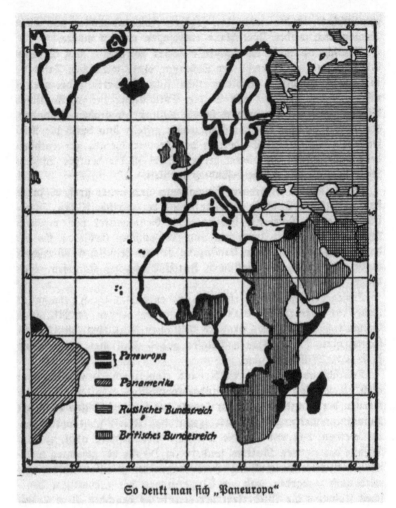

So denkt man sich „Paneuropa"

Figure 2.6 Map of Pan-Europe according to the German geopolitical
theorist Arthur Dix. Source: Arthur Dix, *Was geht uns Afrika an? Das
heutige Afrika in Weltwirtschaft, Weltverkehr, Weltpolitik* (Berlin: Stilke,
1931).

The colonial programme was aggressively pursued in the domestic
arena, drumming home a message of geopolitical injustice afflicting
Germans who – unlike the British, the French and the Belgians – had
no acres of tropical land or legions of coloured people at their feet. The

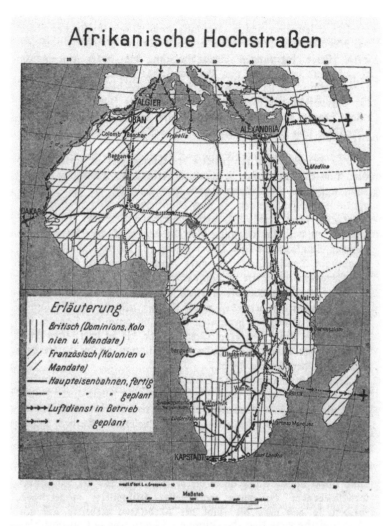

Figure 2.7 Map of Africa with projected highways and routes of transportation. Source: Arthur Dix, *Was geht uns Afrika an? Das heutige Afrika in Weltwirtschaft, Weltverkehr, Weltpolitik* (Berlin: Stilke, 1931).

German Colonial Society chose as its slogan 'Africa for Europe' (*Afrika für Europa*), which was also the title of a pamphlet written by Heinrich Schnee. Not only did the slogan endorse a joint European exploitation of Africa, but it also condemned French placement of African troops on European soil, which in the German view amounted to the opposite programme, an aggressive arousing of 'Africa against Europe'.[54] In *Mein Kampf*, Hitler had warned against the same scenario of Europe being swallowed by the French empire: 'an African state arising on European soil. [...] An immense self-contained area from the Rhine to the Congo, filled with a lower race gradually produced from continuous bastardization'.[55]

In the same spirit, Coudenhove-Kalergi argued that Germany, in return for its reparations payments, should be granted access to its former colonies, whereas Italy on similar terms should be entitled to 'Abyssinia'.[56] The German Social Democrats generally shared these opinions, while also favouring a more far-reaching internationalization of colonial rule. In his 1926 book *Die Vereinigten Staaten von Europa* socialist statistician Wladimir Woytinski argued that a 'United States of Europe' was necessary in order to save world peace and preserve Europe's global hegemony, and that the only agent capable of achieving this was the rising European proletariat. That Woytinski's geopolitical vision was premised on a Marxist analysis did not prevent it from being compatible with conservative and liberal programmes on the colonial issue. Woytinski proposed a complete internationalization of the colonial system. This would, to be sure, enable a regulation of colonial rule that would improve political rights and working conditions for the 'coloured workers'. Yet the main reason for an internationalization of colonialism was economic. 'A European economy without a colonial base is an impossibility', he asserted. Therefore, 'the colonies of the separate members of the Union must become the colonies of the Union as a whole'. Woytinski also shared the view that the colonial problem was not an obstacle to European unification but rather an argument in its favour.[57]

---

[54] Heinrich Schnee, *Afrika für Europa: die kolonial Schuldlüge* (Berlin: Kolonialverlag Sachers and Kuschel, 1924).

[55] Adolf Hitler, *Mein Kampf* (Boston: Houghton and Mifflin, 1943), p. 644.

[56] Richard Coudenhove-Kalergi, 'Reparationen und Kolonien', *Paneuropa*, Vol. 8, No. 1, 1932, p. 11.

[57] Wladimir Woytinski, *Die Vereinigten Staaten von Europa* (Berlin: J. H. W. Dietz Verlagsbuchhandlung, 1926), pp. 157–8.

Redeemed access to colonial territories also remained a priority of German foreign politics throughout the Weimar period. Foreign Minister Gustav Stresemann, reported to have said that the colonial possessions were part of the German soul, stated in 1925 that regained colonial possessions was the main aim – along with adjustments of Germany's eastern frontier – of German foreign policy.[58] He took repeated actions at the League of Nations to argue for Germany's re-entry into the club of colonial powers, and at the Locarno negotiations in 1925 he gained a principled assent of French foreign minister Aristide Briand, who stated that 'there was nobody who in any way wanted to deny this moral right of Germany [to own colonies]'.[59] Apart from fixing Germany's western border with Belgium and France, the Locarno negotiations opened the doors for Germany to the League of Nations and its Mandates Commission, although this was of little practical consequence since it did not entail any redistribution of the mandates as such. However, the talks at Locarno issued in a general atmosphere of appeasement that stimulated French–German collaboration of various kinds. An important initiative was the 'French–German committee for information and documentation', founded by Émile Mayrisch, owner of much of Luxembourg's steel industry, for the purpose of furthering French and German friendship and industrial capacity. This committee is an important part of the genealogy of European integration, as it prepared for many of the ideas that later went into the Schuman declaration, the European Coal and Steel Community and the EU itself.

This increasingly close collaboration between French and German capital automatically raised the matter of inter-European collaboration in Africa. In these discussions, German access to Africa was envisioned

---

[58] Gustav Stresemann, *Vermächtnis: der Nachlass in drei Bänden*, Vol. 2. (ed.) Henry Bernhard (Berlin: Ullstein, 1932), pp. 172, 296, 334–5.

[59] Stresemann, *Vermächtnis*, Vol. 2, pp. 196, 213. For Stresemann, this recognition meant that the allies officially gave up the colonial-guilt lie ('*die koloniale Schuldlüge*'), which in 1919 had justified depriving Germany of its colonies. See also Wolfe W. Schmokel, *Dream of Empire: German Colonialism, 1919–1945* (New Haven: Yale University Press, 1964), p. 83.

either by way of a straight return to Germany of the territories placed under the tutelage of the League of Nations, which in Germany was the favoured option, or through establishing a supranational or Pan-European colonial authority to which the League of Nations would transfer the mandate territories and ultimately all African colonies, which was the programme of the Pan-European organization. Included was also a third option whereby mandate and colonial territories, through negotiated concessions, would be transferred to co-European charter companies (with strong German components), the latter being proposed in 1926 by Hjalmar Schacht, president of the German *Reichsbank* and a tireless advocate of German colonialism in Europe's financial and political circles.[60] All three options made reference to the idea of Eurafrica, which in the late 1920s and early 1930s became a major geopolitical image and ideology, capturing the political imagination throughout the continent, as Eurafrica seemed to provide a remedy to the European crisis, the decline of the West or the destruction of white supremacy.

Schacht's approaches intensified in the depression era and throughout the 1930s, when he also became Minister of Finance in the Nazi government. Large parts of the colonial and business establishment in France reciprocated. Economic powerhouses such as the Mayrisch Committee, the Chamber of Commerce of Paris and the International Chamber of Commerce launched a range of innovative initiatives in order to get German companies involved in the exploitation of the African colonies. In all areas of extraction, production and trade, French capital saw the industrial and banking circles in Germany as attractive or even indispensable partners. As a consequence, from the late 1920s to the late 1930s, a number of French–German economic initiatives and agreements came into being with the explicit purpose of facilitating German access to African resources and of lobbying the governments in Paris, Brussels and London for a political settlement

---

[60] On Schacht's proposal, see Chantal Metzger, 'L'Allemagne et l'Eurafrique', in Marie-Thérèse Bitsch and Gérard Bossuat (eds), *L'Europe unie et l'Afrique: De l'idée d'Eurafrique à la convention de Lomé I* (Brussels: Bruylant, 2005), pp. 60–1.

that would compensate for the colonial losses suffered by Germany through the Treaty of Versailles.[61]

In France, Belgium and Britain, left-wing political leaders such as E. D. Morel (as mentioned above) and Jules Destrée had since the end of the war argued for an internationalization of the colonial system, which they saw as being in the interest of the colonized peoples and in line with US President Wilson's programme.[62] The League of Nations' mandates system was in part a realization of this demand, to the extent that it officially aimed to assist the colonized populations, although it mostly just served to shuffle colonial authority from Germany to Belgium, Britain and France. As the weaknesses of the mandates system became apparent and the economic situation in Europe grew worse, efforts to institutionalize inter-European collaboration in colonial Africa intensified. Insisting, throughout the interwar period, on the necessity of a United States of Europe, Destrée argued in 1929 that a joint exploitation of Africa would create the basis for a European federation and bring peace and prosperity. Destrée strongly supported the Pan-European organization and claimed that he had come up with the idea of a federal European administration of Africa already during World War I.[63]

A key figure on the French side was Albert Sarraut, member of the Pan-European organization, former governor of Indochina and switching between positions as minister of the colonies and minister of

---

[61] See Annie Lacroix-Riz, 'Les relations patronales franco-allemandes à propos de l'empire colonial dans les années 1930', in Hubert Bonin, Catherine Hodeir and Jean François Klein (eds), L'esprit économique imperial (1830–1970): Groupes de pression et réseaux du patronat colonial en France et dans l'empire (Paris: Publications de la SFHOM, 2008), pp. 527–46.

[62] See E. D. Morel's 1920 book The Black Man's Burden: The White Man in Africa from the Fifteenth Century to World War I (reprint, New York: Monthly Review Press, 1969), which argued for the establishment of an international zone in tropical Africa, governed directly by the League of Nations, protecting the African populations from European militarism and capitalism and thus also preempting one of the causes of conflict between Europe's imperial nations. Morel began developing the same argument already in a book published in 1917: Africa and the Peace of Europe (London: National Labour Press, 1917).

[63] Jules Destrée, 'L'Afrique, colonie européenne', in Pour en finir avec la guerre (Brussels: Eglantine, 1931), pp. 49–52.

the navy between 1920 and 1934, after which he became prime minister. He was France's most influential and ardent colonial ideologue, arguing that Europe and the white man were destined to conquer and colonize in the name of human values and solidarity. In 1921, Sarraut proposed to his parliament a plan for long-term investments in infrastructure in the African colonies. More farsighted than others, he argued that such investments would prepare for the decolonization of the overseas territories while at the same time ensuring that they would be kept under French and European influence; history would catch up with Sarraut only in the late 1950s, as the European Economic Community would make colonial arrangements similar to what he proposed. At the time, however, the French Parliament found Sarraut's plan too costly. Sarraut then started to press for what he called 'Eurafrican cooperation', envisioning a thorough Europeanization of colonial Africa, managed by a secretary general who would be reporting to a board of trustees assigned by the governments of interested European states. In his book *Grandeur et servitude coloniales* (1931) Sarraut, explicitly referring to Lothrop Stoddard, wrote that a Eurafrican arrangement was necessary in order to save Europe from 'the rising tide of coloured races' that posed a threefold threat to Europe's world supremacy: loss of economic markets, armed insurrections and ethnic degeneration due to racial mixing.[64] For this purpose, Germany should be given colonial concessions and the noble *mission civilisatrice* be reformed so as to withstand narrow national self-interests.[65]

A stronger proposal along the same lines, albeit with less political leverage, was in the same year put forward by Georges Valois, who drafted a Eurafrican ten-year plan which, as the title made clear, would turn Africa into a 'European construction site' (*Afrique, chantier de l'Europe*), just as Eugène Guernier, as mentioned, wanted to turn Africa into a 'field for European expansion.'[66]

[64] Albert Sarraut, *Grandeur et servitudes colonials* (1931; new edn, Paris: L'Harmattan, 2011), pp. 143–89.
[65] See Yves Montarsolo, 'Albert Sarraut et l'idée d'Eurafrique', in *L'Europe unie et Afrique*, pp. 77–95.
[66] Georges Valois, *L'Afrique, chantier de l'Europe*, Cahiers bleues, No. 111 (Paris: Librairie

These ideas were transformed into political initiatives through French actions within the League of Nations, the International Labour Organization (ILO) and related channels. In 1931 the ILO was charged with the task of examining possible solutions to unemployment in Europe. Its director Albert Thomas, French socialist and devoted Pan-Europeanist, visited Berlin to discuss the matter with chancellor Heinrich Brüning, among others, after which he stated in an interview that 'Europe could be created only by attaching to it a common project for which all would work and from which all would benefit. This project could consist of a general infrastructural improvement [*équipement général*] of Europe and in a certain manner also of an improvement of Africa,' and he suggested that 'Germany could be linked to the development [*mise en valeur*] of North-Africa'.[67] Later in 1931, the assembly of the League of Nations assigned a committee to investigate possibilities for large infrastructural projects in 'European or extra-European territories'. For similar purposes, French leaders Aristide Briand and Pierre Laval met with Brüning and formed a 'Committee for French–German collaboration', the agenda of which included 'collaboration to further the development [*mise en valeur*] of France's African colonies'. At the congress of the French radical-socialist party in November 1931, Sarraut offered Italy and Germany participation in 'the development of the immense Africa, where Europe would find both a large source of prosperity and a partial solution to the problem of migration posed by its increasing population'.[68]

Sarraut was seconded by former premier Joseph Caillaux who issued a set of quasi-official articles and notes, arguing for a Eurafrican solution to the economic crisis. 'The dark continent is called upon to extend and economically support the ancient continent', Caillaux stated in 1931, partly repeating a succinct formula he had coined the year before: 'Europe supported by Africa; Europe reconciled by Africa'.[69]

Valois, 1931); *Note sur L'Afrique, chantier de l'Europe* (Brussels: Institut d'économie européenne, 1931).

[67] Quoted in Ageron, 'L'Idée d'Eurafrique', p. 460.
[68] Ibid., p. 463.
[69] Joseph Caillaux, *D'Agadir à la grande pénitance* (Paris: Flammarion, 1933), p. 125.

For a brief period, then, Eurafrica became an official foreign policy doctrine. A major force behind promoting the Eurafrican idea as a political proposal was the 1931 Great Colonial Exposition in Paris, at which all colonial powers were invited to display their colonial possessions, including native inhabitants (Britain declined the invitation, and Spain and Japan were also absent). The enormously successful exposition in the Vincennes forest offered millions of visitors a Sunday walk through a miniature of a harmonious world order ruled by the European for the benefit of all. The exposition also generated streams of conferences, publications and debates on the future of the colonial system, all of which amounted to, in the words of Catherine Hodeir and Michel Pierre, a temporary 'University of Colonialism'.[70] Top-ranking French politicians argued that European collaboration at the exposition must now be followed by a European collaboration in the world. Paul Reynaud, Sarraut's successor as minister of colonies, explained that 'the colonial reality calls for a European collaboration for which France stands prepared'.[71] Investigating the personal and institutional networks branching out from the exposition, Étienne Deschamps concludes that the event constituted a beacon of colonial optimism in a time when European economy and culture were under severe stress.[72]

At the node of these networks, which to some extent replicated those of the Pan-European organization, was the charismatic presence of marshal Hubert Lyautey, former governor of Morocco and general commissioner of the exposition. Lyautey was regarded as France's colonial master planner, having already transformed the greater cities of Morocco into bi-continental enclaves and in many ways incarnating the Eurafrican idea. At the closing session of the exposition Lyautey argued for a 'Holy Alliance of the colonizing peoples' and for a 'union

---

[70] Catherine Hodeir and Michel Pierre, *L'Exposition coloniale de 1931* (Brussels: André Versaille, 2011), pp. 150–1.
[71] Quoted in Ageron, 'L'Idée d'Eurafrique', p. 457.
[72] Deschamps, 'Quelle Afrique', p. 118.

of all the colonizing nations in a policy of association for the greater moral and material profit of all'.[73]

Another important manifestation of European unity in colonial matters was the 1932 Volta Congress in Rome organized by Italy's Royal Academy. Opened by Mussolini himself, the congress devoted a full day of discussions to Central Africa and the mandates system, with lectures by German diplomat Albrecht Mendelssohn Bartholdy (another Pan-European) and Italian senator Camillo Manfroni, both asserting that Europeans urgently needed to collaborate with one another to make the most of their African colonies.[74]

The same year, Sarraut launched his project in the formal setting of the League of Nations conference on disarmament: 'The French delegation looks toward a future when it is possible that certain European nations which have no colonies may collaborate with colonial nations for the realization of a great work: the development of immense continents like Africa, which are spacious enough to attract the collaborative labour of all European peoples.'[75] In the subsequent negotiations that led to the Four-Power Pact between France, Britain, Germany and Italy, Édouard Daladier, who was prime minister, and Sarraut, having returned as minister of colonies, flaunted their Eurafrican card as a possible path toward future joint European initiatives. As Daladier stated at the time of the negotiations: 'Our country generously offers an opening for others to cooperate in the projects that it is carrying out in Africa.'[76] As we shall see in the next chapter, such initiatives to launch colonial cooperation schemes in Africa, including 'offers' to have also the non-colonial states in Western Europe participate, were to recur after World War II.

By this time, however, the Eurafrican plan of the French government was stuck in a dilemma. Sarraut and Daladier were on the one hand

---

[73] Quoted in Patricia Morton, *Hybrid Modernities: Architecture and Representation at the 1931 Colonial Exposition, Paris* (Cambridge: The MIT Press, 2000), p. 314.

[74] Deschamps, 'Quelle Afrique', p. 105. Orsini di Camerota stressed the importance of the Volta Congress for establishing Eurafrican ideas in Italy (*Eurafrica*, pp. 13–17). A sequel to this congress was held in 1938, at that time entirely devoted to Africa but less interested in European collaboration than in promoting Italian imperialism.

[75] Quoted in Ageron, 'L'Idée d'Eurafrique', p. 465.

[76] Quoted in Montarsolo, 'Albert Sarraut', p. 83.

held back by a domestic colonial *patronat* that rejected the idea of sharing colonial lands with other nations. On the other hand, they were pressed by Italian and German leaders, who greeted such initiatives as an invitation to step up their demands for African space – Italy wanted Ethiopia, Germany its former colonies or at least a substantial piece of Central Africa. Sarraut apparently resolved the situation by proposing what Ageron describes as an 'impossible conference'. He suggested, in the summer of 1933, that European states sit down together with independent African nations such as Egypt, Ethiopia and South Africa, to draft a general plan for Africa's development. According to Sarraut's agenda, European states should be invited to contribute labour, skills, knowledge and capital to African development, while the rights of sovereignty should remain unchanged. The offer was of course unacceptable to Hitler and Mussolini, who could not stomach the idea of serving as labourers, investors or tradesmen in French, Portuguese or Belgian colonies, and this on the same terms as Egyptians or Ethiopians, the latter already designated as Italy's prey.

Sarraut's 'trial balloon', as *The New York Times* put it in April 1934, was thus deflated, and for some time Eurafrica disappeared from the political and diplomatic agenda. In public debate and discourse, however, Eurafrica prevailed – which is of course why *The New York Times* devoted a full-page article to the phenomenon: 'Europe Casts covetous eyes on Africa'. According to its author, Ferdinand Tuohy, Mussolini's Italy was eager to vie with France and Britain for a portion of the continent, and the Four-Power Pact, it was said, may well result in some realization of Sarraut's idea, 'operating side by side with a fresh sharing out of mandates. If so, pecuniary advantages might be held out to Spain and Portugal in return for the making over of their African possessions, especially Portuguese Angola, with which much could be done'.[77]

Although this forecast was wrong, work on Eurafrica continued in offices and formal or informal committees around Europe. Indeed, up

---

[77] 'Europe casts covetous eyes on Africa', *The New York Times*, 8 April 1934.

until 1937, as Anthony Adamthwaite shows, 'Euroafrica' or 'Colonial condominium schemes in Africa were the staple of Franco–German discussions'.[78] Yet, much of this was to result in proposals that were often too utopian to attract serious attention from politicians. From a historical point of view, however, these blueprints merit serious study because they illustrate the Eurafrican project and its underpinnings in its boldest version, and partly also because they are precursors of what was to come after Europeans had suffered yet another world war. Let us therefore briefly outline some of these utopian figurations of Eurafrica in the 1930s.

Damming the Mediterranean: Eurafrica as utopia

At the fourth congress of the Pan-European Union, held in Vienna in May 1935, Max Grünewald, philosopher and rabbi of Mannheim, presented a commissioned report entitled 'Africa and the Problem of Emigration'. The report addressed the most pressing concern in Europe of that period, the twelve-million-strong 'surplus population' for which no employment could be imagined within the foreseeable future. Grünewald's solution was straightforward. A million or so Europeans should, annually, be offered the possibility to settle in Africa.[79] As a modification of and supplement to Grünewald's plan, Pan-European delegate and engineer Artur Biber showed statistics in favour of the establishment of a 'New Europe' in Africa, to be placed under the authority of the League of Nations, populated by three million unemployed Europeans – out of the twelve-million total – and furnished by an investment fund amounting to 1.8 billion Swiss francs, to be provided on loan by all European states interested in supporting the colony by moving part of its surplus population

---

[78] Anthony Adamthwaite, *Grandeur and Misery: France's bid for power in Europe 1914–1940* (London: Arnold, 1995), p. 148.
[79] Max Grünewald, 'Afrika und das Emigrantenproblem', *Paneuropa*, Vol. 11, Nos. 6–8, 1935, pp. 230–2.

southward.[80] Grünewald ended his report by quoting Coudenhove-Kalergi: 'To save Africa for Europe, is to save Europe by way of Africa.'

In 1935, *Paneuropa* also translated and published sections of Guernier's *Afrique: Champ d'expansion de l'Europe*, which began with a fifty-page survey of world migration over the past century. For each European country, Guernier introduced an abundance of demographic data – nativity and mortality rates, unemployment, social stratification, internal and external migration, among others; and for each country he reached the same apparently irrefutable conclusion. Italy, for example, 'will again find itself before the necessity to imagine a way of securing the livelihood of its annual nativity surplus amounting to 455,000 people, a great part of whom, no longer able to cross either the Atlantic, or the Alps, or to live on native territory where the human density has become too high, should start looking toward Africa.'[81]

The problem, as Guernier saw it, was that no single European state owned the resources to organize and finance the required settlements. Therefore, European cooperation was necessary. Guernier suggested a three-step strategy. First, the European states should select the best and brightest of its elite and send them to Africa to draw up concrete plans and projects of development. These elites would then prepare the way for the '*troupes de choc*: engineers, builders, entrepreneurs and builders, who, in providing Africa with its material necessities, will allow the already evolved parts of the indigenous races to improve their standard of living, while at the same time the colonizers arriving from the four corners of Europe will start developing the African land, in order to constitute a complete economic cycle marked by harmony of production and consumption'.[82] Once this new Eurafrican order was set in place, mass-migration of Europeans at an annual rate of

[80] Artur Biber, 'Die Bekämpfung der technolo'gischen Arbeitslosigkeit durch Kolonisation', *Paneuropa*, Vol. 11, Nos. 6–8, 1935, pp. 232–3. Cf. Antoine Fleury, 'Paneurope et l'Afrique', in *L'Europe unie et l'Afrique*, p. 51.

[81] See E. L. Guernier, 'Afrika als Kolonisationsland', *Paneuropa*, Vol. 11, No. 1, 1935, pp. 7–11.

[82] Guernier, *L'Afrique*, p. 266.

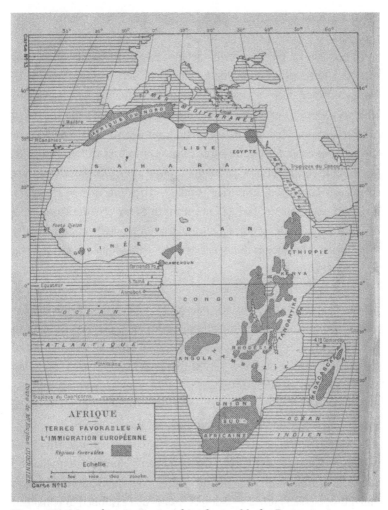

Figure 2.8 Map of territories in Africa favourable for European immigration. Source: Eugène Guernier, *L'Afrique et l'Europe: Atlas* (Paris: Centre de documentation universitaire, 1942).

500,000 would follow, totalling, in thirty to fifty years, twenty million individuals.[83]

In later works, Guernier made detailed maps displaying which areas of Africa were most favourable for European settlers (see Figure 2.8). He also delved deep into political economy, showing how a 'responsible' exploitation of African raw materials along with the increased productivity enabled by key infrastructural investments would cover the start-up costs for relocating such huge numbers of Europeans. In Guernier's work, then, the three main motivations for Eurafrica were seamlessly combined. Eurafrica entailed extraction of raw materials, large-scale settlement of white Europeans in Africa and the ascendance of a third economic, political, cultural and, ultimately, imperial entity – Eurafrica – balancing the Americas (the United States) and Eurasia (the Soviet Union).

This was also the utopian scenario of Orsini di Camerota's *Eurafrica*, in spirit and content closely related to Guernier's manifesto. As mentioned already, these utopian blueprints were far too visionary to be translated into political actions. Still, they serve as testimonials of the cultural atmosphere in a period that understood itself as standing in the twilight of both colonialism and European civilization, and which therefore fantasized about a new dawn, southward geographical expansion, tropical riches and technological leaps.

The most outrageous of such representations of Eurafrica was no doubt German architect Herman Sörgel's blueprint for what he called Atlantropa, which he found superior to Coudenhove-Kalergi's Pan-Europe (see Figure 2.9). Sörgel's Atlantropa exhibited in enhanced forms all the characteristics of the European idea of Eurafrica, while at the same time exaggerating all arguments made in its favour. Sörgel's basic idea was to dam up and contain the net inflow of water into the Mediterranean Sea. A great dam was to be built across the Gibraltar Strait and a network of huge hydroelectric plants at the outlets of all the great rivers flowing into the Mediterranean, the Nile, the Rhône, the

[83] Ibid., pp. 270–1.

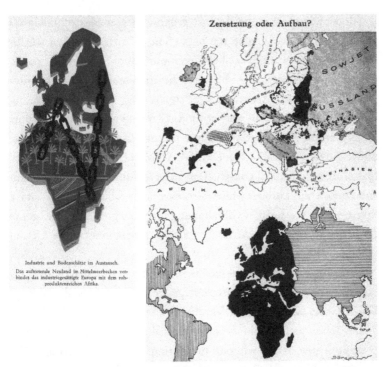

Figure 2.9 Cartographic representations of Atlantropa, as envisioned by Herman Sörgel. Left: the industrial riches of Europe are depicted as complementary to Africa's natural resources. Right: Europe must either construct a Eurafrican unity or face disintegration. Source: Herman Sörgel, *Atlantropa* (Munich: Piloty and Loehle, 1932).

Po, the Tiber, the Ebro, as well as the rivers going into the Black Sea, the Danube, the Dnepr and others. These immense technical works – on the same scale as, or greater than, Stalin's plan to turn Russia's major rivers towards the south – would then lower the sea level of the Mediterranean and also create a territorial bridge between Africa and Europe. Sörgel's idea was to have the sea level decrease by 0.8 metres per year for more than one hundred years, until it would be 200 metres lower than today in the eastern part of the Mediterranean, and 100 metres lower in the western part, the two parts being separated by yet another dam – the Messina dam – stretching from Sicily to Tripoli.

Sörgel was among the first to propose large-scale technological projects that would enable the extraction of Africa's natural wealth while at the same time facilitate communication – railways, roads, telephony and electricity – between the continents. Such infrastructural designs would remain a vital concern for Eurafrican planning up until the early 1960s and beyond. Glancing ahead, we may thus discern an echo of Sörgel's plan in a prestigious engineering venture, under the supervision of French EURATOM president Louis Armand, that proposed, in 1958, constructing a channel tunnel between Britain and continental Europe, which 'also eventually would link up with a tunnel under the Strait of Gibraltar and form the great Eurafrica route connecting Europe with Africa [...] for the development of the African continent'.[84]

Returning to Sörgel, he argued that Atlantropa promised enormous benefits. The project would create large areas of new agricultural land. For instance, to the west of Palestine a stretch of land would rise out of the waters and would be made available to Jewish settlers, thus creating a new Israel without swallowing Palestinian territory. The project would provide Europe with more energy than it could use, and the surplus energy would be used to pump water from the Congo river, led by way of a system of channels through Lake Tchad, in order to irrigate the Sahara, which would thus become agricultural land. Across the new territorial connection between the continents, Africa's natural resources would flow into Europe, while Europe's surplus population would move into and colonize the African continent. The crowning infrastructural accomplishment would be a railroad connecting Berlin and Cape Town and a new capital city of Atlantropa built on new land rising out of the Mediterranean.

But the decisive advantage for Sörgel was that Atlantropa would also create a new European citizen, a superior human being, who would evolve through the consecutive generations' concerted toil and effort to construct their new world. Recall that the realization of

[84] 'English Channel Tunnel spurred', *Christian Science Monitor*, 31 March 1958.

Atlantropa would take hundreds of years, during which all European thought and culture would be profoundly transformed by the great common project, much as the building of communism in Russia would, according to Lenin and Stalin, create a new Soviet human being. Of course, the African people also figured in the equation, as a vast supply of labour for Europe's industry and agriculture. That the sovereignty over the newly created continent was on the side of Europe was signalled by its name. The unified territories of Africa and Europe would be called 'Atlantropa'. Sörgel's technological vision was in his own view the only possible solution to the problems facing Europe: unemployment, overpopulation, lack of energy and natural resources. At one stroke, these difficulties would be resolved. Indeed, the future of the West depended on the project, Sörgel maintained: 'Either: the fall of the West (*Untergang des Abendlandes*), or: Atlantropa as a turning point and new goal.'[85]

Eurafrican appeasement

In the 1930s, Herman Sörgel promoted his project by copying the strategy of Coudenhove-Kalergi, starting an organization of supporters and even launching a political party. Under the subsequent Nazi dictatorship, he sought to convince the leaders of Germany and Italy of the necessity and practicability of his project. However, Mussolini was not enthusiastic about the idea of having Italy's ports dried up. His regime rather relied on geopolitical schemes developed by political geographers collaborating in the journal *Geopolitica*, where Central and Eastern North Africa was claimed as Italy's 'spazio vitale' and the Mediterranean as its 'mare nostrum'. Interestingly, despite the fascist taint of the Italian discourse on Eurafrica, the

---

[85] Herman Sörgel, *Atlantropa* (Munich: Piloty und Loehle; Zürich: Fretz und Wasmuth, 1932), p. 106. For an anlysis of Sörgel's project, see Alexander Gall, *Das Atlantropa-Projekt: Die Geschichte einer gescheiterten Vision. Herman Sörgel und die Absenkung des Mittelmeers* (Frankfurt am Main: Campus Verlag, 1998).

conception itself would remain in place in the post-fascist 1950s and 1960s.[86] (As we shall see, it was easily reactivated in the postwar European integration process.)

Hitler, for his part, had little interest in the all-European collaboration that Sörgel suggested. He devised his own imperial master plan, which presupposed German dominance. Instead of choosing between *Ostpolitik* and *Kolonialpolitik*, Hitler's regime went for both. East Europe would provide *Lebensraum* in the proper sense – that is, areas for German settlement; Africa would serve as a source of natural resources. In a 1936 address, Hitler officially demanded for the first time the restitution of all German colonies, while Schacht, his finance minister, shuttled between Berlin and Paris to negotiate the same programme.

Although many leaders in France and Britain regarded this as an attractive alternative from an economic point of view, they found it geopolitically and strategically dangerous to allow Hitler sovereignty on African territory. Instead, France continued to seek political appeasement through economic concessions, the assumption being that this would strengthen the Nazi regime's moderate arm, such as Schacht and the economic elite, who wanted to cap rearmament and bring Germany into a Western comity of nations. The measures culminated in 1937 when France (under the left-wing Popular Front) and Germany (under the Nazis) signed the 'July 10 Commercial Accords', in which they reciprocally granted one another Most-Favoured Nation Principle, and which also made Germany most-favoured nation in all French colonies as well as in France's mandate areas, Togo and Cameroon. Right up to the start of the war, this economic small-scale Eurafrican arrangement boosted German industry, now with cheaper access to colonial resources, as well as France's colonial economy, which found greater markets.[87] During the Vichy government, this integration of the French Empire and the German *Reich* would be taken

---

[86] Antonsich, '*Geopolitica*', pp. 267–77.
[87] Gordon Dutter, 'Doing business with the Nazis: French economic relations with Germany under the Popular Front', *Journal of Modern History*, Vol. 63, No. 2, 1991, pp. 296–326.

further and evolve into what many French conservatives envisioned as a Eurafrican entity.[88]

The last political effort to revive the Eurafrican idea before World War II was apparently the British prime minister Neville Chamberlain's plan to involve Germany in a grand joint scheme involving Central Africa, which was introduced to Hitler by Britain's ambassador Nevile Henderson in the spring of 1938. 'As before the First World War,' Wm. Roger Louis has summarized this intervention, 'British statesmen attempted to resolve Europe's troubles by an African settlement.'[89] In return for limiting its aggressive claims on Czechoslovakia and Austria, Germany was offered access to a large part of Central Africa, which was to be placed under an international administration with a strong German component. For Chamberlain, the plan intended to open 'an entirely new chapter in the history of African colonial development to be introduced and accepted by the general agreement of the Powers in Africa'.[90] The allied powers thus hoped to barter African territories for the sake of peace in Europe, without concern, of course, for the African populations that would be thrown under Hitler's dictatorship.[91] Rumours of colonial appeasement abounded and as late as 29 October 1938 *The New York Times* reported:

> As a result of reports abroad – particularly Great Britain – that former German colonies soon will be returned to the Reich as part of the general European appeasement sought by Prime Minister Neville Chamberlain and Premier Edouard Daladier, stocks of German shipping concerns and enterprises in the former colonies staged today a sensational boom on the Boerse. Both the gains and the turnover exceeded anything known in the market in recent years.[92]

[88] See Chantal Metzger, *L'empire colonial français dans la stratégie du Troisième Reich (1936-1945)* (Brussels: Peter Lang, 2002).

[89] Wm. Roger Louis, 'Colonial appeasement, 1936-1938', *Revue belge de philologie et d'histoire*, Vol. 49, No. 4, 1971, p. 1175.

[90] Quoted in ibid., p. 1186, from the Minutes of the Committee on Foreign Policy.

[91] Schmokel, *Dream of Empire*, pp. 116–21, 183–4.

[92] 'Stocks in Berlin, London and Paris: Reich shipping and colonial industries boom on reports of regaining possessions', *The New York Times*, 29 October 1938.

In the end though, Hitler rejected the offer. But 1938 also saw a rapid decline in France's appetite for colonial cooperation with Germany; by December opinion polls that just months prior had indicated a solid public support for colonial appeasement of Germany now gave at hand an even more solid rebuttal of this policy.[93]

But this did not mean that all had turned quiet on the Eurafrican appeasement front. Right up until the war broke out, the British labour politician, postwar foreign secretary and – as we shall see in the next chapter – strong Eurafrican advocate Ernest Bevin was hard at work arguing for a 'World Order' (as he termed it) that, through a grand collaborative project for the development of colonial Africa, would advance world peace, economies and living standards across the globe. As one of Bevin's biographers, Francis Williams, recalls, shortly before the war, Bevin made it clear that he:

> envisaged a great United Africa Authority to which all the Colonial Powers in Africa together with the United States should be invited to belong and membership in which should also be offered to Germany and Italy if they would alter their politics of international aggression. British, French and Belgian knowledge of Colonial administration, allied to American capital and the American genius for large scale development plus the technical and research skill of the Germans and the emigrants Italy desperately needed to send abroad could, he argued, turn the underdeveloped areas of Africa into one of the great treasure houses of the world with immense advantage to the status and standard of life of the native people.[94]

During the war itself, Eurafrica, colonial cooperation and appeasement would resume their importance and play an emblematic role in the various plans to integrate Vichy France's African territories into the Third Reich. Of course, these plans did not contain any prospect of a European integration on equal terms. The Nazi conception of Eurafrica usually entailed a redistribution of Britain's African

---

[93] Adamthwaite, *Grandeur and Misery*, p. 148.
[94] Francis Williams, *Ernest Bevin: Portrait of a Great Englishman* (London: Hutchinson, 1952), p. 209.

territories among the Axis powers after an expected victory.[95] For this reason, it diverges from the lineage that we are tracing in this book. Yet it is worth recalling the numerous press reports of the period, especially during the German–Italian campaigns in North Africa, which discussed Eurafrica as a guiding geopolitical vision of the Axis powers. According to *The New York Times* in October 1941, for instance, the German view of 'the future of Europe' included Africa since 'the two continents themselves [were seen as] inseparable, as indicated by the joint designation now in vogue: "Eurafrica"'.[96] Germany's Eurafrican scheme was to be built in close collaboration with fascist Italy and the French Vichy Republic. It was thus also, as we discuss further in the following chapter, a crucial ingredient in the Vichy administration's colonial outlook.

Africa was of course equally important for de Gaulle's Free France and its exiled representatives, many of whom found refuge in Africa with those few colonial administrations that remained loyal to the republic. As the war wore on and an allied victory drew near, the French Congo, Cameroon and Algeria were then turned into launching pads for the postwar French and European order. Indeed, as François Duchêne has it, 'Algiers in the second half of 1943 was a thriving seedbed of ideas for postwar policy'.[97] It was in Algiers, in 1943, that Etienne Hirsch – subsequently one of the negotiators of the European Coal and Steel Community and then President of EURATOM – found his colleague Jean Monnet 'deep in thought in front of a map of Europe laid out on his desk and striped with pencil lines'. As Duchêne quotes Hirsch's recollection, Monnet pointed to the Ruhr and Lorraine regions, noting 'that all the trouble came from that part of the world. It was from their coal and steel that Germany and France forged the instruments of war.' To nip future wars in the bud, therefore, Monnet went on to affirm the necessity

---

[95] Schmokel, *Dream of Empire*, pp. 129–36.

[96] 'Vichy is affected by Soviet losses', *The New York Times*, 16 October 1941.

[97] François Duchêne, *Jean Monnet: The First Statesman of Interdependence* (New York: W. W. Norton, 1994), p. 126.

to somehow 'extract this region from the two countries'.[98] It was also in Algiers in 1943 that René Mayer, at the time heading Free France's commercial fleet and later to become prime minister, successor to Monnet at the head of the ECSC and one of the most influential French officials in European affairs, pondered whether a postwar order in Europe might not have to be centred around an industrial 'Rhenish State' ('Etat Rhénan'), which, however, would have to 'be balanced by the agricultural production of France and the colonies of the federation'. Mayer predicted that this would also bring about 'a solution to the problems posed by the insufficient resourcing of the French colonies'.[99]

Among the fascist governments as well as among the allied states, Eurafrica thus remained a salient representation, and a guiding geopolitical concept, even during World War II. The future of Europe and the idea of European integration could at this point in time not be separated from the notion of some Eurafrican complementarity, upon which the future world order appeared to hinge.

Emerging counter-movements: Concluding remarks

Yet, to bring this into proper perspective, we must return to a topic raised at the beginning of this chapter, namely the colonial presence in the form of black and coloured troops fighting on European territory. If World War I's aftermath constituted the beginnings of Eurafrica, it was also the birth of the anticolonial struggle, in the sense that the 'Wilsonian moment' disappointed the colonized peoples that had been bold enough to expect that Wilson and his allies would make sure that national independence and sovereignty should also apply outside

---

[98] Ibid., p. 126.
[99] René Mayer, 'Un ensemble fédéral occidental: Note de René Mayer', in Gérard Bossuat (ed.), *D'Alger à Rome: Choix des documents* (Louvain-la-Neuve: Ciaco, 1989), pp. 48–9. The proposed 'Rhenish State', would, according to Mayer, consist of France, Germany, the Benelux and possibly also Spain and Italy.

continental Europe.[100] As Mark Mazower puts it, the Vietnamese, Indian and others' attempt to use this moment to bring an end to colonialism met with utter failure, thus leaving intact a perception among Europeans 'that took the durability of empire for granted; few, if any, African or Asian nationalist claims to independence seriously registered'.[101] Hence, for Eurafricanists, it was the USA and USSR that were projected as the chief rivals to Europe's global recovery during the interwar period. The anti-colonial movement would be relaunched in tandem with the formation of the UN in the immediate postwar era. This time, though, and despite many of the UN architects' designs to the contrary – that is, designs to have the UN serve imperial interests and so work in defence of the colonial world order – anti-colonialism proved more resilient and partly successful as India and other Asian colonies' rapid liberations were to prove.[102]

This was thus one competitor that the postwar era's relaunch of Eurafrica was up against. The other was, of course, the emerging Cold War order, an order that initially seemed to work in support of colonial liberation. The immediate postwar years would thus witness three currents that had all, in some rudimentary or ideational form, been present in the interwar years. Eventually, Eurafrica would be the first one of these currents to run out of steam. But for some fifteen years, between 1945 and the early 1960s, Eurafrica was a viable and successful project, one that provided postwar European integration with a purpose and role in the global geopolitical struggle that was set off at the end of World War II. Let us now turn our attention to these crucial years.

---

[100] Erez Manela, *The Wilsonian Moment: Self-Determination and the International Origins of Anticolonial Nationalism* (Oxford: Oxford University Press, 2007).
[101] Mark Mazower, *No Enchanted Palace: The End of Empire and the Ideological Origins of the United Nations* (Princeton: Princeton University Press, 2009), p. 23.
[102] For a full account of this suppressed history, see ibid.

3

Making Europe in Africa: The First Postwar Decade

Immediately after World War II the quest for European integration and unity would make a strong comeback. Equally immediately, though, this mission for unity would have to cope with a divided continent and the ignominious fact that Europe had come under the spell of a rapidly escalating conflict between what were now the world's two lone superpowers. It goes without saying, then, that the evolving Cold War and, with it, the demotion of a world order centred in Europe would function as a formative structure for the ideas and initiatives that drove (Western) European integration in the postwar era. But contrary to the impression given by the great majority of accounts within EU studies, this was not the only such formative framework. For while a war-ravaged and divided Europe was besieged by a superpower conflict largely out of its control, and while its various empires to the east were coming undone, Europeans continued to be in sole control of the African landmass and its enormous wealth of still largely untapped natural resources. Up until 1956, when the Treaty of Rome negotiations commenced, only five African countries (including South Africa and Egypt, where Britain still had troops stationed) had achieved independence. The remainder, which consisted of some 120 million people, was either under direct European colonial rule or indirectly governed by European states as Trust Territories of the United Nations. France and Britain were the main actors; but Belgium and Portugal also possessed considerable areas, whereas Italy and Spain, in particular, played minor roles.

In continuity with the ideational climate during the interwar period, these two formative structures (of superpower preeminence and Europe's African hegemony) would be revived as mutually consti-tuted in the postwar period. Echoing the Kalergian dictum, the gravity of the threat posed by the Soviet and American geopolitical clout would, post-1945, also be conceived as standing in direct proportion to Europe's ability, or inability, to make common cause over its African hinterland. In the minds of many postwar European statesmen, a squeeze from the East and West could be eased through Europe's North–South extension into a Eurafrican Third Force in world politics. Again, many asserted that it was through colonial cooperation, even integration, rather than going it alone, that the exhausted colonial powers in Western Europe were to infuse new energy into their terribly underfinanced empires and so redeem Europe's global stamina.

But for all the ideational continuity, the concrete international and global terrain onto which Eurafrica was to be relaunched had, of course, been radically altered as a result of World War II. Indeed, the starkly more acute sense of international weakness on the part of the Western European powers – a humiliating condition that leaders were to vent almost ad nauseam in the first postwar decade – became much more accentuated as Eurafrica's most potent and tenacious *raison d'être*. As we demonstrate here and in the following chapter, this radical transformation would also bring about a modification of Eurafrica's chief incentives and legitimizing claims. Most of all, it would moderate the utopian impulse and desire that had characterized many of the interwar plans for Eurafrica. As we also show, while Eurafrica clearly reflected a deep-seated ambition to preserve and re-establish pre-war forms of colonial domination, it also harboured a strategy and vision to both accommodate and proactively shape a new world order. As part of the latter, Eurafrica, or a joint European management of the colonial territories, was often sold as reforming, even transcending, traditional and increasingly ill-reputed colonial relations.

As already noted, the viability of the Eurafrican momentum largely rested on the fact that Western European powers, after the war, felt certain that they could remain in uncontested control of the African continent for the foreseeable future. Indeed, in 1945 the British Colonial

Office expected the sub-Saharan Empire to last into the twenty-first century.[1] This stood in diametrical contrast to the developments in Asia where commanding anti-colonial independence movements had already formed and struggles erupted well in advance of the war's end. This resulted in India and Pakistan gaining independence in 1947, followed a year later by Burma and Ceylon, at the same time as an emergency was declared in Malaya. The Netherlands' brutal suppression of Indonesian independence, first declared by Achmad Sukarno in 1945, was defeated in 1949, while France's equally atrocious war in Indochina – launched in 1946, as a result of Paris' refusal to accept Cambodia's, Laos' and Vietnam's independence declarations in 1945 – would ravage on for another five years.

These colonial conflicts co-existed with Asia's rapid transformation into a major theatre of the early Cold War, climaxing with the communist victory in China in 1949 and the Korean War shortly thereafter (1950–3). At the same time, developments in the Middle East and Iran were moving in a similar direction, with colonial and Cold War struggles often inextricably intertwined. Given Africa's (with the crucial exception of Egypt and North Africa in general) relative distance from this nexus of Cold War and anti-colonial struggles, many Europeans thus believed that Eurafrica – or any collaborative effort to reinforce Europe's African possessions – would serve to prevent the push for decolonization in Asia from gaining a foothold on the African continent. In so doing, this would also keep the superpowers at arm's length from African affairs, thereby preventing the Cold War logic from infiltrating Africa.

All these factors contributed significantly to Eurafrica's postwar momentum; they also help explain why the colonial question and

---

[1] Anthony Adamthwaite, 'Britain, France, the United States and Euro-Africa, 1945–1949', in Marie-Thérèse Bitsch and Gérard Bossuat (eds), *L'Europe unie et l'Afrique: De l'idée d'Eurafrique à la convention de Lomé I* (Brussels: Bruylant, 2005), p. 121. For more on this perception of sub-Saharan Africa, see Sally Marks, *The Ebbing of European Ascendancy: An International History of the World 1914–1945* (London: Bloomsbury Academic, 2002), p. 151; and Martin Shipway, *Decolonization and its Impact: A Comparative Approach to the End of the Colonial Empires* (Malden: Blackwell, 2008), p. 116.

Africa were to figure prominently on the agendas of practically all the postwar organizations and institutions of European integration. As historian Yves Montarsolo puts it, 'each time a new "European" institution saw the day, Africa was always at the heart of all concerns'.[2] These new institutions included the European Movement (officially founded in 1948), the Organisation for European Economic Co-operation (OEEC/OECD, 1948), the North Atlantic Treaty Organization (NATO, 1949, seen at the time as an organization of European integration[3]), the Council of Europe (1949), the European Coal and Steel Community (ECSC, 1951), the abortive European Defence Community and appurtenant European Political Community (the EDC Treaty was signed in 1952) and, finally, the European Economic Community (EEC, 1957), which will be the focus of the next chapter.

Such solid high-level organizational and institutional embeddedness stood in sharp contrast to Eurafrica's career in the nebulous organizational landscape of the interwar period. This also combined to relocate much, although by no means all, of the Eurafrican project from its visionary and rather utopian terrain onto a much more practical and hands-on platform. International, intergovernmental and supranational organizational and institutional muscle now both reflected and facilitated a more effective mobilization of political support for European colonial cooperation in Africa. In addition, the issues involved could be subjected to systematic studies and rigorous assessments, addressing and disseminating the imminent and future benefits, as well as the potential pitfalls and trying financial requirements for colonial investments that had to be collectively secured. Besides providing ways of resolving Europe's general geopolitical predicaments, such a problem-solving atmosphere was also conducive to establishing the logical and realistic links between colonial cooperation

[2] Yves Montarsolo, *L'Eurafrique – contrepoint de l'idée d'Europe: Le cas français de la fin de la deuxième guerre mondiale aux négociations des Traités de Rome* (Aix-en-Provence: Publications de l'Université de Provence, 2010), p. 91.
[3] A. H. Robertson, *European Institutions* (The London Institute of World Affairs, London: Stevens & Sons, 1959).

and the resolution of a number of particular predicaments, including Western Europe's dollar deficit, its great demand for raw materials, energy shortage and demographic imbalances.

Later we discuss the ways in which colonial cooperation in Africa was intended to offset such both general and particular problems that Western Europe faced in the immediate postwar period. Setting out by briefly outlining the general developments relating to European colonial empires during the first postwar years, mainly focusing on the Asian scene, we then focus more closely on the two main colonial powers, Britain and France, attending particularly to the increasing importance that they would come to assign to Africa as well as to their attempt at Eurafrican collaboration. Third and finally, we examine how the organizations mentioned earlier, which worked to advance European integration, dealt with the colonial question – especially as it pertained to Africa. As such, this chapter explores the main background and developments that would prepare the ground for Eurafrica's subsequent and successful incorporation into the EEC, which is the topic of the next chapter.

Anti-colonial momentum: Consolidating empires after the war

Strong anti-colonial sentiments and independence movements had been brewing in Asia and the Middle East since well before the war had ended with Japan's defeat in August 1945. As noted in the previous chapter, numerous such movements had formed already in the wake of World War I and its Wilsonian moment, which, at first, had seemed to elevate national self-determination to a universal principle and thus produced the impression 'that a window of opportunity had opened and thrust the issue of colonial liberation to the fore'.[4] While this turned

---

[4] Erez Manela, *The Wilsonian Moment: Self-Determination and the International Origins of Anticolonial Nationalism* (Oxford: Oxford University Press, 2007), p. 220.

out to be a deceptive impression, it served to galvanize and radicalize anti-colonial movements vowing not to let the moment slip a second time once the window reopened in 1945.[5]

Knowing full well what was in the offing, colonial powers were equally engaged in preparing for the opposite development of stemming the tide of independence movements in Asia and the Middle East[6] – and also in North Africa, where anti-colonial uprisings in the Algerian cities of Guelma and Sétif on VE (Victory in Europe) day set off a French military assault that resulted in the killing of somewhere between eight and forty-five thousand Algerians. As Britain's foreign secretary Ernest Bevin declared in the House of Commons in February 1946, echoing Churchill's previous assertion on the matter: 'When I say I am not prepared to sacrifice the British Empire what do I mean? I know that if the British Empire fell, the greatest collection of free nations would go into the limbo of the past, or it would be a disaster.'[7] Britain's initial imperial consolidation in 1945 and 1946 actually effectuated a significant imperial expansion in Asia. For their part, France and the Netherlands were determined to regain the colonial possessions in Southeast Asia that had been occupied by Japan.[8] Up until 1950, moreover, Italy also aspired to regain part of its African empire that Britain had wrested from Mussolini during the war.[9]

Most important, given the focus of this study, is that the pro-colonial preparations also occasioned forceful collaborative actions on the part

[5]   Ibid., pp. 224–5.
[6]   A. J. Stockwell, 'Imperialism and nationalism in South-East Asia', in Judith M. Brown and Wm. Roger Louis (eds), *The Oxford History of the British Empire, Volume IV: The Twentieth Century* (Oxford: Oxford University Press, 1999), pp. 476–80.
[7]   Quoted in John Saville, *The Politics of Continuity: British Foreign Policy and the Labour Government, 1945–46* (London: Verso, 1993), p. 4.
[8]   For a full account of the developments in Britain's Asian Empire between 1945 and 1949, see Christopher Bayly and Tim Harper, *Forgotten Wars: The End of Britain's Asian Empire* (London: Allen Lane, 2007). For an in-depth, comparative study of the fate of Europe's colonial empires and their respective attempts at restoration in the immediate postwar period, see Shipway, *Decolonization and its Impact.*
[9]   Antonio Varsori, 'Italy in the International System: From Great Power Illusion to the Reality of a Middle Rank Power: 1945–57', in Michael Dockrill (ed.), *Europe within the Global System 1938–1960: Great Britain, France, Italy and Germany: From Great Powers to Regional Powers* (Bochum: Universitätsverlag Dr N. Brockmeyer, 1995).

of European powers. A case in point is Britain's military interventions in both Vietnam (Indochina) and Indonesia (Netherlands East Indies) in 1945.[10] These were conducted to pave the way for France's and the Netherlands' restoration of the colonial control that had been lost during the war. Viewed with scepticism in Washington, Britain's decision rested with the firm belief that the rebuilding of the French and Dutch empires in Asia would be imperative for Britain's ability to hold on to its own Asian possessions – the lifeline of dollar earnings coming from Malaya's rubber and tin production, for one, could simply not be lost at this critical hour.[11] 'The frontiers of Malaya', said Britain's ambassador to Thailand, 'are on the Mekong'.[12]

It was thus absolutely necessary to swiftly establish a common Western front in Asia, capable of thwarting the general momentum of anti-colonial movements that were already receiving important boosts from the approaching Indian independence and the communist struggle in China. But the unswerving commitment to France's reacquisition of Indochina was equally determined by London's conviction that its postwar aims inside Europe itself, but also, as we shall see later, in Africa, could only be realized if a strong compact with France was upheld. In 1947, for instance, Britain and France signed the Treaty of Dunkirk, which established a defensive pact to safeguard against any future German aggression and to promote cooperation in the economic sphere. From the British perspective, then, Western unity in Asia and unity in Western Europe were, quite strictly, two sides of the same strategic and economic coin.[13]

Due to Britain and France's dire financial situation (by now relying on US assistance) and their already terribly overstretched armed forces,

---

[10] For an in-depth account, see Bayly and Harper, *Forgotten Wars*, Ch. 4. See also Marilyn B. Young, *The Vietnam Wars 1945–1990* (New York: Harper Perennial, 1991), pp. 11–12.

[11] See Mark Atwood Lawrence, 'Forging the "Great Combination": Britain and the Indochina Problem, 1945–1950', in Mark Atwood Lawrence and Fredrik Logevall (eds), *The First Vietnam War: Colonial Conflict and Cold War Crisis* (Cambridge: Harvard University Press, 2007). See also Fredrik Logevall, *Embers of War: The Fall of an Empire and the Making of America's Vietnam* (New York: Random House, 2012), pp. 112–15.

[12] Quoted in Lawrence, 'Forging the "Great Combination"', p. 122.

[13] Ibid., pp. 108–9.

it was equally clear that the long-term viability of such a Western front in Asia depended on the US lending its wholehearted commitment to the endeavour. To achieve this, which turned out to be a difficult task, Britain and France did everything they could to frame the colonial problematic in Cold War terms of a communist plot to oust Western powers from Southeast Asia. 'Our aim', Bevin declared in a parliamentary debate in September 1948, 'is to provide every estate with the maximum number of trained and armed defenders. It will be a terrific task to put an end to these terrorist gangs. The trouble is due mainly to Chinese Communists, who have been specially assigned to go into the country and organize trouble.' In what could hardly be read as anything but a plea for US assistance, Bevin went on to warn that '[i]f this policy of stirring up civil war goes on as it has been going on ever since the war ended, first in one territory and then in another, no one can foresee the end to which it will lead those that promote it.'[14]

Following years of arduous work of persuasion, London and Paris finally succeeded in having Washington embark on what would soon turn out to be an American bankrolling of the French war in Indochina.[15] But the breakthrough with the Americans came only in the autumn of 1949, four years into the war, and Washington's formal recognition of the French puppet regime under Emperor Bao Dai took until February 1950. As late as spring 1949 the US State Department had expressed strong misgivings about the US embroiling itself on the side of the French in Indochina, pointing to the Bao Dai government as a mere pawn and the war as almost certainly a futile and extremely wasteful enterprise.[16] Due to the wait, Britain had to sustain much of what it least wanted – namely, sharp and persistent criticism from Asian national movements and leaders for supporting the brutal colonial regimes of France and the Netherlands, Nehru going as far as comparing Britain's

---

[14] 'Bevin for 3d force as world balance', *The New York Times*, 16 September 1948.
[15] For an in-depth account of the US involvement in the French war in Indochina 1950–1954, see e.g. Irwin Wall, *The United States and the Making of Postwar France* (Cambridge: Cambridge University Press, 1991); and Logevall, *Embers of War*.
[16] Ibid., p. 212.

military intervention on behalf of France in Vietnam to Nazi Germany and Fascist Italy's intervention in the Spanish civil war. Increasingly, moreover, anti-colonial forces in Asia were working in concert. In January 1949, nineteen Asian countries organized what was, according to *The New York Times*, 'the first official all-Asian political conference in history', representing 'more than half of the world's population'. Rallying in support of Indonesian independence from the Dutch onslaught and resoundingly condemning European colonialism, the conference was regarded by many in the West as 'the first step in the development of an Asian bloc'.[17]

In London, such strident criticism was seen as potentially indicating that its Asian strategy was in jeopardy. The strategy in question aimed to nurture friendly future relations with those Asian countries (mainly India) that were gaining independence from Britain – so as to preserve a certain amount of postcolonial leverage – while simultaneously making sure not to stir anti-colonial nationalism in those Southeast Asian colonies that Britain was determined to keep, mainly Malaya, Singapore and Hong Kong. Since Britain's backing of France in Indochina, despite attempts at a low profile, was there for everyone to see, its backfiring impact on the larger strategy made it imperative for London to recede swiftly into a back-seat role once Washington had assumed the driver's seat. Being able to rest assured that Washington was fully committed to the task in Indochina, Whitehall was now, as Mark Lawrence puts it, finally 'free to give highest priority to its anxieties about antagonizing Asian opinion', with Bevin henceforth hard at work to tone down any indications of a Western accord on Indochina.[18] By January 1950 Britain had dispensed with US policy and had gone ahead and recognized Communist China as a precautionary move to protect Hong Kong. During the Battle of Dien Bien Phu in 1954, where the conclusive Vietminh victory would come to decide the subsequent and rapid French departure from Indochina,

---

[17] 'Indonesia issue spreads', *The New York Times*, 23 January 1949.
[18] Lawrence, 'Forging the "Great Combination"', p. 126.

it was thus only logical that London should decline Washington's bid to have Britain join an effort to come to the rescue of the battered French forces.[19] That is to say, with a wholesale US commitment to Vietnam being clinched well in advance of the looming French collapse, Britain had already declared its mission accomplished and moved on to concentrate its diminishing resources and global reach on more pressing tasks.

A third world power: The British response

Looking into such tasks is also tantamount to sensing the centrality of Africa, in general, and Eurafrica, in particular, for Britain and France's handling of their weakening positions in Asia during the first postwar decade. Concurrently with Britain and France finding themselves forced to scale back their engagement in Southeast Asia and the Middle East, they began to perceive of Africa not only as a defensive fallback option but also, and most importantly, as a great opportunity to reinvigorate their respective colonial enterprises and hence their standings as great powers.

For the British postwar Labour government (under Clement Attlee and his dominant foreign secretary Ernest Bevin),[20] which assumed office in July 1945, the essential and, indeed, decisive importance of Africa was clear from the outset. By autumn 1945, Moscow's bid (later dropped), as part of the peace settlement, to be provided with a Mediterranean port in Tripolitania – the western half of British-occupied

---

[19] Stockwell, 'Imperialism and nationalism in South-East Asia', p. 485; see also Edward Fursdon, *The European Defence Community: A History* (London: Macmillan, 1980), pp. 261–2; Kevin Ruane, *The Rise and Fall of the European Defence Community: Anglo-American Relations and the Crisis of European Defence, 1950–55* (Houndmills: Macmillan, 2000).

[20] According to David Dilks, 'Bevin enjoyed an initiative in the making of foreign policy which no Foreign Secretary since the days of Sir Edward Grey [who served 1905–1916] had exercised.' David Dilks, 'Britain and Europe, 1948–1950: The Prime Minister, the Foreign Secretary and the Cabinet', in Raymond Poidevin (ed.), *Origins of the European Integration (March 1948 – May 1950)* (Bruxelles: Bruylant et al., 1986), p. 391.

Libya (formerly under Italian colonial rule) – triggered deep suspicion in the Foreign Office, Bevin being certain that this signalled the Soviets' determination to convert the Mediterranean into a 'Russian lake' and then continue to seize a stake in the natural riches in sub-Saharan Africa, particularly the uranium in the Belgian Congo.[21]

Such fears were aggravated by the realization shortly thereafter that Britain's two pivotal military installations in the Middle East – Palestine and the Canal Zone in Egypt – could no longer be considered safe bets. Should a withdrawal from these base sites come to pass, both political and military leaders agreed, the Russians would waste no time establishing themselves in Egypt and Palestine. Since such a reversal would leave the door to the entire African continent wide open, it was impossible, from a British standpoint, to exaggerate the cataclysmal consequences it would entail. Russian control over Egypt and Palestine, the British Chiefs of Staff warned in April 1946, 'would prejudice our position both in North-West Africa [...] and in the Indian Ocean. It would be the first step in a direct threat to our main support area of Southern Africa.'[22] Besides Britain, the Commonwealth as a whole shared this grave concern. At the Commonwealth's Prime Minister's meeting in London in the spring of 1948 the bottom line agreement was crystal clear: 'Russia should be excluded from Africa at whatever cost.'[23]

When British troops withdrew from Palestine in April 1948 (the founding of the State of Israel being proclaimed a month later) this just served to strengthen London's resolve to stay put in the Canal Zone. However, and most importantly, it also served to intensify the ongoing search for alternative base sites and strategies, including alternatives to the Canal Zone itself. Practically all of this centred on Africa, and,

---

[21] Geoffrey Parker, *Western Geopolitical Thought in the Twentieth Century* (London: Croom Helm, 1985), pp. 136–7; Wm. Roger Louis, *The British Empire in the Middle East 1945–1951: Arab Nationalism, The United States, and Postwar Imperialism* (Oxford: Oxford University Press, 1984), pp. 29, 271.

[22] Quoted in Louis, *The British Empire in the Middle East*, p. 28.

[23] Alan Bullock, *Ernest Bevin: Foreign Secretary, 1945–1951* (London: Heinemann, 1983), p. 235.

as Louis puts it, much of it echoed the spirit of the late nineteenth century's scramble for Africa: '[T]he map of tropical Africa would be painted a new shade of British red from Mombasa to Lagos, with the vital centre in the Sudan. In the Sudan rail or air links could be provided, if the Egyptians were amenable, to Cairo and Cape Town.'[24] In addition, Kenya (and possibly Tanganyika too) was seen by Attlee, as suggested in 1946, as the primary candidate for hosting a new main base for the protection of Britain's imperial interests, serving first as a backup to Egypt and ultimately as its replacement.[25] Since Bevin and the military still coveted the Middle East as a long-term strategic bastion, they viewed Attlee's Kenyan replacement plan with scepticism. Even so, Bevin was all in on Africa's growing strategic and economic importance and did not view the Middle East and tropical Africa in either–or terms; for him it was rather a both–and situation.

Yet, if there was one part that was growing in importance, the tendency in 1946 was clearly in favour of Africa. 'Despite drastic changes in her position abroad', *The New York Times* wrote in October 1947, 'Great Britain remains a powerful imperial nation.' To be sure, the report went on, India was lost, Palestine on its way and, while still strong, its ties to the Middle East and the Far East were certainly also showing signs of strain. In contrast to this development however, the *Times* could also confirm that 'Britain's interests in Africa – from Kenya, the Sudan and Nigeria right down to the Cape – are expanding.'[26] Indeed, in 1947 Africa was taking the place of India 'as one of the ultimate justifications of the British Empire', and, with it, the primary function of the Middle East in Britain's global strategy, although still key and still the irreplaceable king of oil, was shifting from one of assuring the commercial and strategic link between Europe and Asia to one of facilitating the security of Africa.[27]

---

[24] Louis, *The British Empire in the Middle East*, p. 109.

[25] Bullock, *Ernest Bevin*, p. 243. See also 'Attlee aides scan East Africa bases', *The New York Times*, 8 October 1946.

[26] 'Britain holds to Near East despite her empire change', *The New York Times*, 20 October 1947.

[27] Louis, *The British Empire in the Middle East*, p. 16; John Gallagher, *The Decline, Revival and Fall of the British Empire* (Cambridge: Cambridge University Press, 1982), pp. 145–9.

Britain's strong-minded commitment to the revival of African colonialism was owed chiefly to the belief in the continent's magnificent economic potential – Bevin being 'hypnotized' by its mineral riches. As such, it presented Britain with a priceless opportunity to resolve its appalling financial situation, its overall economic decline and, not least, its embarrassing dependence on the USA.[28] This manifested in Britain's unparalleled investment in its African colonies in the early postwar years; and as Britain's economic situation showed further signs of structural weakness after 1947, this precipitated, as Butler puts it, 'a brief, but unprecedented fixation with drawing on colonial resources.'[29]

Africa's splendid economic prospects notwithstanding, Britain's initial enthusiasm could not rest with this alone. The presumed viability of the enterprise was also intimately bound up with an equally presumed temporal buffer. In sharp contrast to the Asian scene, then, Britain felt it could work under the assumption that its African plans had time on their side, given that the type of malevolent nationalist and communist currents materializing elsewhere in the Empire still were seen to be at a safe distance from tropical Africa. 'With regard to the African and his aspirations', it was asserted in *International Affairs* in 1948, 'rapid political evolution is not of much concern to him; nor is it his primary need.' Rather, what the African was said to be seeking, and what Britain should provide for, was 'nourishment for his body and his mind.'[30] 'Africa', to use John Gallagher's depiction, 'would be the surrogate for India, more docile, more malleable, more pious.'[31] As Louis alludes to, this created a much-needed sense of African invincibility for the British. Until the early 1950s, Africa was the place where 'a permanent line of British defence could and should be decisively

[28] L. J. Butler, *Britain and Empire: Adjusting to a Post-Imperial World* (London: I. B. Tauris, 2002), pp. 81–5; H. V. Brasted, Carl Bridge and John Kent, 'Cold War, informal empire and the transfer of power: Some "paradoxes" of British decolonisation resolved?', in Dockrill (ed.), *Europe within the Global System 1938–1960*, pp. 17–18, 25–6, 29; Shipway, *Decolonization and its Impact*, pp. 114–26.

[29] Butler, *Britain and Empire*, p. 82.

[30] Louis Kraft, 'Pan-Africanism: Political, economic, strategic or scientific?', *International Affairs*, Vol. 24, No. 2, 1948, p. 225.

[31] Gallagher, *The Decline, Revival and Fall of the British Empire*, p. 146.

drawn', the place 'where the British Empire might be maintained indefinitely'.[32] In Bevin's mind, as his biographer Alan Bullock has it, 'African independence was the agenda of the next generation.'[33]

But if the temporal buffer was in place, at least for the time being, the sustainability of Britain's colonial regeneration in Africa also required European support and cooperation; this in order to reap economic scale benefits with regard to trade and technology on the one hand, and to serve as a necessary buffer against American involvement in Africa on the other. Until 1949, such Eurafrican colonial cooperation formed the backbone of Bevin's and the British Labour government's bid for establishing a 'Third World Power' or 'Third Force' that would grow to become equal in strength to both the USA and the Soviet Union.[34] Bevin also referred to this scenario as the 'three great Monroes' around which the postwar world was set to be structured.[35] While the brunt of the initiative, and part of Bevin's 'Grand Design', was with Britain, the leadership was to rest with a solid British–French coalition that would soon, if everything went to plan, attract the participation of other Western European states. Commencing in 1945, and with antecedents in Britain and Free France's cooperation in West Africa during the war, the Eurafrican Third Force conception would rapidly come to dominate the strategic and economic planning of the British Foreign Office.[36]

---

[32] Louis, *The British Empire in the Middle East*, pp. 108–9, 16. See also Michael Collins, 'Decolonization and the "Federal Moment"', *Diplomacy & Statecraft*, Vol. 24, No. 1, 2013, pp. 26–8.

[33] Bullock, *Ernest Bevin*, p. 610.

[34] John Kent, 'Bevin's imperialism and the idea of Euro-Africa, 1945–49', in Michael Dockrill and John W. Young (eds), *British Foreign Policy, 1945–56* (Houndmills: Macmillan, 1989). For a full account on the relations between Britain and France as regards Africa, spanning the period from 1939 to 1956, see John Kent, *The Internationalization of Colonialism: Britain, France, and Black Africa, 1939–1956* (Oxford: Clarendon Press, 1992). See also Anne Deighton, 'Ernest Bevin and the idea of *Euro-Africa* from the interwar to the postwar period', in Bitsch and Bossuat (eds), *L'Europe unie et l'Afrique*; Anne Deighton, 'Entente Neo-Coloniale?: Ernest Bevin and the proposals for an Anglo-French Third World Power', *Diplomacy and Statecraft*, Vol. 17, No. 4, 2006, pp. 835–52; John W. Young, *Britain and European Unity, 1945–1999* (Houndmills: Macmillan 2nd edn, 2000), pp. 1–25; and Dilks, 'Britain and Europe, 1948–1950'.

[35] Parker, *Western Geopolitical Thought in the Twentieth Century*, p. 136; Deighton, 'Ernest Bevin and the idea of *Euro-Africa*', p. 110.

[36] Kent, 'Bevin's imperialism and the idea of Euro-Africa'.

In the summer of 1945 Britain's new Labour government was eager to craft a strategy with which it could quickly close what was deemed a transient power gap *vis-à-vis* the USA. As the preeminent scholar on the topic, John Kent, establishes, for this to become feasible it required Western European partners, foremost France. In addition, it required the inclusion of the propitious colonial regions in Africa, where the USA had no foothold and whose future stability, in stark contrast to Southeast Asia, did not call for American assistance. But although this 'concept of a Euro-African entity', as Kent terms it, immediately attained the status of established doctrine within Bevin's Foreign Office, and although a modest programme of technical cooperation in Africa between Britain and France had been operational since as early as November 1945 – in parallel with numerous other initiatives at lower levels – Bevin's big push for the Eurafrican Third Force did not begin until 1947.

Apart from the surging economic importance being assigned to Africa in 1947, this also, as mentioned earlier, was due to London's realization that its intra-European efforts to strengthen Britain's leadership in Western Europe had failed to materialize. Expanding trade and economic exchange between Britain and France and within Western Europe as a whole was thus seen as an insufficient remedy for Britain's broader economic problems, its accelerating dollar deficit and hence its continued dependence on the USA. Another factor that needs to be mentioned was tied to Bevin's quest, also getting under way in 1947, to acquire the trusteeship over Cyrenaica (the eastern part of Libya); this in order to safeguard a base option that could compensate for Britain's weakening position in the Eastern Mediterranean and the Middle East. Since this necessitated an understanding with both France and Italy (apart from the UN), it added to the momentum for European cooperation in Africa.[37]

Rather than cooperation *inside* Europe, to which many within the British government had become increasingly sceptical, focus was from

---

[37] Ibid., pp. 48–56.

now on placed more firmly on European cooperation *outside* Europe.[38] Indeed, as Anne Deighton has revealed, within the British foreign policy establishment there was also a perception maintaining that 'it might be easier to create an African Union under European guidance rather than unify in Europe itself'.[39] In accordance with Coudenhove-Kalergi's and Sarraut's respective formulas, a Western European bloc, or a 'Third World Power' on a par with the USA and the Soviet Union, was then to emerge chiefly as a result of a successful European joint venture in Africa.[40] Or as the Chancellor of Exchequer, Stafford Cripps, spelled out before the African Governor's Conference in November 1947:

> The economies of Western Europe and Tropical Africa are so closely interlocked in mutual trade, in the supply of capital and in currency systems that their problems of overseas balance are essentially one. Tropical Africa is already contributing much, both in physical supplies of food and raw materials and in quite substantial net earnings of dollars from the sterling area pool. The further development of African resources is of the same crucial importance to the rehabilitation and strengthening of Western Europe as the restoration of European productive power is to the future progress and prosperity of Africa. Each needs and is needed by the other. In Africa indeed is to be found a great potential for new strength and vigour in the Western European economy and the stronger that economy becomes the better of course Africa will fare.[41]

Under the headline 'Cripps says colonies hold key to survival', *The New York Times* underscored that Cripps' contention had 'been widely accepted by the country's top economists and business men'.[42]

---

[38] Ibid., p. 52.

[39] Deighton, 'Ernest Bevin and the idea of *Euro-Africa*', p. 110n. 22. In some Commonwealth policy circles during the 1940s, such African Union-leaning European cooperation in Africa was also urged under the banner of 'Pan-Africanism'; see e.g. Kraft, 'Pan-Africanism'.

[40] For the interwar roots of the Eurafrican Third World Power project as conceived in Great Britain, see Deighton, 'Ernest Bevin and the idea of *Euro-Africa*'; David Russell, '"The Jolly Old Empire": Labour, the Commonwealth and Europe, 1945–51', in Alex May (ed.), *Britain, the Commonwealth and Europe: The Commonwealth and Britain's Applications to join the European Communities* (Houndmills: Macmillan, 2001), p. 18; and Saville, *The Politics of Continuity*, pp. 93–6.

[41] Quoted in Kent, 'Bevin's imperialism', pp. 58–9.

[42] 'Cripps says colonies hold key to survival', *The New York Times*, 13 November 1947.

A few months earlier, *The Christian Science Monitor* had also commented on the Eurafrican scheme that was in the offing, beginning its almost full-page coverage as follows: 'The resources of Africa, with the surface hardly scratched, appear increasingly suited to development of the Dark Continent into a hinterland for a new western European grouping that may balance the United States and Russia.' Marvelling at the expert testimonies in circulation at the time concerning sub-Saharan Africa's enormous and still largely untouched riches in everything from foodstuff to minerals, the *Monitor* also noted that this part of Africa presented Europe with yet another asset in the form of a 'population' that, 'unlike the Arabs', constituted 'less of a political problem'. But for Western Europe to truly succeed in realizing this great opportunity it required an equally great effort at European cooperation and coordination in the African colonies. According to this American daily, a few promising signs of such coordination could already be glimpsed, and hence its upbeat conclusion: 'The response of Britain, France, and Belgium to this potential of the future has made its first news. The "course of empire" does not belong to this day. Today it is "the course of co-ordination" – and it is apparently going to grow on a new north–south line. The Eurafrica Atlantic era of world balance appears to be dawning.'[43]

Stafford Cripps' address was preceded by high-level discussions between London and Paris in spring 1947, where Bevin and President Auriol had first met and converged on the key value of colonial cooperation in Africa for the creation of a Western European bloc less constrained by US interests. Subsequently, Bevin notified the French premier Paul Ramadier that he would like their countries to initiate economic cooperation in Africa. The French reaction was very positive, Paris returning the favour by disclosing an even bolder agenda for African colonial cooperation, one that went beyond Bevin's expectations. Accordingly, by autumn 1947 the time was ripe for an agreement between the two countries on a long-term cooperation

---

[43] 'Resources scarcely scratched', *The Christian Science Monitor*, 17 June 1947.

plan for Africa, comprising both political and economic issues. Both Bevin and his French colleague Georges Bidault took the matter to be of such magnitude that it was now to be managed at the highest ministerial level;[44] it 'was now part of major foreign policy', as Britain's Colonial Secretary Arthur Creech Jones underscored.[45] This sparked a flurry of high-level activity on both sides of the Channel. France proposed talks to clear the way for colonial cooperation in the areas of intercolonial trade, development, infrastructure and pricing of agricultural commodities – an initiative that led to the setting up of an Anglo–French working party on economic cooperation in West Africa towards the end of 1947.[46]

In 1948 the planning for a Eurafrican bloc reached its climax. Britain set out to engage other European countries, but also South Africa, as participants in the Eurafrican enterprise. Belgium was already part of the plan, whereas Italy now became a key focus. As already mentioned, this was connected with Britain's interest in Cyrenaica. But in 1948, Britain's bid for a trusteeship had expanded to encompass Libya in its entirety. Since Italy, Libya's former colonizer, was seeking the trusteeship over Tripolitania, Britain's tender clearly had to include a severance payment to Rome. Among other things, this was to offer Italy wholesale accession to Western Europe's colonial cooperation in Africa, and, among the particulars, it was also to offer Britain's African colonies as an emigration outlet for Italy's many unemployed.[47] In general terms, Rome welcomed all available openings for European collaboration in Africa. As World War II had rolled back Mussolini's colonial push, which was a source of great national pride during the fascist period, Italy's postwar governments sought to re-establish international prestige by supporting all efforts towards European and US-led regional integration, which Rome saw as opportunities for asserting its economic presence in North Africa and furthering its 'Mediterranean

44 Kent, 'Bevin's imperialism', p. 58.
45 Quoted in ibid., p. 59.
46 Ibid., p. 59; Deighton, 'Entente Neo-Coloniale?', pp. 841–2.
47 Kent, 'Bevin's imperialism', pp. 60–1, 64.

vocation'. Bevin's Eurafrican plan – as well as the Eurafrican proposals that would follow in the 1950s – was thus of primary importance to the reconstruction of Italy's position in foreign affairs.[48] In the spring of 1948, moreover, the British Foreign Office went ahead and announced its plans for an African Development Council, representing Belgium, Britain, France, Italy, Portugal and South Africa and to be operative under the auspices of the Committee of European Economic Co-operation (the precursor of the OEEC and OECD).

By this time the Eurafrican plan also featured prominently in the world press.[49] 'France and Great Britain are in permanent consultations to realise an economic Eurafrica, an element of equilibrium between the US and the USSR', Stafford Cripps told journalists in Paris on 11 February 1948.[50] This was a follow-up to Bevin's wide-ranging address to the House of Commons in January in which he stated that the time was 'ripe for a consolidation of Western Europe'. Bevin then went on to 'the subject of the organisation in respect of a Western Union', and here we must quote at length:

> I would emphasise that I am not concerned only with Europe as a geographical conception. Europe has extended its influence throughout the world [...]. In the first place, we turn our eyes to Africa, where great responsibilities are shared by us with South Africa, France, Belgium and Portugal [...]. The organisation of Western Europe must be economically supported. That involves the closest possible collaboration with the Commonwealth and with overseas territories, not only British but French, Dutch, Belgian and Portuguese. [...] They have raw materials, food and resources which can be turned to very great common advantage, both to the people of the territories themselves, to Europe, and to the world as a whole. The other two great world Powers,

---

[48] See Alessandro Brogi, *Questions of Self-Esteem: The United States and the Cold War Choices in France and Italy, 1944–1958* (Westport: Praeger, 2002), pp. 191–210; Ruth Ben-Ghiat, 'Modernity is just over there: Colonialism and Italian national identity', *Interventions*, Vol. 8, No. 3, 2006, pp. 380–92.

[49] Deighton, 'Entente Neo-Coloniale?', p. 842.

[50] Cripps' interview was quoted globally; see, for instance, 'African bloc as balance with U.S.A. and Soviet', *The Canberra Times*, 12 February 1948. See also Montarsolo, *L'Eurafrique – contrepoint de l'idée d'Europe*, p. 26.

the United States and Soviet Russia, have tremendous resources. There is no need of conflict with them in this matter at all. If Western Europe is to achieve its balance of payments and to get a world equilibrium, it is essential that those resources should be developed and made available [...]. There is no conflict between the social and economic development of those overseas territories to the advantage of their people, and their development as a source of supplies for Western Europe, as a contributor, as I have indicated, so essential to the balance of payments.[51]

Bevin's speech, seen as tremendously important at the time, won a broad backing also from the Conservatives in the House.[52] Under the bold caption 'Historic policy shift announced by Britain', *The New York Times* blazoned abroad London's European mission to erect a 'Third World Power' that, thanks to its overseas raw material riches, confidently could aim to achieve parity with both the US and the Soviet Union.[53] Indeed, if such a Western Union took charge of the development of the African colonies, Bevin asserted in the autumn of 1948, 'we could have the U.S. dependent on us, and eating out of our hand, in four or five years. Two great mountains of manganese are in Sierra Leone, etc. US is very barren of essential minerals and in Africa we have them all.'[54]

Yet, for all the cocksureness and determination to achieve independence from the USA, the Eurafrican concert fizzled out in 1949. All of a sudden, Britain opted out of the European bloc and instead decided that its fortunes would be better served by an Atlantic alliance and trade with the Commonwealth and Empire. In France, at the same time, President Auriol rejected Prime Minister Ramadier's and Foreign Secretary Bidault's plans for an agreement with Britain on colonial Africa, as he feared this would hamper the autonomy of

---

[51]	'Address given by Ernest Bevin to the House of Commons', 22 January 1948, CVCE (*Centre Virtuel de la Connaissance sur l'Europe*), www.cvce.eu/viewer/-/content/7bc0ecbd-c50e-4035-8e36-ed70bfbd204c/en

[52]	Deighton, 'Entente Neo-Coloniale?', p. 844.

[53]	'Historic Policy Shift Announced by Britain', *The New York Times*, 25 January 1948.

[54]	Quoted in Kent, 'Bevin's Imperialism', p. 66.

the newly reconstructed French Union. Colliding French and British interests, including the incompatibility of their respective colonial governance structures and philosophies, as well as their diverging views on European integration, also played a part in the demise of the French–British Eurafrican scheme. So did the collision within the British government between the Foreign and Colonial Offices. Not that the Colonial Office opposed European colonial cooperation per se, but it advocated a very different arrangement, one that would operate under the auspices of the OEEC and so include states that did not have colonies. The Colonial Office was adamant that European cooperation in Africa be built in close partnership with the Africans themselves so as to ward off any incriminating suspicions of colonial exploitation and European supremacy. But as Kent also explains, much of London's U-turn stemmed from the Labour government's mounting scepticism to European economic cooperation as a remedy for Britain's own economic problems. Having already dispensed with the idea of a European customs union as ill suited to British interests, and with Britain and Western Europe's economy taking a turn for the worse in 1949, London saw itself as being in no position to assume responsibilities for assisting the continent. As a direct result of this, Kent shows, 'any formal sharing of colonial export markets had to be ruled out' and, accordingly, 'Euro–African links were now seen as hindering British efforts to achieve equilibrium between the dollar and sterling areas'.[55] As Britain's balance of payments and sterling–dollar crises spiralled out of control in 1949, forcing a sharp devaluation in the autumn of 1949, this, according to Kent, served the final nail in Britain's Eurafrican coffin. Having little choice but to ask Washington for assistance further confirmed that Atlantic alliance was to be Britain's new strategy of choice.[56]

This did not mean that all Anglo–French colonial cooperation in Africa vanished from history in 1949. During the 1950s, for instance,

---

[55] Ibid., p. 69; see also Young, *Britain and European Unity*, pp. 22–3.
[56] Kent, 'Bevin's Imperialism', p. 70. For Britain and Bevin's change in perception on Eurafrica, see also Deighton, 'Ernest Bevin and the idea of *Euro-Africa*'; and Adamthwaite, 'Britain, France, the United States and Euro-Africa, 1945–1949'.

such collaboration was quite successful in preventing the UN from gaining a foothold in African colonial affairs.[57] Another case in point, of course, is the Suez Crisis, or the Anglo–French (and Israeli) war against Nasser's Egypt in 1956 (as we discuss further in the next chapter). From the British perspective, however, these and other joint efforts were geared towards advancing Britain's independent room to manoeuvre in Africa and the Middle East – not to craft common European colonial policies – and were thus perfectly in line with the decision in 1949 to discard the Eurafrican plans. Important too, then, was that London's strategic and economic substitution of Atlantic alliance, the Commonwealth and Empire for Eurafrica and Western Europe also determined Britain's more general reluctance to European integration in the 1950s. From the late 1940s onwards, British governments would attribute enormous importance to the economic and trade relations with the Empire and Commonwealth, and to its special relationship with the USA; and London thus feared that being part of European integration on the continent, particularly of the supranational kind, would severely hamper and compromise these relations and thereby also Britain's standing as an independent world power.[58]

Africa first! The French response

If Britain's new global strategy required an estrangement from European integration in general, and Eurafrican cooperation in particular, the strategy on the part of France called for the opposite. Yet, the basic reasons for the differences in orientation, including the reasons for parting company over colonial cooperation in Africa, rested with very similar colonial objectives. Whereas Britain saw European integration as an impediment to colonial trade and investment in Africa, France was realizing that European, or Eurafrican, integration was becoming

---

[57] See Kent, *The Internationalization of Colonialism*.
[58] See e.g. Young, *Britain and European Unity*, pp. 22–4.

increasingly necessary in order to expand colonial trade and secure the absolutely vital investments in Africa that France was in no position to muster on its own.

The French Empire, as noted earlier, came out of the war barely a shadow of its interwar standing. To be sure, since the organization of Free France's resistance in large part rested on its fallback position in Africa, Brazzaville being the symbolic capital of Free France and Algiers (from 1943) its headquarters, Gaullist propaganda could claim that the Empire had saved the Republic.[59] This was a glorious picture from which the key figures were retouched – that is, the huge number of colonial troops who fought for Free France. In reality though, the greater part of the Empire – as in the imperial leadership – betrayed the Republic. It was Vichy, not de Gaulle's Free France, who with a few exceptions won the Empire's loyalty after the defeat in 1940. Hence, when de Gaulle proclaimed from London, in the summer of 1940, that 'The Crime of this Armistice is to have capitulated as if France did not have an Empire',[60] he was lambasting an enemy, Vichy, who already treated the Empire as basically the only game in town. For Vichy, the Empire was by far its most vaunted asset, its true claim to legitimacy and its big bargaining chip against Germany to restore national honour and make up for the defeat.[61] More important, de Gaulle was appealing to a leadership in the colonies who had already turned its anti-republican back on him and freely pledged their allegiance to Vichy.[62] Adding to the shameful string of events, the Vichy regime pro-actively sought Germany's colonial cooperation in Africa. As Robert Paxton has shown, it only took a month or so after the defeat before Vichy 'tried to

---

[59] See Henri Laurentie's address at the Chaillot Palace on 26 January 1945: 'L'empire au secours de la métropole', in Patrice Liquière (ed.), *Restaurer, reformer, agir: la France en 1945* (Paris: La documentation française, 1995), pp. 41–51.

[60] Quoted in Eric T. Jennings, *Vichy in the Tropics: Pétain's National Revolution in Madagascar, Guadeloupe, and Indochina, 1940–44* (Stanford: Stanford University Press, 2001), p. 9.

[61] See further Martin Thomas, *The French Empire at War 1940–45* (Manchester: Manchester University Press, 1998); Robert O. Paxton, *Vichy France: Old Guard and New Order 1940–1944* (New York: Columbia University Press, 1972, 2001).

[62] Jennings, *Vichy in the Tropics*, pp. 9–30.

interest the Germans in making France the colonial and maritime link to an African "hinterland" for the New Europe'.[63] By offering Germany both strategic and economically lucrative stakes in the French Empire, it was hoped that Germany would consent to Vichy's military struggle against Free France in Africa, its plans at making inroads into British colonies and to Vichy's overall aim of preserving as much as possible of its imperial autonomy. But Eurafrican colonial cooperation with Germany was also seen as a means to usher in more of a partnership between Germany and France in Europe proper.[64]

From the defeat to the Germans in 1940 until the liberation in 1944, the two rival French regimes of Vichy and Free France fought a civil war in an Empire they both claimed as their own. Yet what emerged from the ashes of defeat, humiliation and the mutual accusations of treachery was nothing less than 'the consolidation of an unprecedented imperialist consensus in French domestic politics'. Indeed, directly after the war, and save for the Communists, 'none of France's major political parties even paid lip service to the gradual disengagement from colonial territories that was so much a feature of British imperial policy after 1945'.[65] Thus asked Raymond Aron in 1945: 'What are the essential objectives of all French foreign policy today?' His answer was as unequivocal as the question was rhetorical: 'The first is the maintenance of the integrity of the French Empire; the second is the permanent strengthening of France *vis-à-vis* Germany'.[66]

Important steps towards this consolidation, or 'maintenance', were taken already at the Brazzaville Conference in January and February of

[63] Paxton, *Vichy France*, pp. 58–9.

[64] Julian Jackson, *France: The Dark Years 1940–1944* (Oxford: Oxford University Press, 2001), pp. 172–89. For a further discussion of Eurafrica's importance in Vichy France, see Julia Nordblad, 'The un-European idea: Vichy and Eurafrica in the historiography of Europeanism', *The European Legacy*, Vol. 19, 2014, forthcoming. For an interesting proposal that was put forward in 1942, envisioning a future political and economic integration of Europe and Africa under German–French leadership, see René Viard, *L'Eurafrique: Pour une nouvelle économie européenne* (Paris: Férnand Sorlot, 1942).

[65] Martin Thomas, 'French imperial reconstruction and the development of the Indochina War, 1945–1950', in Lawrence and Logevall (eds), *The First Vietnam War*, p. 130.

[66] Raymond Aron, 'Reflections of the foreign policy of France', *International Affairs*, Vol. 21, No. 4, 1945, p. 445.

1944, where the Free France leadership and the colonial representatives in Africa sought to stake out the future of the French Empire, focusing primarily on sub-Saharan Africa. (It was on the basis of the Brazzaville Declaration that the Fourth Republic redesignated the French Empire as the French Union in 1946.) Brazzaville set out from an awareness of an imperial crisis, where parts of the empire's clout, most acutely in the Levant (soon to be lost), but also in Indochina, were already crumbling. As Brazzaville's main champion and chief architect, the Ministry of Colonies' Director of Political Affairs Henri Laurentie – subsequently a strong advocate for French–British and wider European colonial cooperation in Africa[67] – summarized in a memorandum to de Gaulle in December 1944: 'Deprived of the means to exercise our power – army, air force, navy – we decided to replace them with the ideas and sentiments needed to revive and confirm France's rights to a colonial empire. It was in this spirit that the Brazzaville Conference was conceived and organized.'[68]

For Laurentie, as Martin Shipway explains, the colonial problems were so grave that French policy following Brazzaville had to be shaped and articulated as being up against 'a general problem', since, as he added, 'we are looking at colonial revolution'. Although he recognized 'the colonial peoples' desire for independence' and thus the need for a reformed French policy that could partly accommodate such desires while at the same time succeeding in preserving the empire, the general solution to the 'general problem' nonetheless turned out to be one almost solely focused on 'imperial restoration'.[69]

Free France's colonial minister (and future prime minister) René Pleven, who firmly presided over the meeting, made this very clear when he stated that 'the African peoples want no other liberty than that of France'.[70] Such was also the unequivocal message conveyed by

---

[67] Kent, *The Internationalization of Colonialism*, pp. 187–8.
[68] Quoted in Martin Shipway, *The Road to War: France and Vietnam, 1944–1947* (New York: Berghahn Books, 1996/2003), p. 76.
[69] Ibid., pp. 78, 81, 82.
[70] Quoted in Paul Nugent, *Africa Since Independence: A Comparative History* (Houndmills: Palgrave, 2004), p. 42.

the final resolution of the Brazzaville Conference: '[T]he aims of the work of colonisation which France is pursuing in her colonies exclude any idea of autonomy and any possibility of development outside the French empire *bloc*; the attainment of self-government in the colonies even in the most distant future must be excluded.'[71]

This is not to imply that colonial policy was altogether static. Brazzaville also comprised discussions and measures that called for reform and which addressed the growing plight of the colonial peoples, including the offence of forced labour, appalling living conditions and lack of political representation. For the most part, however, initiatives towards reform were indeterminate and never challenged the overarching objective of reaffirming French imperial sovereignty. Rather, the reform agenda emerging from Brazzaville foremost served 'to provide moral rearmament for a revitalized empire.'[72] And while the sense of imperial crisis and disorder, even revolution, expressed in Brazzaville was real enough, it had little bearing on the sub-Saharan African scene, which, although clearly fraught with mounting and visible discontent, was still worlds apart from the situation in Indochina, the Levant and North Africa.[73]

Immediately after the war, the reconquest of Indochina in 1945–1946 was instrumental in pushing Brazzaville's reform agenda further into the background, cementing a 'colonial consensus' in France that, from now on, would spawn an ever more unabashed attitude and brutal means to ensure French imperial ascendancy.[74] For our purposes here, though, it is important to qualify this colonial consensus further.

---

[71] Les recommandations de la conférence de Brazzaville, 6 February 1944. Assemblée nationale, France; www.assemblee-nationale.fr/histoire/discours-de-brazzaville.asp#recommandations (accessed 2 August 2013). See also Hubert Luethy, *France Against Herself* (New York: Frederick A. Praeger, 1955), p. 218.

[72] Nugent, *Africa Since Independence*, p. 41. For an in-depth account of France's colonial policy in the immediate postwar period, see D. Bruce Marshall, *The French Colonial Myth and Constitution-Making in the Fourth Republic* (New Haven: Yale University Press, 1973).

[73] Nugent, *Africa Since Independence*, pp. 44–5; Thomas, 'French imperial reconstruction', p. 139.

[74] Tony Smith, 'The French colonial consensus and people's war, 1946–58', *Journal of Contemporary History*, Vol. 9, No. 4, 1974, pp. 217–47.

Because for all the visible and seeming consensual determination to hold on to Indochina, the accord was, in actuality, shaky at best. Moreover, as Laurent Cesari convincingly argues, this was in no small measure due to it being in conflict with France's far higher priorities in Africa, with key figures, such as subsequent premier Pierre Mendès France and François Mitterrand (overseas minister, minister of the interior and minister of justice in several governments between 1950 and 1957), calling early on for a 'retreat to Africa'. Soon enough, even the staunchest advocates of the war would concede that the real stakes in the conflict did not revolve around Indochina's strategic or economic importance per se. There was thus widespread agreement that Indochina's utility was diminishing rapidly, and this was made starkly apparent by France's dramatic reduction and withdrawal of both private and public investments in Indochina, most of which were being relocated to North and West Africa. Rather, the fear was that quitting Indochina would make France look weak and so encourage rebellion in North Africa.[75] Akin to the changes in the British colonial disposition at the time, although pursued with a far greater steadfastness, the real colonial consensus in postwar France was to crystallize around Africa. Thus, already at the Brazzaville Conference, René Pleven, realizing that France needed the assistance of its European partners, took the opportunity to reopen the Eurafrican discussion.[76]

France's plans to develop its colonial possessions south of the Mediterranean evolved in tandem with the many initiatives for an internationalization of the colonial system in Africa, from Bevin's proposal for a French–British management of Africa and onwards. The most influential of these plans was made by Eirik Labonne, whose maximalist version of a future geopolitical entity stretching from the

[75] Laurent Cesari, 'The declining value of Indochina: France and the economics of empire, 1950–1955', in Lawrence and Logevall (eds), *The First Vietnam War*, pp. 176–95.
[76] Thomas, *The French Empire at War 1940–45*, p. 25; Speech by Mr Corniglion-Molinier, Debates in plenary session, The European Parliament, 11 May 1960, Draft Convention on the election of the European Parliament by direct universal suffrage, 30 April 1960, compiled by the European Parliament, *The Case for Elections to the European Parliament by Direct Universal Suffrage* (DG for Parliamentary Documentation and Information, 1969), pp. 142–3.

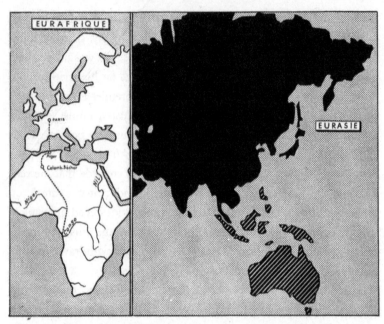

Figure 3.1 Map of Eurafrica and Eurasia. Source: Eirik Labonne, *Politique industrielle et stratégique de l'Union Française. Les Z.O.I.A. Zones d'organisation industrielle et stratégique africaines* (Paris: Révue Militaire d'Information, 1955).

Congo to the Rhine set the terms of the French debate throughout the 1950s (see Figure 3.1). A former resident general in Morocco and Tunisia, and ambassador to Moscow during World War II, Labonne's master plan for integrating France's African colonies into some five industrial and strategic zones (Zones d'Organisation Industrielle et strategique Africaines, ZOIA) was influenced by large-scale infrastructure and development programmes such as the Tennessee Valley Authority in the USA of the New Deal era and Stalin's Magnitogorsk. Referring to the Soviet experience, Labonne stated his ambition in 1948: 'For us, for the French Union, for the European Union, the Atlas mountains should be our Ural and Africa our Siberia.'[77]

---

[77] Eirik Labonne, *Politique économique de l'Union Française – Industrialisation et armement*. Deux conférences à l'Ecole nationale d'administration (Paris: Atelier d'Impressions S.L.N, 1948), p. 40.

Launched as a series of lectures at the École nationale d'administration in 1948 and 1949, Labonne's initiative was, in 1950, officially institutionalized as a governmental committee (the Comité ZOIA or, simply, the Comité Labonne) chaired by the prime minister, and with Labonne as deputy chair and coordinator of a number of scientific teams and subgroups that laid out a master plan for a future Eurafrica. Labonne's first main idea was to focus on energy supplies (coal, oil, hydro-energy, uranium), these being indispensable for any industrial development. Second, he identified a set of geographically limited 'zones of industrial and strategic organisation' – that is, areas that were suitably located for mining, processing, manufacturing or general economic growth and simultaneously of strategic importance in an emerging Cold War context (Figures 3.2 and 3.3). The greatest efforts went into outlining Zone 1 and Zone 2, centred around Colomb-Bechar on the Algerian–Moroccan border and Tebessa on the Algerian–Tunisian border, respectively. The other three zones were to be built around the projected Konkouré dam and bauxite mines in Guinea, the Kouilou dam project in the French Congo and the coal fields of Madagascar's Sakoa region.[78] As vital parts of France's and Western Europe's defence strategy, these ZOIAs would provide France with territorial depth and an opportunity for dispersal of military forces and supplies. In economic terms the zones would provide the French and European economy with a scale sufficiently large to compete on the world market with processed raw materials (steel, aluminium, petrochemical products, for instance), thus turning the French Union into what Labonne called an 'autarchic' economic sphere, such as the USA, the Soviet Union and the British Commonwealth already possessed.

Third, in understanding the gigantic investments of money and labour needed, Labonne promoted collaboration of several dimensions. His plan entailed a far-reaching integration of France's civil and military forces. Labonne therefore welcomed France's withdrawal from

---

[78] Eirik Labonne, *Politique industrielle et stratégique de l'Union Française. Les Z.O.I.A. Zones d'organisation industrielle et stratégique africaines* (Paris: Révue Militaire d'Information, 1955), pp. 10–13, 26–9.

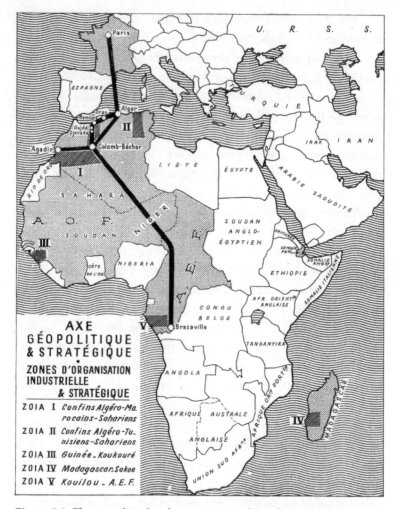

Figure 3.2 The geopolitical and strategic axis of Eurafrica, and the
   five projected industrial and strategic zones in Africa, as conceived
   by the Labonne committee. Source: Eirik Labonne, *Politique
   industrielle et stratégique de l'Union Française. Les Z.O.I.A. Zones
   d'organisation industrielle et stratégique africaines* (Paris: Révue Militaire
   d'Information, 1955).

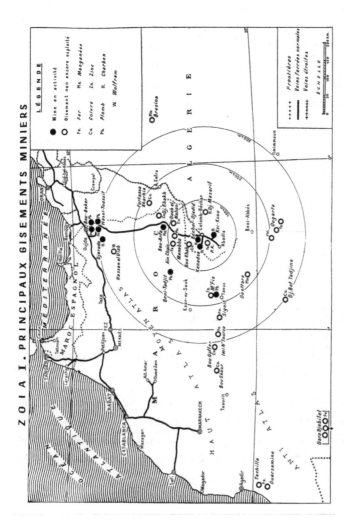

Figure 3.3 Africa's Industrial Zone number 1, centred around Colomb-Bechar, Algeria. Source: Eirik Labonne, *Politique industrielle et stratégique de l'Union Française. Les Z.O.I.A. Zones d'organisation industrielle et stratégique africaines* (Paris: Révue Militaire d'Information, 1955).

Indochina as this made troops available for African development, and he proposed the creation of an organization (Bureau Africain de Travaux Industriels Militaires) that would coordinate the role of the 'three armies' (land, sea, air) in Africa's industrialization. Yet, even if France's worlds of money and soldiery joined forces, their resources would not suffice. This is why Labonne conceived of the ZOIAs as an international undertaking, calling for a pooling of capital from the Marshall Plan and for the constitution of pan-European consortiums.[79]

Through the act of modernizing and industrializing Africa, formerly antagonistic European nations would come together in an act of practical solidarity, Labonne asserted, echoing the Eurafrican utopias of Coudenhove-Kalergi, Sörgel, Valois, Guernier, Sarraut and Orsini di Camerota of the interwar period. As Labonne explained, Europe was becoming increasingly isolated from the rouble, dollar and sterling zones:

> In this isolation, Africa remains for France more than ever a supreme opportunity to pull the Western nations of Europe, Germany included, into the orbit of a vast zone characterised by diversity and relative independence. Such European participation – financial, technical and human – in the organisms destined to promote African industrialisation constitutes one of the rare means, at once precise and rapid, through which may be established under our aegis that European solidarity which is one of the true pillars of peace.[80]

Labonne's plan was more detailed and, save for budgetary matters, practicable than those of any of his predecessors. As mentioned, his plan also enjoyed political support at the highest governmental level. In 1952, the government instituted a Bureau for African industry (the Bureau d'Organisation des Ensembles Industriels Africaines, BIA) headed by the engineer Louis Armand, later to become the first

---

[79] Eirik Labonne, *Politique économique de l'Union Française – Industrialisation et équipement stratégique*. Étude – Programme (Paris: [unidentified publisher], 1949), pp. 30–2.

[80] Labonne, *Politique économique de l'Union Française – Industrialisation et équipement stratégique*, pp. 10–11.

president of EURATOM, in an effort to increase investments and promote industrialization of Africa in accord with Labonne's plan.[81] Like Labonne, Armand realized the need for foreign investments in French Africa, and he was especially keen on exploiting the resources of Sahara.[82]

Labonne's and Armand's organizations provided a platform that throughout the 1950s guided investments and policies aiming to modernize the French Union, which eventually led to the reorganization of the Sahara region in 1957 and the establishment of the Common Organization of the Sahara Regions (OCRS), which we discuss in the next chapter.[83] Most of the proposed industrial complexes remained on the drawing table, however. The dilemma was that – even as one-fifth of France's public spending in 1955 went to the Overseas[84] – the level of investments, skills and expertise was insufficient, which is why the rescue of the French Union seemed to depend on the establishment of a European union that would partly take charge of the colonies and in return would flourish thanks to the immense but unexploited resources of Africa. In support of this calculation, French Eurafricanists relied on

---

[81] For a brief descpription of the tasks of BIA in relation to Labonne's programme, see Louis Armand, 'Pourquoi un ensemble industriel au Sahara', article in two parts, *Union Française et Parlement*, Vol. 4, No. 39, June 1953, pp. 12–13; and Vol. 5, No. 40–1, July–August 1953, pp. 7–8.

[82] Louis Armand, *Le Sahara, L'Afrique et L'Europe*. Conférence prononcé le vendredi 25 février 1955 (Lyon: Société d'économie politique et d'économie sociale, 1955). Armand promoted Jean-Michel de Lattre's detailed report on the legal aspects of foreign investments in the French Union: *La mise en valeur de l'ensemble eurafricain français et la participation des capitaux étrangers: Sociétés à participation étrangère; Compagnies à charte* (Paris: Libraire générale de droit et de jurisprudence, 1954).

[83] Several organizations were thus founded in collaboration with or inspired by the Comité Labonne and Armand's BIA, such as the Bureau de Recherches de Pétrole (BRP), the Commissariat à l'Energie Atomique, the Bureau de Recherches Minières of Algeria, the Bureau Minier de la France d'Outre-mer, the Comité d'Expansion de la région de Colomb-Bechar, the Association Eurafricaine Minière et Industrielle (ASSEMI) and the Consortium européen pour le développement des ressources naturelles de l'Afrique (Consafrique) – the latter two being particularly interesting as they were explicitly pan-European consortiums of European bankers and industrialists with an interest in African raw materials. See Jean-Michel de Lattre, 'Sahara, clé de voûte de l'ensemble eurafricain français', *Politique étrangère*, Vol. 22, No. 4, 1957, pp. 364–66.

[84] The figure was calculated by Pierre Moussa in his book *Les chances économiques de la communauté franco-africaine* (Paris: Armand Collin, 1957), which provided a detailed balance sheet of the costs and benefits of the empire for metropolitan France.

the argument of geopolitics, according to which only larger economic and political entities were able to enjoy independence, autonomy and prosperity. What Siberia meant to the Soviet Union, what the Western plains and mountains meant to the USA, and what China and India sought to accomplish with their great industrial leaps, must now be executed in Africa by the nations of Western Europe, Armand argued.[85] This is the reason why the strongest promoters of a rapid exploitation and development of Africa's raw materials were typically also strong promoters of European integration.

A case in point is François Mitterrand. A supporter of Labonne's plans, he deplored the scant resources that since 1946 had been devised for the modernization of Africa, whereas the war in Indochina had cost ten times as much.[86] Enumerating all the riches yet to be extracted ('iron, manganese, coal, gold, diamonds, copper, bauxite, salt, phosphates, maybe uranium, maybe oil'), he argued that Africa must come first ('Afrique d'abord') and that Paris, in being the capital of French Africa, also held the key to the future of Europe:

> From the Congo to the Rhine the third continental nation will find its equilibrium around our metropolis. Europe itself can do nothing without France. What can it do to the East? The South opens itself generously to its people, its machines, its commodities, its capital, but all the routes leading there passes through us. Once again, the French itinerary determines that of Europe.[87]

Mitterrand found it scandalous that the French quarrelled among themselves about whether to side with the Eastern or the Western bloc. There was obviously a superior alternative: 'the colossal bloc that extends from Lille to Brazzaville and from Abéché to Dakar'. This was for Mitterrand 'the one and only incontestable historical reality: Eurafrican France'. However, he, too, understood that the

---

[85] Armand, *Le Sahara*, p. 19.
[86] François Mitterrand, *Aux Frontières de l'Union Française* (Paris: René Julliard, 1953), pp. 24–5. (Africa had since 1946 received 350 billion francs and Indochina more than 4,000 billion, according to Mitterrand.)
[87] Ibid., p. 35.

development of this entity demanded European input of capital and skills. Thus, precisely because of the combination of France's imperial and geopolitical potential and France's inability to realize this potential on its own, the country was predestined to assume leadership in the process of European integration.[88]

France's efforts to modernize Africa proved both instrumental and indispensable for its colonial and foreign policy in the 1950s, the European integration process in particular also in more concrete terms. As these plans apparently demonstrated France's high ambitions for Africa's development and concern for the welfare of its populations, they provided France's political and diplomatic corps with a strong argument against decolonization and for continued presence in Africa.

Developments in Cameroon illustrate this, as evinced in pioneering research by Thomas Deltombe, Manuel Domergue and Jacob Tatsitsa. Governing on a UN mandate, France here faced resistance from a major independence movement, the Union of the Peoples of Cameroon (UPC, or Union des populations du Cameroun) led by Ruben Um Nyobé. In response to such anti-colonial opposition and to preempt an anticipated long-term scenario where France's rule would be succeeded by a sovereign Cameroon, France decided in 1950 to consolidate its control of Cameroon's industrial, commercial and strategic infrastructure. The territory became a vital field for strategic and industrial planning in accord with Labonne's Eurafrican principles. The main agent putting this into practice was Roland Pré, governor of Guinea (1948–51) and France's high commissioner in Cameroon (1954–6). Pré administered a swift expansion of Guinean bauxite mining along with the construction of an aluminium smelter with supporting power plants in Cameroon (the so-called Enelcam–Alucam combine in Edea), all of which served to entrench French and European interests and to justify the increased presence of military forces to protect the new instalments and root out the UPC, which, since 1955, conducted an armed struggle of liberation. Eurafrican planning and militarized colonial repression

[88] Ibid., pp. 34–55, 206–11.

fused seamlessly and successfully. Nyobé was assassinated in 1958 and, as the pro-French leader Ahmadou Ahidjo was brought into power, the integrity of French interests was secured even as Cameroon became independent in 1960, all of which was applauded by an international community convinced by the economically and politically noble cause of France's Eurafrican policy.[89] Indeed, the first ingot of aluminium was tapped from the Edea plant only weeks before the agreement on associating the African colonies to the EEC.[90]

Algeria was a far more critical case, as we shall see later. As political unrest was growing in Algeria, in 1955 the French government commissioned Labonne to make a quick draft programme to improve industrialization, employment opportunities and strategic organization of the Colomb-Bechar region.[91] Labonne's committee and its various offshoots thus became instrumental for France's effort to resolve the Algerian conflict, to counter decolonization and consolidate its presence in Africa, while they also warranted the credibility and attractiveness of France's Eurafrican bid in negotiations on European integration.

In modelling what historian Dirk van Laak terms an 'imperial infrastructure', the above-mentioned large-scale plans thus furnished a programme for a colonialism of modernization and development that, thanks to its urgent economic and strategic motivation, could count on approval from many who sought to strengthen the case for some future European union.[92] This was post-World War II policy, to be sure, and it evolved in a geopolitical context very different from the Eurafrican schemes of the interwar period. Yet, the underlying attitude

---

[89] Thomas Deltombe, Manuel Domergue and Jacob Tatsitsa, *Kamerun! Une guerre cachée aux origines de la Francafrique, 1948–1971* (Paris: La Découverte, 2011), pp. 96–186.

[90] This event was headline news in France's press and seen as proof of France's efforts to modernize its empire; see 'Le prémier lingot d'aluminium de l'Afrique française a été coulé au Cameroun', *Le Monde*, 3–4 February 1957.

[91] Labonne, *Politique industrielle et stratégique de l'Union Française. Les Z.O.I.A.*, pp. 27–9.

[92] For the notion of 'imperial infrastructure' and its relation to the 'infrastructure of imperialism', see Dirk van Laak, *Imperiale Infrastruktur: Deutsche Planungen für eine Erschließung Afrikas, 1880 bis 1960* (Paderborn: Ferdinand Schöningh, 2004), pp. 15–39.

of unequal complementarity remained the same. 'It is in Africa that Europe will be made,' Jean Michel de Lattre wrote in a 1955 article promoting Labonne's plan.[93] Returning to the same issue in 1957 he asserted that 'in order to provide Europe with a future, three elements are missing: space, energy, raw materials. Africa can provide these; in return, Europe can deliver people, technology, capital.'[94] Such views found strong support also in the numerous publications, journals, magazines and pressure groups, which became increasingly convinced that European integration provided the best way to consolidate the Eurafrican project and develop France's colonial system.[95]

As we see, then, France's uncompromising determination to restore its Empire while at the same time being fully aware of its own dismal weakness and the growing anti-colonial sentiments provide important clues as to why France would be the most tenacious standard-bearer for the relaunching of Eurafrica after World War II. For how else could French weakness be squared with French grandeur? As examined earlier, the mostly abortive Anglo–French colonial collaboration in Africa can be seen as the first major postwar attempt at Eurafrican consolidation. As Labonne's example indicates, such consolidation apparently had history on its side, as it conformed to a number of economic, geopolitical and strategic imperatives. During the 1950s, many more efforts along the same lines would be added, the most important one converging on the Treaty of Rome negotiations in

---

[93] Jean-Michel de Lattre, 'Les grands ensembles africains', *Politique étrangère*, Vol. 20, No. 5, 1955, p. 543.

[94] de Lattre, 'Sahara', p. 378.

[95] The main organs were *Marchés coloniaux* and *Union française et parlement* – and also, to some extent, the Algiers-based journal *Eurafrique: Revue générale d'action africaine et méditerranéenne* – in which Eurafrica was promoted by all the major voices in France's and Europe's colonial circles as being of utmost economic, cultural and economic importance. Linked to these venues were numerous civil society initiatives, organizations and associations on both sides of the Mediterranean and with varying degrees of political and economic leverage. In 1957, many of these organizations and associations would organize in 'Eurafrica committees' (Comités Eurafrique), with their own publication, *Cahiers économiques et de liaison des Comités Eurafrique*, and with strong support at the top political level. For instance, the presidency of the French committee was held by Jacques Soustelle, governor of Algeria, and Félix Houphouët-Boigny. The French committee also counted Louis Armand, Eirik Labonne and most other French Eurafricanists among its honorary members.

1956–7. While this is the subject matter of the next chapter, it is now high time to move beyond the immediate context of France and Britain's efforts to modernize their empires and instead focus our attention on how the colonial question, and Africa in particular, were dealt with in the various European organizations that sprang up in the late 1940s and early 1950s.

Internationalizing the colonies: The European movement

Let us begin where most EU studies' accounts on postwar European integration begin – namely, with the Congress of Europe, which took place in The Hague in May 1948. The Congress was held on the initiative of the International Committee of the Movements for European Unity, an umbrella organization established in 1947 to coordinate a number of movements and bodies of various political persuasions who advocated European integration (excluding communists and the far right); the organization changed name to the European Movement in October 1948. The event gathered several hundred prominent Europeans, ranging from intellectuals and trade unions to church leaders, businessmen and high rank statesmen – including Winston Churchill (who chaired the event), Paul-Henri Spaak, Konrad Adenauer, Alcide De Gasperi, Paul Reynaud, Anthony Eden, Paul van Zeeland, Paul Ramadier, Harold Macmillan and Pierre-Henri Teitgen, to mention but a few. Most importantly, the Congress of Europe heralded the establishment of the Council of Europe the following year.

While the Congress and the European Movement's subsequent flurry of activities are nearly always referred to in the literature – to a greater or lesser extent – the discussion is almost exclusively focused on the European Movement's intra-European concerns. Among other things, this comprises questions of peace-building in Europe and reconciliation between recent enemies, the German question, the future of nation-states and nationalism in Europe, the mounting Cold

War division of Europe and, not least, the contentious question of whether a united Europe was to be governed according to federal, supranational or intergovernmental principles. Rarely, if ever, though, are the European Movement's positions on the colonial question addressed. This is puzzling indeed, particularly considering that the colonial question featured prominently in the Movement's discussions.[96] Also, to think that this should not have been the case is entirely counter-intuitive, given what we have just recounted concerning the tremendous importance that Britain and France assigned to their colonial empires after the war – something that also held true for Belgium and the Netherlands.

As indicated, most of the European Movement and the Congress of Europe's participant groupings (among them Coudenhove-Kalergi's new organization, the European Parliamentary Union) adhered to the Eurafrican tenet concerning the necessity of developing African colonies for the collective benefit of a war-torn Western Europe striving to emerge as a 'third force' in world politics.[97] 'If we wish to rebuild', said Hendrik Brugmans, the leader of the European Union of Federalists (EUF) and one of the staunchest third force advocates, 'we urgently need "living space" – if you will forgive the expression – on a bigger scale than that of the old, so-called autonomous nations.'[98] In an article in British Labour's *Daily Herald* a year prior to the Congress, appealing to Ernest Bevin, Brugmans affirmed the indispensability of Europe's independence between the superpowers, adding that the European Union must include the overseas territories that were associated with its members.[99]

---

[96] For an exception, see Wolfgang Schmale, 'Before self-reflexivity: Imperialism and colonialism in the early discourses of European integration', in Menno Spiering and Michael Wintle (eds), *European Identity and the Second World War* (Houndmills: Palgrave Macmillan, 2011), pp. 190–8.

[97] Jean-Marie Palayret, 'Les mouvements proeuropéens et la question de l'Eurafrique, du Congrès de La Haye à la Convention de Yaoundé (1948–1963)', in Bitsch and Bossuat (eds), *L'Europe unie et l'Afrique*, pp. 185–229.

[98] Quoted and documented in Alan Hick, 'The European Union of Federalists (EUF)', in Walter Lipgens (ed.), *Documents on the History of European Integration*, Vol. 4 (Berlin: Walter de Gruyter, 1991), p. 16.

[99] Documented in ibid., pp. 17–18.

During the deliberations in The Hague in May 1948, such views were commonplace, the Congress' Political Report serving as a good illustration. One of the Congress' most important documents, it was drawn up by its International Committee, which was influenced by the British, French and Benelux foreign ministers. The report established that the integration of Germany into a European Union was to be achieved, in part, by means of a joint control of the country's heavy industry. 'On her side', the report went on, 'Germany would gain full access to the resources of other European nations and to the raw materials of their overseas territories.' This synergy rested on the foregone conclusion that, as the report spells it out under the heading 'Overseas Territories', 'The European Union must, of course, include in its orbit the extensions, dependencies and associated territories of the European Powers in Africa and elsewhere, and must preserve the existing constitutional ties which unite them.'[100]

In the Congress' Political Resolution, moreover, it was unanimously agreed that the future European union or federation 'must assist in assuring the economic, political and cultural advancement of the populations of the overseas territories associated with it'.[101] Similarly, the Economic and Social Resolution '[d]eclares that this Union must maintain and progressively adjust the economic ties which at present link the countries of Europe with the Dominions and associated States or dependent territories overseas'.[102]

We should also briefly attend to the Congress' Closing Plenary Session and its unanimous adoption of the final document, entitled 'Message to Europeans', which had been drawn up by the Swiss author and staunch federalist Denis de Rougemont. In the fourth paragraph of this very short document (just over one page) the following message was delivered: 'Together with the overseas peoples associated

---

[100] Quoted in Alan Hick, 'The "European Movement"', in Lipgens (ed.), *Documents on the History of European Integration*, pp. 335–6.

[101] European Movement, *Europe Unites: The Hague Congress and After* (London: Hollis and Carter, 1949), p. 38.

[102] Ibid., pp. 68–9.

with our destinies, we can to-morrow build the greatest political formation and the greatest economic unit our age has seen.'[103]

Among scores of other examples underlining the salience of the colonial question within the European Movements, we could turn, finally, to the European Union of Federalists' (EUF) subsequent (and failed) attempt to federalize the Council of Europe, which was established a year after the Congress of Europe, almost to the day, on 5 May 1949. At its Extraordinary General Assembly in Paris in October 1949, the EUF adopted its 'Draft of a Federal Pact', to be submitted to the Council of Europe's Consultative Assembly. Expressing grave concerns over what was seen as a botched unification of Europe, something that the EUF attributed to the failure to recast Europe in a federal or supranational mould, the Pact was drafted with the utmost urgency. As the Preamble warned, 'the political, economic, social and military position of Europe is rapidly approaching the critical point after which there will be no further possibility of preventing the final collapse of our civilization.' This urgency is also reflected in the Pact's approach to the colonial territories. As maintained by the EUF, 'Europe as an entity will be viable only if the links which unite it with countries and dependent territories scattered all over the globe are taken into account.' The necessity of incorporating the colonies into the European Federation is primarily economically motivated:

> The object of federalizing Europe is not only to establish a world equilibrium, but also to provide for Europe, together with its associated countries and dependent territories overseas, a favourable place in the economy of the world. This last result will not be achieved unless Europe, with its associated countries and dependent territories overseas, develops all its resources so as to raise the standard of living of all the peoples concerned, and to re-establish the balance of payments between Europe and the rest of the world.

This provided, the Pact could also go on to proclaim that 'The era of national ownership of colonial territories is past. […] From now

---

[103] Ibid., p. 94.

onwards a common European policy of development for certain regions of Africa should be taken in hand, for the benefit of all the peoples concerned.' In closing, the EUF emphasized that 'the Council of Europe must be asked to study as a matter of urgency, in consultation with all the interested parties, this question which is so vital for the successful building of Europe'.[104]

Cooperation overseas: The Council of Europe and the OEEC

While the Council of Europe (CE) failed entirely to embody the federal principles advocated by the EUF and many other parties within the European Movement, it immediately succeeded in turning colonial cooperation in Africa into one of the organization's defining priorities – a fact largely forgotten today.[105] The unanimous adoption of the Strasbourg Plan by the CE's Consultative Assembly in 1952 provides ample testimony to this. Before probing the Strasbourg Plan, however, we need to say something about the organization that had been instrumental in the preparatory work for the Plan, namely the Organisation for European Economic Co-operation (OEEC, subsequently the OECD), which has already been mentioned in passing above in the context of Britain's efforts to increase European colonial cooperation in Africa.

The OEEC was formed in April 1948 for the purpose of administering the US Marshall Plan – or the European Recovery Program.[106]

---

[104] Quoted and documented in Hick, 'The European Union of Federalists (EUF)', pp. 84–90.

[105] See Palayret, 'Les mouvements proeuropéens et la question de l'Eurafrique', pp. 200–13; Uwe Kitzinger, *The Challenge of the Common Market* (Oxford: Basil Blackwell, 1962), pp. 90–1; Robert W. Heywood, 'West European Community and the Eurafrica concept in the 1950s', *Journal of European Integration*, Vol. 4, No. 2, 1981, pp. 199–210; Karis Muller, '"Concentric Circles" at the periphery of the European Union', *Australian Journal of Politics and History*, Vol. 46, No. 3, 2000, pp. 322–35; A. H. Robertson, 'The Council of Europe and the United Nations', in Berhanykun Andemicael (ed.) *Regionalism and the United Nations* (New York: United Nations Institute for Training and Research, 1979), pp. 506–7.

[106] The signing of the Convention for European Economic Co-operation formally established the OEEC (on 16 April 1948) and the organization originally consisted of eighteen member countries and territories.

While portions of its funds were used to assist individual recipient states in their work to boost financial stability in their respective colonial empires,[107] the OEEC also immediately decided to form an Overseas Territories Working Group in order to promote European cooperation in colonial affairs, particularly towards Africa.

In its extensive report from 1951, focusing on investments in the colonial territories south of the Sahara, the OEEC described itself as 'one of the media through which Member countries' overseas territories pursue their policy of co-operation'.[108] But it also maintained that the necessary public and private investment in overseas territories by no means should be limited to those OEEC members with colonial territories. Rather, all members should be encouraged to contribute: 'It is in the interest of the whole free world that the [colonial] territories, which form part of it, should endeavour to speed up and increase the production of scarce materials.'[109] Although formulated in less utopian terms, the report echoes the interwar period's plans for Eurafrica in its focus on large-scale infrastructural projects, water control, agriculture and 'constructional work, on a heavier scale' – e.g. 'Vast stretches of mosquito-infested swamp must be drained.'[110] Important too is that the report is completely void of indications that colonialism in Africa might some day come to an end; on the contrary, Eurafrican planning is unreservedly described as 'a long-term task' in an African terrain characterized by 'political security'. In combination with rising raw material prices and the necessity of increased industrial production, such political security, the report goes on, had helped generate the current 'tendency for capital to move towards Africa'. Therefore, 'Every advantage must be taken of this tendency.' In conclusion, however, the report makes sure to

---

[107] OEEC, *Investments in Overseas Territories in Africa, South of the Sahara* (Paris: OEEC, 1951), pp. 51, 75; Frances M. B. Lynch, *France and the International Economy: From Vichy to the Treaty of Rome* (London: Routledge, 1997), p. 192.
[108] OEEC, *Investments in Overseas Territories in Africa*, p. 9.
[109] Ibid., p. 20.
[110] Ibid., p. 21.

underscore yet again that, 'quite apart from the present situation, [...] the development of the territories is essentially a long-term task'.[111]

For its part, the Council of Europe's Strasbourg Plan set out to resolve one of Western Europe's most pressing problems at the time, namely its chronic and paralysing dollar deficit, which the (by now) discontinued Marshall aid had done little to settle. The answer? Africa! As explained by the French CE representative, M. Saller, during the CE's Consultative Assembly debate on the Plan: '[N]o European Political Community can survive without the support and co-operation of overseas countries having constitutional links with Europe. This is an ever-present economic reality which Europe must perforce recognize if she is not to be doomed to perish.'[112]

By way of joint large-scale investments in the exploitation of the African colonies' vast yet largely untapped natural resources, Western Europe would be able to reduce its dependence on dollar imports of raw materials. As established by the Plan: 'The economies of the overseas territories, which are large producers of raw materials, and the industrialised economies of the European countries are on the whole complementary.'[113] As West German representative Johannes Semler, heading the CE's Committee on Economic Relations with Overseas Territories, pleaded for the Plan before the Assembly, he quoted from a speech made a week earlier by former French prime minister Paul Reynaud, now chairman of the CE's Committee on Economic Questions: 'We must also, if free Europe is to be made viable, jointly exploit the riches of the African continent, and try to find there those raw materials which we are getting from the dollar area, and for which we are unable to pay.'[114] In so doing, this would facilitate Western

---

[111] Ibid., pp. 72, 79.
[112] Council of Europe, *The Strasbourg Plan* (Strasbourg: Secretariat-General Council of Europe, 1952), p. 151. We could note that Jean Monnet had been an early advocate of precisely this line of policy; see e.g. 'U.S. to prod Europe for self-recovery', *The New York Times*, 16 July 1948.
[113] Council of Europe, *The Strasbourg Plan*, p. 16.
[114] Ibid., p. 135.

Europe's transition into 'a third economic group standing midway between the Communist and the dollar areas'.[115]

However, since the large-scale investments required could not be shouldered by the colonial powers alone, the Plan was adamant in stressing the indispensability of all Council members (by now fourteen countries) contributing. As pointed out by the UK representative Lord Layton, 'it is clear that we have to think of these overseas territories not as the possessions of any one country [...]; they have to be integrated with all the countries of Europe and all the overseas territories'. This chimed with practically all of the representatives. For instance, Denmark's Hermond Lannung emphasized 'the overriding importance of greater co-operation and of a major joint European effort in Africa if we do not wish to see Africa lost to European influence, culture, trade, etc. and, in the long run, for that influence to be replaced by that of another continent'. Europe had just lost the 'battle of Asia', Lannung asserted, and now its nations needed to unite in order to not also lose 'the battle of Africa'. 'Here we have before us a great concrete and practical task which calls for the utmost collaboration of us all.'[116]

For this project to become viable, obviously, West German, but also Scandinavian, capital and industrial clout was greatly sought after. According to the Plan, all parties stood to gain from such a collaborative approach: 'If European countries without colonial responsibilities contribute to the development of overseas territories it will then be possible to open these overseas markets to them.' With limited access to its traditional markets in the east – now within the Soviet orbit of control – the Plan argued, such a scenario should provide West Germany, in particular, with an important incentive to look to Africa as an outlet for its 'tractors, cranes, bridges, dredges, machine tools, etc.'[117]

As during the interwar Eurafrica debate, the topic of European emigration to Africa also figured prominently in the Strasbourg Plan, since 'over-population' still was seen as 'one of Europe's most critical

---

[115] Ibid., p. 15.
[116] Ibid., pp. 140, 154.
[117] Ibid., pp. 54–7, 175, 190, 64, 54.

human and social problems'.[118] Save for Italy's demand to provide for mass emigration to African colonies, however, the majority opinion within the CE's Assembly opted for a more moderate approach, mostly advocating emigration of select groups of people with certain skills.[119]

While the Strasbourg Plan, after several years of deliberation, was basically rejected by the CE's Committee of Ministers – a quite natural fate given the EC's intergovernmental character – its content and spirit was still very much representative of the Eurafrican momentum during the 1950s. Let us not spoil this chance to create 'Eurafrica as a third global force', exhorted the major French magazine *L'Observateur* in October 1952 in reference to the Strasbourg Plan.[120] Also, the Committee's rejection did not slow down the Assembly's activity on the matter; on the contrary, the work and debate continued unabated during the 1950s. In response to the rejection, for instance, the Assembly proceeded to set up a 'Study Group for the Development of Africa'.[121] We should note too that in its review of the Strasbourg Plan, which was published in 1954 and commissioned by the CE's Committee of Ministers, the OEEC observed 'with satisfaction that the aims laid down in the Strasbourg Plan by the Consultative Assembly of the Council of Europe largely agree with those of the Organization'. Here, the OEEC also affirmed that 'there can be no doubt of the community of interests which exists between Member countries and the overseas countries covered by the Strasbourg Plan', adding: 'The governments of Member countries are therefore in full agreement with these objectives [...]. The Strasbourg Plan rightly insists on the importance of economic co-operation between all Member countries and the overseas territories dependent on certain of them.'[122]

---

[118] Ibid., p. 58.
[119] For a more extensive account of the issue of European migration to Africa in the context of postwar Eurafrican integration, see Peo Hansen and Stefan Jonsson, 'Demographic colonialism: EU–African migration management and the Legacy of Eurafrica', *Globalizations*, Vol. 8, No. 3, 2011, pp. 261–76.
[120] P. M. Dessinges, 'Le Conseil de l'Europe et l'Afrique', *L'Observateur*, No. 126, 9 October 1952.
[121] Robertson, 'The Council of Europe and the United Nations', pp. 506–7.
[122] OEEC, *Comments on the Strasbourg Plan* (Paris: OEEC, May 1954), pp. 9–10.

In this context it is also important to mention the European League for Economic Co-operation (ELEC), which was established in 1946 for the specific purpose of promoting colonial cooperation between Western European states. An economic organization, think-tank and lobbying group, ELEC gathered key political and economic actors in Europe and had close ties to the OEEC. As Laura Kottos has shown, ELEC was not only influential in shaping the content of the Strasbourg Plan as such; it was also instrumental in keeping its spirit alive after it had been formally rejected. Most crucially, however, ELEC's perseverance and the fact that many of its members also functioned as key players in the Treaty of Rome negotiations would combine to facilitate the institution of the EEC's colonial association regime subsequently agreed upon in Rome in 1957. As Kottos is able to demonstrate, then, despite the Strasbourg Plan's formal demise within the Council of Europe, some of its key components were to be resurrected as part of the EEC's association of the members' colonial territories.[123]

NATO's Eurafrican outfit

If the OEEC and the CE's efforts mainly focused on the economic aspects of colonial cooperation – albeit always embedded in the prevailing geopolitical discourse and objectives – the establishment of NATO, also in 1949, would involve a modest yet very concrete strategic application of Eurafrica. As the NATO Treaty (signed on 4 April 1949) specified in its Article 6, 'an armed attack on one or more of the Parties is deemed to include an attack: on the territory of any of the Parties in Europe or North America, [and] on the Algerian Departments of France'.

---

[123] Laura Kottos, 'A "European Commonwealth": Britain, the European League for Economic Co-operation, and European debates on empire, 1947–1957', *Journal of Contemporary European Studies*, Vol. 20, No. 4, 2012, pp. 497–515. For support of Kottos' thesis, see 'Översikter och meddelanden', *Statsvetenskaplig tidskrift*, Vol. 64, No. 5, 1961, pp. 316–18.

The incorporation of French Algeria rested with a French demand or, better, an ultimatum. Indeed, if the USA, which very much disapproved of Algeria's inclusion, had not succumbed, France would most likely have refused to join NATO, something that in turn would have jeopardized the whole project, given the absolute centrality of France's participation.[124]

France's original bid, forwarded during the negotiations in the summer of 1948, went even further, asking for the inclusion of North Africa in its entirety, covering not only Algeria but also northern Egypt, the Suez Canal, all of Tunisia as well as the northern parts of Morocco. For a while, this French demand prompted Belgium to ask for Congo's inclusion into NATO as well.[125] In the draft treaty, France actually managed to have its tender acknowledged, although dissenting views were appended to the draft. Such dissent would soon be voiced more generally in the ensuing negotiations towards the end of the year. Nonetheless, France did receive some qualified support from Britain, with its US ambassador, Oliver Franks, stating that 'while the British government would probably not wish to continue to press for inclusion of all of Africa north of 30° it would want the part west Libya included'. As the late Escott Reid explains, the real purpose of this was that 'the British were prepared to compromise on excluding all of Africa except Algeria'.[126] While still not ready to formally back down from its original bid, France's immediate response was nonetheless quite indicative of the fact that it was Algeria that constituted the heart of the matter. At the beginning of January 1949, Foreign Minister Robert Schuman clarified this in his talks with the Canadian ambassador to France, Georges Vanier, informing him that:

> [I]t would be quite impossible for any French government to accept the idea of excluding Algeria which was part of metropolitan France, on political grounds of course because no French government could

---

[124] Lawrence Kaplan, *The United States and NATO: The Formative Years* (Lexington: The University Press of Kentucky, 1984), p. 118.

[125] John W. Young, *Britain, France and the Unity of Europe 1945–1951* (Leicester: Leicester University Press, 1984), p. 103.

[126] Escott Reid, *Time of Fear and Hope: The Making of the North Atlantic Treaty 1947–1949* (Toronto: McClelland and Stewart, 1977), p. 214.

possibly propose this to Parliament, but also on purely strategic grounds because the general defence of France could not be envisaged without the inclusion of Algeria as a base for defensive action as well as for purposes of retreat. [...] It would even be difficult for the government to accept the exclusion of Tunisia and Morocco, but that of Algeria quite impossible.[127]

Schuman's strategic point regarding the 'inclusion of Algeria as a base for defensive action as well as for purposes of retreat' reflected the Eurafrican sentiments that were predominant in France, not least within its military circles and the Labonne Committee. As we shall discuss further in the next chapter, the strategic argument in favour of Eurafrica drew from the lessons of France's failure to utilize North Africa precisely 'as a base for defensive action as well as for purposes of retreat' during the German attack in 1940; but it also drew from the lesson that, eventually, as the war progressed, North Africa would come to assume such a strategic role, thus facilitating the liberation of Europe. As illustrated by Labonne's programme for constructing industrial and strategic zones in Africa, the postwar reasoning for a strategic Eurafrica concept thus sought to drive home the point that the only way to sustain or deter a Soviet attack on the continent was to reconstruct Western Europe and North Africa as an integral whole.[128]

With the French government making it very clear that Algerian inclusion was an ultimatum while at the same time clarifying that it would not push NATO's African extension any further than Algeria, its partners, save for the USA and Canada, were also getting ready to accept France's demand.[129] The main objections raised by Washington revolved around two main concerns: (1) 'that the inclusion of Algeria would bring up the whole controversial problem of overseas territories'; and (2) that the US military was 'fearful lest the pact might

---

[127] Ibid., p. 215–16.
[128] See e.g. Claude d'Abzac-Epezy and Philippe Vial, 'In search of a European consciousness: French military elites and the idea of Europe, 1947–54', in Ann Deighton (ed.), *Building Postwar Europe: National Decision-Makers and European Institutions, 1948–63* (Houndmills: Palgrave Macmillan, 1995).
[129] Reid, *Time of Fear and Hope*, p. 216.

be called into operation in the event of native tribal troubles in these areas', also referred to as 'native uprisings'.[130] Before long, though, the USA decided to budge and let the French request stand. This happened shortly after Canada had judged the French position unyielding and so opted to accept Algeria's inclusion, the Canadian chief negotiator reporting home that as far as he was concerned 'the inclusion of Algeria would make no real difference in the operation of the treaty'.[131] As we show in the next chapter when discussing the implications of Article 6 in the context of the Algerian war, such a conclusion was soon proven to have been quite off the mark.

Africa as an essential European task: The Schuman Declaration

On 9 May 1950, almost exactly a year after the establishment of NATO, French foreign minister Robert Schuman presented what was to become known as the Schuman Declaration, or Schuman Plan, announcing the Franco–German aim to jointly regulate extraction and production of coal and steel. The Schuman Plan – which, besides Jean Monnet's work, benefitted greatly from American input and backing – gave birth to the European Coal and Steel Community (ECSC) in the Treaty of Paris a year later, comprising France, West Germany, Italy and the Benelux countries (but not Britain). Not only did the ECSC create a common market for coal and steel among the six members, but also, most significantly and symbolically, it vested the control over production with a supranational High Authority (the precursor of the European Commission). With coal and steel constituting the basis for

---

[130] Quoted in ibid., p. 216.
[131] Quite remarkably, Reid and Lawrence Kaplan basically agree that this prediction was borne out by future events, Reid concluding that, 'By skilful diplomacy, France had won a victory on the Algerian issue but the victory did not have much substance.' For his part, Kaplan claims that, 'In the long run Algeria was to mean little; the portions of North Africa identified clearly and specifically in Article 6 became irrelevant after Algeria won its independence' (Reid, *Time of Fear and Hope*, pp. 216–17; Kaplan, *The United States and NATO*, p. 118).

arms production, this arrangement was said to be designed so as to tie France and West Germany together, or as it was stated in the Schuman Plan, 'to make it plain that any war between France and Germany becomes not merely unthinkable, but materially impossible'.[132] Due to its peace message and *supranational* design, the Schuman Plan, and not least Robert Schuman himself, is a source of pride within today's EU policy parlance and the 'whiggish' EU scholarship.[133] Since 1985, moreover, the EU officially celebrates 9 May as 'Europe Day' in the 'spirit of peace and solidarity', no mention being made of the fact that while Robert Schuman made his 9 May plea for 'World peace', France was fighting an extremely brutal colonial war in Indochina.

As for Eurafrican institutionalization, the ECSC offered little on paper and was limited to the stipulation in paragraph 79 of the Paris Treaty, whereby 'Each High Contracting Party binds itself to extend to the other member States the preferential measures which it enjoys with respect to coal and steel in the non-European territories subject to its jurisdiction.'[134] In the opinion of the Committee on Economic Affairs and Development of the Council of Europe's Parliamentary Assembly, this stipulation was seen as holding out 'some prospects' in favour of 'the Eurafrican conception'.[135] According to Vernon McKay, also commenting at the time, Article 79 owed in part to German and Italian steel producers wanting admittance to markets in France's African colonies, and to Italy and the Netherlands' wish to gain access to the iron ore deposits in Gabon and Mauritania.[136] More precisely, Italy demanded that the ECSC incorporated France's colonial areas so as to ensure Italy the cheapest possible iron ore imports from

---

[132] European Union, 'Declaration of 9 May 1950', *Europa* (official website of the European Union), http://europa.eu/abc/symbols/9-may/decl_en.htm

[133] We owe the coining of this term (in the context of EU scholarship) to Mark Gilbert, 'Narrating the process: Questioning the progressive story of European integration', *Journal of Common Market Studies*, Vol. 46, No. 3, 2008, pp. 641–62.

[134] Treaty establishing the European Coal and Steel Community, Paris, 18 April 1951; the treaty entered into force on 23 July 1952.

[135] Council of Europe, Parliamentary Assembly, Opinion Committee on Economic Affairs and Development, 'Draft Treaty embodying the Statute of the European Community, adopted by the Ad Hoc Assembly', Doc 127, 7 May 1953, p. 3.

[136] Vernon McKay, *Africa in World Politics* (New York: Harper & Row, 1963), p. 144.

the mines in eastern Algeria. Since this would have required some tough adjustments within the French Union and its complicated tariff system, France was not ready to accommodate Rome's request.[137] As Ernst Haas noted in *The Uniting of Europe*, this 'almost resulted in Italian withdrawal from the negotiations and only a bilateral accord with France saved the situation'.[138] The compromise, brokered by none less than Jean Monnet himself, thus specified that while the French overseas territories and Algeria were to remain outside the ECSC, France was to grant its partners, Italy in particular, the same 'preferential measures which it enjoys with respect to coal and steel in the non-European territories subject to its jurisdiction' – as stipulated in the treaty's Article 79.[139]

But this was not the only colonial matter that could have derailed the ECSC negotiations. Italy also demanded that France made sure it capped Algerian labour immigration into its mining, coal and steel industries. Italy, who was desperate to secure outlets for its allegedly huge 'surplus population' of unemployed, thus wanted the ECSC Treaty to allow preferential treatment for Italian labour migrants in (foremost) France's heavy industry. France, who had no interest in enacting measures that would risk stoking the conflict further in Algeria, resolutely turned down this request. In fact, 'the French delegation threatened to refuse further cooperation with the proceedings in case the Italian proposals would be supported by the others'.[140] Since the guaranteeing of free movement for its miners and coal and steel workers within the ECSC area was deemed indispensable and so could

---

[137] Gérard Bossuat, *L'Europe des Français, 1943–1959: La IVe République aux sources de l'Europe communautaire* (Paris: Publ. de la Sorbonne, 1996), p. 174; Seung-Ryeol Kim, 'France's agony between "*Vocation Européenne et Mondiale*": The Union Française as an obstacle in the French policy of supranational European integration, 1952–1954', *Journal of European Integration History*, Vol. 8, No. 1, 2002, p. 63.

[138] Ernst B. Haas, *The Uniting of Europe: Political, Social, and Economic Forces 1950–1957* (Notre Dame: University of Notre Dame Press, 1958), p. 249.

[139] Kim, 'France's agony between "*Vocation Européenne et Mondiale*"', p. 63; see also William Diebold Jr., *The Schuman Plan: A Study in Economic Cooperation, 1950–1959* (New York: Council on Foreign Relations, Frederick A. Praeger, 1959), p. 134.

[140] S. A. W. Goedings, *Labor Migration in an Integrating Europe: National Migration Policies and the Free Movement of Workers, 1950–1968* (The Hague: Sdu Uitgevers, 2005), p. 131.

not be allowed to stall over the Algerian migration issue, Rome soon yielded to Paris' position; and consequently the matter was left to the discretion of the member state governments. However, as we shall see in the next chapter, the Algerian migration issue was to reappear as an even more contentious issue towards the end of the Treaty of Rome negotiations.

These colonial hurdles notwithstanding, the treaty, as mentioned, only included one article with pertinence to the colonial issue. Yet, the Schuman Declaration itself spoke in more assertive terms: 'With increased resources Europe will be able to pursue the achievement of one of its essential tasks, namely, the development of the African continent.'[141] Apparently, Schuman picked up on a suggestion made by René Mayer, then Minister of Justice, and Jean Monnet, both of them keen Eurafricanists, that France could give Africa as a 'dowry to Europe' and as a way to 'seduce the Germans'.[142]

[141] European Union, 'Declaration of 9 May 1950'. Somewhere down the road, the Schuman Declaration's bold assertion concerning Africa appears to have become a sensitive, or perhaps embarrassing, topic in certain circles. In the English translation of Robert Schuman's *Pour l'Europe* (Paris: Nagel Editions, 1963), the Schuman Declaration is reprinted – and retouched – in an annex with the Africa-passage deleted, and this without any information as to why this has been done; Robert Schuman, *For Europe* (Avignon: Institut Robert Schuman pour l'Europe, 2000), Annex, p. 103. The European Movement's official website proceeds in the same fashion, although here the deletion is marked (yet never explained) with three periods inside square brackets; www.europeanmovement.eu/index.php?id=6790 (accessed 13 September 2013). While it is not far-fetched to assume that today both the Institut Robert Schuman pour l'Europe and the European Movement have a vested interest in trying to conceal the Schuman Declaration's manifest colonial outlook, it is much harder to explain why Leiden University's Schuman Plan Collection has also chosen (without any explanation) to delete the Schuman Declaration passage on Africa (as it appears on its European Union History website); www.hum.leiden.edu/history/eu-history/historical/schuman.html (accessed 13 September 2013). In the words of Etienne Deschamps, the silence of historians on the Eurafrican dimension of Schuman's thinking on Europe 'remains astounding'; see Deschamps, 'Robert Schuman, un apôtre oublié de l'Eurafrique?', in Sylvain Schirman (ed.), *Quelles architectures pour quelle Europe: Des projets d'une Europe unie à l'Union européenne (1945–1992)*, (Brussels: Peter Lang, 2011), p. 75.

[142] The immediate mastermind behind the passage on Africa in Schuman's declaration, according to McKay, was none less than the 'Father of Europe' himself, Jean Monnet, also the chief architect of the ECSC; see McKay, *Africa in World Politics*, p. 139. However, sources closer to the political scene show that it was proposed by René Mayer, Minister of Justice and representative of Algerian Constantine who, with Monnet's approval, added it to the final draft of Schuman's declaration; see Pierre Uri, *Penser pour l'action: Un fondateur de l'Europe* (Paris: O. Jacob, 1991), p. 80; Jean Monnet, *Memoirs*, trans. Richard Mayne (New York: Doubleday, 1978), p. 300; and, for a discussion of

As such, of course, the Schuman Declaration's Eurafrican passage followed from the historical pattern sketched here. Since the 1920s, community and collaboration of Europe's states had presupposed their collaboration in Africa too. Now, as both the Council of Europe and the ECSC were established, their protagonists obviously felt it important to signal that these organizations and institutions of European integration enabled the more far-reaching collaboration that had for long occupied debates on foreign policy and geopolitics. Schuman himself was convinced that such a collaboration was necessary and had to be a part of any form of European integration. As we shall see later, he would become an even more ardent promoter of the Eurafrican idea as this towards the mid-1950s appeared to him as the only viable strategy for containing the African territories within a geopolitical sphere controlled by France and Europe.[143]

A month after the Schuman Declaration, the French government followed up their initiative in a note proposing a 'European fund for the economic and social development of Africa' to be set up in liaison with the creation of the coal and steel community. The concrete format envisaged by the French government was basically that which would later be realized with the European Economic Community: all interested European partners – Germany above all – were invited to contribute to the development of France's colonial possessions in Africa, and in return for opening the overseas territories to foreign investors the French government expected European markets to be gradually opened for African products.[144]

Many European intellectuals picked up the signal from the Schuman declaration, among them influential Austrian writer on foreign policy,

these accounts, Thomas Moser, *Europäische Integration, Dekolonisation, Eurafrika: Eine historische Analyse über die Entstehungsbedingungen der Eurafrikanischen Gemeinschaft von der Weltwirtschaftskrise bis zum Jaunde-Vertrag, 1929–1963* (Baden-Baden: Nomos Verlagsgesellschaft, 2000), pp. 169–77.

[143] Deschamps, 'Robert Schuman, un apôtre oublié de l'Eurafrique?', pp. 84–91.

[144] 'Note sur le développement du continent africain en liaison avec la réalisation du pool européen de l'acier et du charbon', 15/20 June 1950. Reprinted in Bernard Bruneteau (ed.), *Histoire de l'idée européenne au premier XXe siècle à travers les textes* (Paris: Armand Colin, 2006), pp. 252–5.

Anton Zischka. In his view, the Franco–German coal and steel agreement was but the first step in a process leading to a common exploitation of Africa's resources. Africa, argued Zischka in the title of his book, was 'Europas Gemeinschaftsaufgabe Nr. 1' ('Europe's number one common priority')[145] (see Figure 3.4). Similarly, German weekly *Der Spiegel* reported immediately after Schuman's speech that the African option, lost for Germany after World War I, was now again open for West German industrialists seeking to extend their mining and processing investments to northern Africa. An old dream was thus revived: 'Der Eurafrika-Konzern'.[146] In 1954, Gustav-Adolf Gedat, formerly a fellow traveller of the Nazis and now a prominent politician in Adenauer's party, wrote an influential treatise stating that 'Europe's future lies in Africa'[147] (see Figure 3.5). French writer Pierre Nord expressed the same conviction: '[I]t is in Africa that the French-German reconciliation, the first condition of Europe, may begin.'[148] As *The New York Times* reported in early 1953, this was also a prevalent opinion within the West German Economics Ministry, where the 'pooling of Western Europe's coal and steel' was seen as a sure gateway to new and larger markets: 'European industry, in combination, it is believed, will be able to achieve what an official of the Ministry called the "ultimate goal" of opening Africa to industrialization and thus creating a market there.'[149] Or as one unnamed 'great industrialist', also quoted in the *Times*, put it shortly after the Schuman Declaration had been made:

> Under the Schuman plan the latent riches of the African continent would be intensively exploited. American companies with dollar capital would buy in Europe part of the equivalent needed in Africa. Thereby,

---

[145] Anton Zischka, *Afrika: Europas Gemeinschaftsaufgabe Nr. 1* (Oldenburg: Gerhard Stalling Verlag, 1951).

[146] 'Schumanplan: Kombinat Europa', *Der Spiegel*, No. 20, 18 May 1950, pp. 13–17.

[147] Gustav-Adolf Gedat, *Europas Zukunft liegt in Afrika* (Stuttgart: Steinkopf, 1954). In 1938, Gedat had published a first book on the geopolitical and religious struggle over the African continent: *Was wird aus diesem Afrika: Erlebter Kampf um einen Erdteil* (Stuttgart: Steinkopf, 1938).

[148] Pierre Nord, *L'Eurafrique, notre dernière chance* (Paris: Arthème Fayard, 1955), p. 12.

[149] 'West German outlook is clouded by coming role in allied defence', *The New York Times*, 6 January 1953.

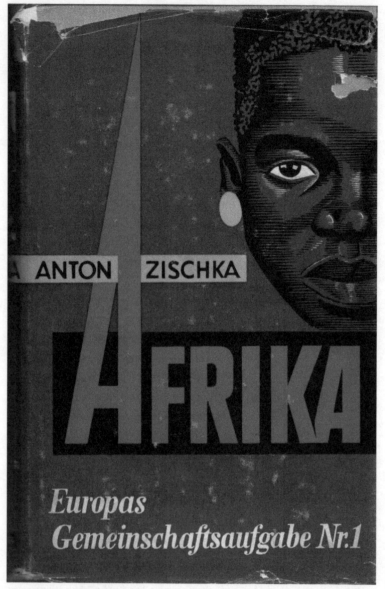

Figure 3.4 Cover of Anton Zischka, *Afrika: Europas Gemeinschaftsaufgabe Nr. 1* (Oldenburg: Gerhard Stalling Verlag, 1951).

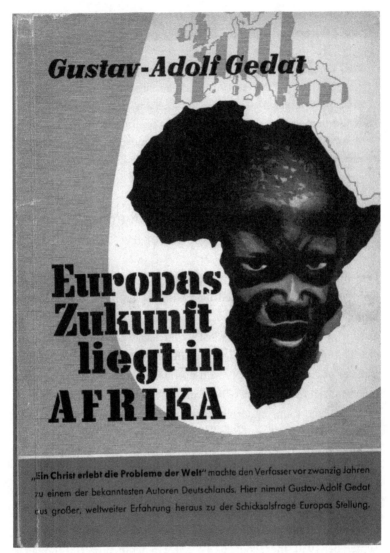

Figure 3.5 Cover of Gustav-Adolf Gedat, *Europas Zukunft liegt in Afrika* (Stuttgart: Steinkopf, 1954).

Europe could earn enough to close the dollar gap [...]. Marshall aid would become superfluous. Expanding markets created in Africa could absorb the growing exportable surplus of Europe. This would keep Europe fully employed. In Africa, production of low-cost food raw materials purchasable in non-dollar currencies would become available to cover needs in Europe. Africa is close to Europe. She would become the goal of home-seekers from overcrowded Europe as America was before World War I. Several millions of refugees from east Europe, several millions in Italy would find an outlet in Africa.[150]

Servicing the empire: The European Defence Community

Less than two months after the Schuman Plan was proclaimed, the Cold War confrontation intensified with the outbreak of the Korean War. This forced an increase in defence spending across Western Europe and the USA. Having lost its nuclear weapons monopoly the year before, this also compelled Washington to embark on a substantial transfer of troops to Europe, with numbers increasing from less than one hundred thousand in 1950 to more than one-quarter of a million in 1952. Even more important, Washington made sure it notified its allies about the urgency of going ahead with West German rearmament in some form – although this, of course, would have to stop short of an independent West German army. Despite US reinforcements, these were still far from sufficient in the event of a Soviet assault on Western Europe, for which German manpower was deemed essential. 'With Germany', President Truman stated at the NATO Council meeting in September 1950, 'there could be a defence in depth, powerful enough to offer effective resistance to aggression from the East [...] Any map will show it, and a little arithmetic will prove what the addition of German manpower means to the strength of the joint defence of Europe.'[151]

---

[150] 'Schuman Program is hailed by Swiss', *The New York Times*, 15 May 1950.
[151] Quoted in Fursdon, *The European Defence Community*, p. 83.

While the former items were fairly straightforward, although financially burdensome, the latter – about arming West Germany, which had been discussed since well before Korea and had always been flatly rebuffed by France – would prove much more difficult to achieve, at once pitting Washington's pressure on Paris to accept German rearmament against Paris' countermove to first obtain Washington's assistance in consolidating France's meagre military standing in Europe as well as its precarious imperial clout. Since Washington was already on board in Indochina, and since the rebuilding of French military strength in Europe was vital to US strategy, Paris' demands were not problems *per se*; they were already subjects for ongoing negotiations. The problem was rather to reach a swift agreement with France on German rearmament within NATO, something that all the other NATO partners were to stand solidly behind by September of 1950.

At the New York foreign ministers' meeting of the 'Big Three' (the USA, UK and France) in September, French foreign minister Schuman had informed his partners that he too recognized the need for German troop involvement in Western defence, but since this would be impossible to sell to the French public and Parliament France had little choice but to stand firm in its refusal to allow for an immediate German rearmament.[152] At the same time though, France also took seriously the US threat of deciding to go ahead without awaiting France's consent. But with France constituting a centrepiece in the USA's European defence architecture and since Washington was staunchly in favour of European integration, the Americans opted for not alienating France any further and instead convinced Paris that it should take the initiative and put forth a proposal for the others to consider.[153]

On 24 October 1950, the French government under René Pleven rose to the occasion and presented a plan to Parliament (again built on ideas of Jean Monnet)[154] for the establishment of a European Army.

---

[152] Marc Trachtenberg, *A Constructed Peace: The Making of the European Settlement, 1945–1963* (Princeton: Princeton University Press, 1999), p. 109.
[153] Wall, *The United States and the Making of Postwar France*, pp. 188–99.
[154] For Jean Monnet's influence on the Pleven Plan, see Fursdon, *The European Defence*

This became the so-called Pleven Plan, the rudiments of which would subsequently make up the abortive European Defence Community, signed into treaty in Paris in May 1952 by the six members of the ECSC. Since the other NATO members mainly viewed the Pleven Plan as little more than a tactic to delay German rearmament – according to Eisenhower it was as 'cockeyed an idea as a dope fiend would have figured out'[155] – the plan stalled in bitter debate and had to go through a new set of difficult negotiations. French diplomats even conceded to their British colleagues that, although clearly affirming West Germany's military contribution in principle, the Pleven Plan was intended to block a speedy German rearmament.[156] Nonetheless, and to cut a very long and convoluted negotiations story short, once France had accepted that the EDC was to operate within the framework of NATO, the US decided to commit to the largely French-oriented EDC.[157] Soon after, the new Eisenhower administration would elevate the EDC into the most imperative objective as far as the European Cold War theatre was concerned; indeed, as Edward Fursdon puts it, for the Americans 'there was no other European policy'. By the same token, the Eisenhower administration was to throw the whole weight of its influence in favour of a swift ratification of the treaty.[158]

According to the treaty, the EDC was to be a supranational community (yet with an intergovernmental Council), conferred with binding decision-making powers – some of which were to involve majority voting – common institutions, common armed forces and a common budget.[159] Modelled on the Schuman Plan and the ECSC's

Community, pp. 84–8.

[155] Quoted in Sebastian Rosato, *Europe United: Power Politics and the Making of the European Community* (Ithaca: Cornell University Press, 2011), p. 131.

[156] Ibid., p. 131; see also Trachtenberg, *A Constructed Peace*, pp. 110–11.

[157] Wall, *The United States and the Making of Postwar France*, p. 203.

[158] Fursdon, *The European Defence Community*, p. 271; see also Wall, *The United States and the Making of Postwar France*, pp. 263–96; Trachtenberg, *A Constructed Peace*, pp. 122–5; Geir Lundestad, *"Empire" by Integration: The United States and European Integration, 1945–1997* (Oxford: Oxford University Press, 1998), pp. 45–8.

[159] European Defense Community Treaty. Signed at Paris, 27 May 1952. Unofficial translation. Archive of European Integration, University of Pittsburgh, http://aei.pitt.edu/id/eprint/5201. (Traité instituant la Communauté européenne de défense (Paris, 27 mai

institutional structure, the EDC's principal element consisted of its common army, which was to be employed in the event of an armed attack against any one of the member states. This supranational 'European Army' was to be made up by a total of forty divisions, whereby fourteen would be French, twelve German, eleven Italian and three from the Benelux countries. In order to ensure the objective of integrating national armies, and hence the supranational European Army, no army corps was allowed to contain more than one division from the same country; in addition to this the general staff was to be integrated and senior officers recruited from all the member states.

Crucial too was of course that member states could not, as specified in Article 9 of the treaty, 'recruit or maintain national armed forces' outside the common army framework. Hence, there would be German soldiers in Western Europe again, but no sovereign German army. At the request of France, however, the treaty's Article 10 afforded an equally crucial exception to this rule by laying down that 'member States may recruit and maintain national armed forces intended for use in the non-European territories with respect to which they assume defense responsibilities, as well as units stationed in their countries which are required for the maintenance of these forces and for their relief'.

At first sight, this may give the impression that the EDC, in contrast to the Council of Europe, NATO and other European integration enterprises, was rather de-linked from colonial matters. After all, the treaty established a clear-cut separation between a European Defence Community whose scope of operation was delimited to the European turf (west of the Elbe), on the one side, and France's extra-European military engagements, on the other. Despite repeated (and ultimately successful) French requests to tamper with this separation by having protocols added to the treaty that gave France additional and exclusive rights – in contravention of the treaty's original federal ambition – to withdraw troops from the EDC for service in the colonies, some of the

1952). Mémorial du Grand-Duché de Luxembourg. Journal officiel du Grand-Duché de Luxembourg. Recueil de législation. 05.05.1954, n° 24. Luxembourg: Service Central de Législation.)

major studies on the topic nonetheless convey this impression that the EDC only concerned intra-European affairs. That is, these studies do not even provide a hint at the possibility of a colonial and thus a wider global dimension to the EDC saga.[160]

That the EDC episode somehow can be approached as reducible to the developments on the European Cold War scene and to Franco-German relations, in particular, has been thoroughly put to rest by, among others, Jasmine Aimaq, Kevin Ruane and Irwin Wall's research into French–American relations over the EDC. As Wall is able to demonstrate, the negotiation struggle over EDC was indissolubly linked with France's colonial struggle, particularly in Indochina:

> Indochina and EDC became the two poles of American policy in France, each dependent upon the other; for only French success in Indochina could allow a restrengthened France in Europe, able to take a confident place in the integrated European army alongside a militarily restored Germany. It was thus American policy as much as French that collapsed at Dien Bien Phu.[161]

In a situation where Washington's entire European policy had been made to hinge on a swift ratification of a European Defence Community that, in turn, hinged on (the false promise of) a congenial French government determined to secure parliamentary approval for the treaty, Indochina emerged as a key bargaining chip in the hands of the French. It did so too, because in addition to the EDC being the chief US objective in Europe, a pro-Western Indochina was its top priority in

---

[160] See, for instance, Simon Duke, *The Elusive Quest for European Security: From EDC to CFSP* (Houndmills: Macmillan, 2000); Craig Parsons, *A Certain Idea of Europe* (Ithaca: Cornell University Press, 2003); Rosato, *Europe United*. In Parsons, the part on the EDC sets out from the premise that 'All accounts agree that the French debate over German rearmament arose in response to massive geopolitical pressure' (p. 68). Yet such 'geopolitical pressure' is understood as resulting entirely from bipolar tensions between the USA and the Soviet Union, and is thus not made to encompass the enormous pressure France found itself under in Indochina and, increasingly so, in North Africa and elsewhere in the French Union, all of which coincided with the EDC imbroglio.

[161] Wall, *The United States and the Making of Postwar France*, p. 235.

Asia. The fact that, as Ruane notes, 'both objectives depended to a large degree on the French' was 'an irony not lost on US policymakers'.[162]

By posing stability in Indochina as a prerequisite for parliamentary approval, Paris managed to exploit this equation to its advantage in the increasingly hostile negotiations with Washington between 1952 and 1954. In other words, France was able to have the US commit to shouldering more and more of the financial burden for the Indochina war – close to 80 per cent by early 1954 – in exchange for France's repeated, but never fulfilled, promises to ensure a ratification of the EDC that French governments and parliament, post-1952, wanted less and less. As Jasmine Aimaq demonstrates, this was indeed a 'chronic theme' in the EDC negotiations, the French constantly lamenting the fact that they were unable to garner enough domestic support for the EDC unless they were lent assistance in Indochina.[163] And while this agonized the Americans tremendously, 'it proved impossible to cut off funds in Indochina to make the French ratify EDC; given Washington's anti-communism, Paris held the upper hand'.[164]

As Aimaq also reveals in her original study *For Europe or Empire?*, the intimate nexus of the EDC and France's colonial objectives would become further accentuated and so culminate during the partly overlapping Dien Bien Phu crisis (13 March–7 May 1954) and the UN Geneva Conference – which convened from 26 April until 21 July 1954, concluding with a peace accord on Indochina (the Geneva Agreements) that, among other things, withdrew French troops from the north and temporarily divided the country at the 17th parallel. Here, with France on the brink of collapse at Dien Bien Phu, the premier Joseph Laniel made it blatantly clear to the Americans that if they were to tolerate a French defeat they would also have to suffer the

---

[162] Ruane, *The Rise and Fall of the European Defence Community*, p. 83.
[163] Jasmine Aimaq, *For Europe or Empire? French Colonial Ambitions and the European Army Plan* (Lund: Lund University Press, 1996), p. 234.
[164] Wall, *The United States and the Making of Postwar France*, pp. 268. See also William I. Hitchcock, *France Restored: Cold War Diplomacy and the Quest for Leadership in Europe, 1944–1954* (Chapel Hill: The University of North Carolina Press, 1998), pp. 179–81.

consequences of the EDC's defeat; 'France would not deliver both.'[165] A few months earlier, it was exactly such a situation that US Secretary of State John Foster Dulles had alluded to when warning that 'we must be on our guard lest Indochina also carry [the] European Defence Community down the drain.'[166]

The USA seriously contemplated intervention to save France at Dien Bien Phu, but in the end Washington decided to keep out, much due to, as we noted earlier, British refusal to participate but also after concluding that a defeat would not seriously disrupt the overall US strategy. But with the fall of Dien Bien Phu to the Vietminh the French government under Laniel also fell, and with the new government under Pierre Mendès France not only did French Indochina policy change in a way detrimental to US objectives – meaning a rapid peace accord with Vietminh and French withdrawal – but also the EDC prospects were to deteriorate even further. Once again Dulles' prediction seemed to have been confirmed; just months prior the Secretary had deemed the Laniel government 'our main reliance both for EDC and Indochina', adding that whichever government came after 'would not only have a mandate to end the war in Indochina on any terms, but also to oppose French ratification of EDC.'[167]

The day after the Geneva peace settlement was signed on 21 July the USA decided to terminate all deliveries going to the French in Indochina. A little over a month later, on 30 August, the EDC was laid to rest by the French National Assembly with 319 votes to 264; this was undertaken on a procedural motion and thus without a substantial debate. As if to vindicate Washington's worst suspicions, Mendès France – who wanted the treaty dismissed[168] – did not even put his government on the line over the vote, but rather chose to stay in a false neutral and so refrained from stating anything in support of the treaty. Shortly thereafter, the one question that had occasioned the EDC

[165] Aimaq, *For Europe or Empire?*, pp. 227, 225.
[166] Quoted in Ruane, *The Rise and Fall of the European Defence Community*, p. 85.
[167] Quoted in ibid., p. 90.
[168] Hitchcock, *France Restored*, pp. 194–96.

in the first place, namely West German rearmament, found a swift resolution through the Paris agreements of October 1954, whereby West Germany (with a few restrictions attached) was admitted into the Western European Union and NATO.[169]

In focusing on Indochina, Aimaq is able to reorient the EDC from its narrow European Cold War milieu onto its proper and much broader global terrain. But in answering the question posed by the title of her book – *For Europe or Empire?* – she takes the case much further, arguing that for France the European army plan was never primarily about preventing German rearmament within NATO. By the same token, neither was it chiefly about utilizing Indochina as a means to stall or delay German armament. Standing the received scholarly wisdom on its head, Aimaq instead contends that, by and large, the EDC was a means by which France could exert leverage against the USA in order to continue the fight for control in Indochina. Above all, then, the army plan was contrived not for European objectives, but rather for imperial ones. As Aimaq states it, France used Europe for Empire.

This is not the place to determine whether Aimaq's line of reasoning fully corroborates such a very bold claim. However, we do need to reconnect briefly with Laurent Cesari's insights that we touched upon earlier when discussing colonial policy in postwar France more generally. To recapitulate, we highlighted Cesari's cogent point concerning the declining economic and strategic value that the majority within France's political establishment were to assign to Indochina from the early 1950s and onward. By the same token, there was also a growing agreement that the Indochina war was militarily unwinnable and that the goal instead should be to obtain a 'graceful exit' and to shore up France's military capabilities in Africa, foremost in Algeria where a crisis was looming – hence Mendès France's call for a 'retreat to Africa' from Indochina.[170] 'Africa, especially North Africa', Cesari clarifies, 'was the really useful part of the French Empire. Opponents

---

[169] This was approved by the French Parliament at the end of December 1954; West Germany was formally admitted to NATO at a ceremony in Paris on 9 May 1955.

[170] Cesari, 'The declining value of Indochina', pp. 175–95.

of the Indochina war such as Mendès France supported Eurafrican colonialism'. As for strategic value specifically, moreover, 'North Africa was almost equal to that of Europe'.[171]

However, by no means does this lead Cesari to depreciate Indochina's key role and function in the EDC negotiations. But in contrast to Aimaq's thesis he does not see France's utilization of Indochina as being tantamount to it choosing Empire, as in its *Asian* empire, over Europe. Rather, he manages to make the case that France used the Indochina bargaining chip in the EDC negotiations for the purpose of strengthening its standing both in Europe proper and in its Eurafrican prolongation. France thus secured US funding for the war under the pretext of not being able to ratify the EDC while having most of its armed forces tied down in Indochina. This predicament was then also used as a forceful argument against ratifying the EDC *before* Indochina had been successfully pacified and troops shipped back to Europe, since such a premature decision would have resulted in having more German divisions than French serving in the European Army. But as Cesari can show, while Washington, from 1952 and onward, started to pour money into the French war effort, Paris 'in no way planned for a decisive military victory over the DRV [Democratic Republic of Vietnam], whatever [it] might have said to the Americans in this regard'.[172] Rather, a chief objective in receiving American aid was to use parts of it to build up its European and Eurafrican defence capabilities and its arms industry, which in turn would help France procure large dollar revenues from increased arms exports.

As a result of this ingenious manoeuvre, which also allowed France to relieve its own budget of some spending that otherwise would have gone to Indochina, the war soon emerged as a 'dollars-earning machine'.[173] Once the war had ended, Mendès France confirmed this before the National Assembly, stating that 'we have found in the Indochina war the equivalent of resources that normally our exports

[171] Ibid., p. 179.
[172] Ibid., p. 187.
[173] Ibid., p. 186.

should procure for us. […] The end of the hostilities in Indochina will result in a diminution of our dollar reserves.'[174]

So while Cesari's account confirms the centrality of Indochina in the struggle over the EDC, it throws doubt on Aimaq's claim concerning the centrality of Indochina in French strategic planning. The years 1950-4 were rather marked by an internal French struggle between those clinging to a more global colonial outlook, and where the retention of Indochina of course was vital, and those advocating the Eurafrican path. According to Cesari, this struggle ended with the Geneva peace agreement and France's subsequent ceding of control to the USA in South Vietnam. When the new French premier Edgar Faure, on 10 May 1955, decided to give up on trying to persuade the Americans about the risks involved in supporting Ngo Dinh Diem, South Vietnam's newly appointed prime minister, Cesari picks this as the 'symbolic date marking the definite victory of supporters of Eurafrica over rivals with global ambitions for France'.[175]

The point here, though, is not to decide which of Aimaq's and Cesari's accounts is the more accurate – the complexities surrounding the EDC are simply beyond our scope. Rather, the point is to show that the EDC drama, much like other European integration schemes at the time, is impossible to comprehend outside the global colonial context.

Africans in European Parliaments? The European Political Community

In closing, we should also say something about the equally strong colonial imprint on the abortive European Political Community (EPC), which was to function as the EDC's political authority and super-structure. According to the EDC Treaty (Article 38), the EPC was to 'be conceived so as to be capable of constituting one of the elements of

---

[174] Quoted in Wall, *The United States and the Making of Postwar France*, p. 282.
[175] Cesari, 'The declining value of Indochina', pp. 194-5.

an ultimate Federal or confederal structure, based upon the principle
of the separation of powers and including, particularly, a bicameral
representative system'. It was the ECSC's Parliamentary Assembly (the
precursor of the European Parliament) that was commissioned to
prepare a draft treaty to establish a European Political Community; the
work was conducted in collaboration with members of the Council of
Europe's Consultative Assembly and under the leadership of the ECSC
Assembly's president and former Belgian premier Paul-Henri Spaak.
This grouping, named the Ad Hoc Assembly, went on to adopt what
many took to be a very bold and far-reaching draft treaty in March
1953.[176]

As set out in Article 1 of the draft treaty, 'The present Treaty sets up
a EUROPEAN COMMUNITY of a supra-national character', assigned
with a 'mission', as stipulated in Article 2, 'to ensure the co-ordination
of the foreign policy of Member States in questions likely to involve
the existence, the security or prosperity of the Community'. As also
specified, 'The Community, together with the European Coal and Steel
Community and the European Defence Community, shall constitute
a single legal entity' (Article 5), which basically meant that the EPC,
besides engaging with its own aims and objectives, would assume the
authorities and tasks of the ECSC and EDC. Important, too, was that
in terms of financial competence the draft treaty authorized the EPC
to levy its own taxes (Article 77). The Community budget was thus not
only to rely on member states' contributions, but was also allocated a
means of independent financial leverage. Politically, this was even more
strongly expressed in the EPC's institutional framework, which, due
to its supranational character, invested the two-chamber parliament
– a directly elected People's Chamber and a Senate elected by the
parliaments of the member states – and the Executive Council with
far-reaching powers. Such powers, alongside a range of other issues,
were to be debated and amended ad infinitum during the rocky road of

---

[176] Ad Hoc Assembly, *Draft Treaty Embodying the Statute of the European Community*
(Paris: Secretariat of the Constitutional Committee, 1953).

negotiations that both preceded and followed the Ad Hoc Assembly's formal adoption of the draft treaty in the spring of 1953.

There was also to be much dissension over the draft treaty's stated objective that the EPC should work towards 'the progressive establishment of a common market' among the six member states (Article 2). What caused this was the Netherlands' accompanying proposal, the so-called Beyen Plan – named after its initiator and Dutch foreign minister Johan Willem Beyen – that was put forth already in 1952, prior to the ad hoc committee's adoption of the draft treaty. In order to ensure the advance towards a true political union, the Beyen Plan wanted the EPC's common market to include an expansive range of common policies, including a fully fledged customs union that would abolish internal tariffs and quotas as well establishing a common external trade policy. Since the Dutch government presented the Beyen Plan as a condition for going along with the EPC, France's flat rejection of the plan has led many accounts of the EPC to conclude that this also constituted the chief reason why no agreement ever could be reached on the EPC. According to Seung-Ryeol Kim and Yves Montarsolo, however, this is a premature conclusion. In meticulously sifting the archival evidence, both Kim and Montarsolo are able to demonstrate that the pivotal matter on which the EPC negotiations was made to hinge and continuously tread water rested with the French inability to decide how the empire, or French Union, would fit into the new European Political Community.[177]

Sharing many similarities with the intra-French divergence over colonial matters as relating to the EDC, the fault lines with regard to the EPC ran between those (mainly Gaullists, such as Michel Debré, and prominent officials at the Quai d'Orsay, the French foreign ministry) who feared that the supranational, and eventually federal, character of the EPC would be to the detriment of the French Union and France's global role, and those (including Schuman and Pierre Henri Teitgen's

---

[177] Kim, 'France's agony between *"Vocation Européenne et Mondiale"*', p. 64; Montarsolo, *L'Eurafrique*, pp. 91–194.

Christian Democrats [MRP], Guy Mollet's Socialists, Conservatives like Paul Reynaud of the Council of Europe and, of course, Monnet) who thought European integration and the EPC could work to the benefit of France's colonial objectives.

But in contrast to the EDC, the EPC draft treaty actually made provisions for the full incorporation of France's colonial territories into the new community, albeit leaving it up to France to determine the extent to which this would apply. In commenting on the EPC draft treaty, the Council of Europe's Committee on Economic Questions, headed by Paul Reynaud, welcomed these provisions, stating that:

> The Committee re-affirms its belief in the conception of the Strasbourg Plan that neither the Six nor the Fifteen (Eighteen) [referring to the CE members] form an adequate framework for a solution of the European economic problem in its broader aspects and that the area of freer trade should be extended as far outside Western Europe as possible. In this connection the Eurafrican conception of the Draft Treaty, although more wholeheartedly developed in a few remarkable statements before the Ad Hoc Assembly than in the Treaty itself, should be greeted as a step in the right direction. The hope may be expressed that the member countries concerned will, as a rule, be in a position to make laws, recommendations and all other decisions of the Community applicable to the non-European territories, as foreseen in the second paragraph of Article 101 of the Draft Treaty.[178]

Due to the marked disagreements in Paris, the colonial question, or the French Union, soon emerged as the main crux of the negotiations, both internally in France and between the six. In other words, due to the treaty's provisions regarding incorporation of 'overseas' or 'non-European territories', including their political representation and economic and, ultimately, trade relations, France was now put in a situation where it had to make some very difficult choices and decisions.

---

[178] Council of Europe, Parliamentary Assembly, 'Opinion (Appendix to the Rec. 45) of the Committee on Economic Questions [1] on certain economic aspects of the Draft Treaty embodying the Statute of the European Community', 11 May 1953.

This, though, was not a question of whether the colonies should be in or out of the EPC; instead, the matter revolved almost exclusively around under what political forms and principles and to what extent they should be brought into the EPC, a state of affairs that just made the issue even more intricate.[179] The influential Gaullist and deeply Euro-sceptic Michel Debré, on the one side, and the staunch Euro-advocate and MRP leader Pierre Henri Teitgen, on the other, were thus in agreement on the incontrovertible necessity of the full incorporation of the colonial territories into the EPC. They also agreed that the French Union was absolutely vital to France, or that, as Teitgen put it, 'France was not only a European power but also a world power, whose interests went beyond the framework of the European continent', which, in consequence, meant that the bond between the metropole and the overseas was 'indivisible'.[180]

But whereas Teitgen, Schuman, Monnet and the like felt that such indivisibility could be made quite compatible with the supranational structure of the EPC, Debré, his Gaullists and powerful officials at the Quai would have none of it and so were determined to settle for nothing less than the scrapping of the community's supranational and federal ambitions in favour of a strictly intergovernmental or confederal arrangement. In their view, supranationalism namely risked severing the overseas territories from France, since it would pave the way for the other member states to benefit economically from France's overseas territories without being obligated to offer anything in return. As such it would deprive France of its preferential trading system and access to colonial markets, while at the same time continue to saddle her with the lone investment responsibilities.[181]

The political risks were equally serious. With Indochina, Tunisia, Morocco and others calling for independence, there was a strong sense that if the African territories gained representation in the

---

[179] Kim, 'France's agony between "*Vocation Européenne et Mondiale*", p. 67.
[180] Quoted in ibid., p. 66.
[181] Montarsolo, *L'Eurafrique*, pp. 137–9, 154–8; Kim, 'France's agony between "*Vocation Européenne et Mondiale*"', pp. 69–70.

EPC's powerful and directly elected parliament (People's Chamber), they might very well utilize such a position to break ranks with the metropole. By allowing France's sovereignty to be diluted in a supranational European community, this would fundamentally threaten the cohesion of the French Union and, with it, France's global influence. According to this particular outlook, Kim shows, 'it was to be expected that the relationship between the European community and the Union Française would supersede the existing connections between France and its overseas areas'.[182] In order to prevent Monnet's supranational 'adventure' from unfolding into such a 'nightmare', as Debré described it, measures needed to be taken to divest the EPC of its supranational mandate and its parliament of all its 'governmental and legislative power'. In its place, Debré wanted a Europe made up of 'a coalition of national authorities' or 'an association of sovereignties'.[183]

To say that many within the MRP and the Socialists opposed such views is not tantamount to saying that they bought the draft treaty and its supranational blueprint wholesale. They too, of course, realized that the EPC could entail negative consequences for the French Union and so needed to be equipped with certain safeguards against adverse infringements on French colonial sovereignty. But their basic approach was that it should be possible to strike a fruitful balance between supranational European integration and France's colonial undertakings. In this context, Socialist leader Guy Mollet – a major Eurafrica proponent – argued that since France would not be able to muster the much-needed overseas investments on its own, European collaboration in this area was to be welcomed. To set this in motion, Mollet, together with others, called for the rapid establishment of a joint European investment bank for the French colonies.[184]

Important to mention, too, is that a few African voices influenced the EPC debate, most importantly that of the French deputy from Senegal, Léopold Sédar Senghor (subsequently the first president of

---

[182] Kim, 'France's agony between "*Vocation Européenne et Mondiale*"', p. 73.
[183] Ibid., pp. 69, 73.
[184] Ibid., pp. 74–5.

Senegal), representing the Senegalese Democratic Bloc, which he had founded in 1948. Senghor was also a member of the EPC's Ad Hoc Assembly (as part of the subgroup 'Co-opted Members') and as such he spoke as one of the most unreserved advocates of the draft treaty.[185] This advocacy also formed part of Senghor's Eurafrican platform, which was partly inspired by Anton Zischka whom Senghor quoted frequently in his parliamentary interventions. He saw the overseas territories' full and unconditional incorporation into the EPC as necessary as it was indisputable. As Senghor explained, metropolitan France with 42 million inhabitants would not be able to take the guiding role in Europe, but 'Eurafrican France with 88 million inhabitants would be able to play the role as guide and animator of the European Union precisely by emancipating the peoples of the Overseas territories'.[186] In contrast to most others, Senghor therefore considered political representation for the peoples in the overseas territories to be a necessary prerequisite, insisting that twenty seats (out of a total of 281) in the People's Chamber be earmarked for the overseas.[187] What Gaullists and Quai officials feared would enable overseas deputies to challenge the metropole and sow division in the French Union, Senghor took to be a condition for the Union's future survival.

But Senghor's position on overseas representation in a supranational EPC did not garner any enthusiasm with the other camp either. This was particularly true for Georges Bidault of the MRP, who was the minister of foreign affairs in 1953–4. Bidault replaced Robert Schuman at the demand of the Gaullists who knew Bidault as a sceptic of both the EDC and the EPC and thus as Schuman's opposite, although they both belonged to the same party.[188] But Bidault, who would become the central

---

[185] See for instance Senghor's intervention in L'Assemblée nationale 18 November 1953: 'La politique européenne', *Liberté II: Nation et voie africaine du socialisme* (Paris: Le Seuil, 1971), pp. 117–24.

[186] Senghor, 'L'Eurafrique: Unité economique de l'avenir' (L'Assemblée nationale, 17 January 1952), *Liberté II*, p. 91.

[187] Montarsolo, *L'Eurafrique*, pp. 115–18; Kim, 'France's agony between "Vocation Européenne et Mondiale"', pp. 66–7.

[188] R. E. M. Irving, *Christian Democracy in France* (London: George Allen & Unwin, 1973), pp. 171, 174–5, 181.

figure in the EPC tussle, was no advocate of a rollback of European integration as such; rather, he ended up defending certain aspects of what had gone before, he straddled other issues, but most of all he made sure he demonstrated his aversion to the supranational character and federal intentions of the EPC draft treaty. As he told the National Assembly in March 1953: 'We have to make Europe without unmaking France.' 'We speak on behalf of 120 million people', he continued, adding most crucially: 'We must pursue two objectives which are not contradictory: the consolidation of the French Union and the construction of Europe.'[189]

But how this was to be accomplished in concrete terms never found agreement among the French, an impasse that, needless to say, was to rub off on the row of fruitless EPC negotiations between the six. Instead, what ensued in the months prior to the EDC's demise was, first, a further strengthening of the French confederal and anti-supranational position – straining the European talks even further. The day prior to the foreign ministers' conference in The Hague in November 1953, *The New York Times* thus wrote that 'M. Bidault has insisted that the political community should not be of a federal character and should be strictly confined to the coal and steel pool and the proposed European army. It would thus have little supranational power.' The *Times* also referred to Bidault's rejection of any future federal encroachments on the French Union.[190] The latter reflected a second tendency of an intensified intra-French debate concerning the importance of creating a balance between France's European role and its global role, the sticking point always being the colonial question or the French Union.[191]

---

[189] Quoted in Irving, *Christian Democracy in France*, p. 182; see also Kim, 'France's agony between "*Vocation Européenne et Mondiale*", pp. 75–7.

[190] 'Continental unity hinging on France', *The New York Times*, 26 November 1953.

[191] Montarsolo, *L'Eurafrique*, pp. 191–4; Kim, 'France's agony between "*Vocation Européenne et Mondiale*", pp. 82–3.

Europe's last chance: Concluding remarks

Since the EPC was ditched in direct consequence of the collapse of the EDC, the EPC negotiations were never formally concluded; and neither did the internal French debate reach a settlement. France was thus stuck agonizing, as Kim puts it, between its *'vocation européenne'* and its *'vocation mondiale'*. And despite Bidault and scores of others' repeated promises, the search for a balance between the two had only produced a frustrating impasse and a growing cleft within France's political establishment. Yet, as our discussion of the European Defence Community – the EPC's older sibling – should have indicated, in the autumn of 1954 there were also signs that this impasse was nearing a resolution. In other words, instead of continuing along a hopeless path of trying to strike a balance between *two* missions framed as separate at best – as in France's European role *and* its global role – but which more often than not were treated as mutually exclusive – as in *'vocation européenne'* or *'vocation mondiale'* – there were indications that many in France, not least the Socialists under Guy Mollet, were getting ready to seriously reconnect with the Eurafrican path of approaching the two as necessarily constituting *one* relation of 'interdependence'. Eurafrica thus inevitably remained on the agenda, the failure of EDC and EPC turning out to be a mere *faux pas* on what many French and European intellectuals and politicians saw as the trail of historical necessity. The scenario was summarized in a book by Pierre Nord entitled *L'Eurafrique, notre dernière chance* (Eurafrica, our last chance) (see Figure 3.6). Politically disunited, economically weak and militarily impossible to defend, Western Europe was crushed between the USSR and the USA, Nord contended:

> Only Eurafrica is a complete economic, political and military solution. It is *the* solution for Europe. Economically, Eurafrica may very rapidly become a power equal to the USSR and the US, between which it will ensure the equilibrium. Economically and militarily, Eurafrica will be a nuclear power. In its immense territories, which no enemy can occupy, destroy or obliterate, it will produce atomic bombs. Which is

to say that nobody will attack it. Yet, what we want is peace, nothing but peace.'[192]

How this endeavour was to play out during European integration's next big test is the topic of the next chapter.

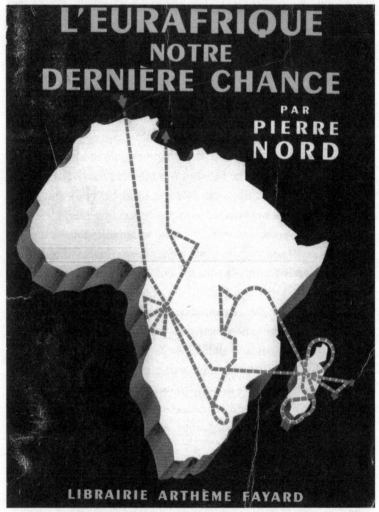

Figure 3.6 Cover of Pierre Nord, *L'Eurafrique, notre dernière chance* (Paris: Arthème Fayard, 1955).

---

[192] Nord, *L'Eurafrique, notre dernière chance*, pp. 114–15.

4

The Eurafrican Relaunch: The Treaty of Rome Negotiations, 1955–1957

After the French Parliament had buried the European Defence Community (EDC) in August 1954, it took less than a year before a new initiative was taken to 'relaunch' European integration. This process would culminate in the signing of the Treaties of Rome on 25 March 1957, which founded the European Economic Community (EEC) and the European Atomic Energy Community (EURATOM). The setting for *La relance Européenne* was Messina, Sicily, where the foreign ministers of the six members of the European Coal and Steel Community (ECSC) met for three days in June 1955 to discuss a set of options for the Community's future development. Foremost on the agenda for the Messina Conference were plans to establish a common market – for which the Beyen Plan, as mentioned previously in relation to the European Political Community (EPC), was to serve as a starting point – and cooperation in atomic energy. The proposals were presented by the Belgian foreign minister Paul-Henri Spaak, who also accepted the invitation to commence and lead the ensuing intergovernmental committee.[1] This work resulted in the so-called Spaak Report, which was delivered to the six governments of the ECSC in April 1956 and subsequently discussed at the Venice Conference for the foreign ministers of the six governments on 29–30 May.[2]

---

[1] Spaak, nicknamed 'Mr Europe', had previously been president of the UN's first General Assembly (1946), prime minister (1947–9), chairman of the OEEC Council (1948–50), president of the Parliamentary Assembly of the Council of Europe (1949–51), president of the Common Assembly of the European Coal and Steel Community (1952–4) and subsequently he would take the helm of NATO (1957–1961).

[2] *Rapport des chefs de délégation aux Ministres des affaires etrangères* (*The Brussels Report on the General Common Market*; Brussels, 21 April 1956). The principal drafters of the

Given the importance that European integration (as in the OEEC, CE, ECSC, EDC and EPC) up to this point had assigned to the colonial question and to Africa, in particular, it might strike some as quite remarkable that neither the Messina Conference nor the Spaak Report took any notice of issues pertaining to colonial territories. This becomes even more remarkable, perhaps, when considered in view of the fact that the EEC's prospective association of colonial territories would become the toughest question to resolve in the actual treaty negotiations. However, the absence of colonial matters in the Spaak Report was not indicative of their anticipated insignificance for the ensuing negotiations. Neither should France's subsequent request for colonial association be seen as a 'last-minute demand', as some scholars have tended to frame it.[3] On the contrary, the omission was a conscious decision on the part of the report's authors who knew full well that France could not enter serious negotiations without some type of proviso for its colonial empire. As Pierre Uri, the chief drafter of the report, recalled at a later point, it was on the explicit demand of Félix Gaillard, head of the French delegation to the intergovernmental commission created in Messina to chaperone the Spaak Report, that the colonial issue was to be left out, on the understanding that it was up to the French to decide when to take the initiative.[4]

Spaak Report were the head of the report group, Pierre Uri (France), and Hans von der Groeben (West Germany). An unofficial and abridged English translation was issued as *The Brussels Report on the General Common Market* (Luxembourg: Information Service High Authority of The European Community for Coal and Steel, June 1956).

[3] E.g. Alan S. Milward, *The European Rescue of the Nation-State* (London: Routledge, 2000), p. 218.

[4] See Pierre Uri's discussion at the 1987 conference marking the 30th anniversary of the signing of the Treaties of Rome, in Enrico Serra (ed.), *Il Rilanco dell'Europa e i trattati di Roma/La Relance européenne et les traités de Rome: Actes du colloque de Rome, 25–28 mars 1987* (Brussels: Bruylant, 1989), p. 190. See also CVCE (Centre Virtuel de la Connaissance sur l'Europe) 'Association of the Overseas Countries and Territories' (2011), p. 3. www.cvce.eu/obj/Association_of_the_Overseas_Countries_and_Territories-en-02904be2-7409-421d-8ee2-f393eb409fef.html (accessed 19 April 2012). Furthermore, the French government under Guy Mollet had not been a participant at Messina, having assumed office only in January 1956, and so clearly needed time to assess the Spaak Report and iron out internal divergences of opinion as concerned the Empire's, or the French Union's, status within a future common market.

The origin and initiative of the idea to include French and Belgian Africa in the Common Market can be traced to Pierre Moussa, director of Economic Affairs at the Ministry of Overseas France, and an expert on the economy of the French Union.[5] In early May 1956, as part of the preparation for the foreign ministers' meeting in Venice at the end of the month, Moussa submitted a note to his minister, Gaston Defferre, signalling the importance of the colonial issue for the upcoming negotiations.[6] Concurrently, the interministerial committee of the French government met to discuss the French response to the Spaak proposal. Here, as previously during the EDC and EPC deliberations, officials within the Finance and Foreign Ministries put forth qualms as to the advantages of incorporating the colonies into a common market since 'a Eurafrican economic union' may risk robbing France of its economic and 'political preeminence in her overseas countries'. For one, it was argued, a common market could well spark divisions between the colonial territories, so that some of them may choose not to participate in the 'Eurafrican common market'.[7]

However, these objections soon receded into the background as Moussa's initiative garnered support at the highest level. On 17 May, Defferre submitted a note to Guy Mollet, demanding that the French government should not enter the Common Market without the colonies being on board.[8] On the same day he approached Maurice Faure, the head of the French delegation, and Foreign Minister

---

[5] Around the same time, as Laura Kottos explains, Moussa was charged by Gaston Defferre to develop a plan for the inclusion of the French colonies into the Common Market; see Laura Kottos, 'A "European Commonwealth": Britain, the European League for Economic Co-operation, and European debates on empire, 1947–1957', *Journal of Contemporary European Studies*, Vol. 20, No. 4, 2012, pp. 497–515. Pierre Moussa, *Les chances économiques de la communauté franco-africaine* (Paris: Armand Collin, 1957).

[6] ANOM (Archives Nationaux Outre-Mer), AFFPOL 2317, 'Les TOM et le projet de Marché commun européen', 3 May 1956, signed by Pierre Moussa. Cited in Yves Montarsolo, *L'Eurafrique – contrepoint de l'idée d'Europe: Le cas français de la fin de la deuxième guerre mondiale aux négociations des Traités de Rome* (Aix-en-Provence: Publications de l'Université de Provence, 2010), p. 200. See also Moussa's memoirs, *Les roues de la fortune. Souvenirs d'un financier* (Paris: Fayard, 1989), pp. 60–70.

[7] HAEU (Historical Archives of the European Union), SGCICEE 3112, 'Note sommaire et provisoire concernant la compatibilité entre un marché commun de la zone franc et un marché commun européen'.

[8] Gaston Defferre, 'Lettre à Guy Mollet', 17 May 1956; in Gérard Bossuat (ed.), *D'Alger à Rome (1943–1957): Choix de documents* (Louvain-la-Neuve: Ciaco, 1989), pp. 167–77.

Christian Pineau with the same message.[9] In his letter to Mollet, Defferre stated that he wished, first, 'that the overseas territories be integrated into the *Eurafrican* common market and, second, that the OCTs [overseas countries and territories] enter into this common market while benefitting from special clauses justified by their state of underdevelopment'.[10] Two options were considered, only to be discarded: first, that metropolitan France entered the Common Market without the OCTs. Since this would lead to a fast rupture of economic ties, and then to political secession, it was deemed unacceptable for France, 'which cannot sacrifice its African vocation for its European vocation'. As a second option metropolitan France could enter into a European common market, on the one side, and keep the French–African unity (the French Union) intact, on the other. This was ruled out as untenable, because the French economy would be subjected to competition from the five partners, while at the same time needing to continue investing in the OCTs. This would entail a situation where France would end up running a chronic trade and budget deficit.

This provided, the only real alternative, according to Defferre, was to enter the Common Market *with* the OCTs. However, even this entailed potential disadvantages that had to be anticipated and managed with special provisions, one of which needed to ensure strict curbs on migration between the continents. As Defferre argued:

> Given the overpopulation and underemployment in certain European countries such as Italy, it is likely that this free circulation risks leading to rather important population movements toward the OCTs. For reasons less economic than human, it is necessary to guard oneself against an excessive flow which could lead to psychologically unfavourable reactions, which could nourish the evolution of nativist social structures and lead to clashes between Africans and Europeans, clashes of which we have but too many examples in North Africa. Thus, it is not possible to assume the principle of the free circulation of people between Europe and Africa without precautions. For that

---

[9] Montarsolo, *L'Eurafrique*, p. 204.
[10] Defferre, 'Lettre à Guy Mollet', 17 May 1956, p. 168; our emphasis.

matter, I think it is likely that, for analogous reasons, our European partners will themselves raise this question, animated by the desire to guard themselves against an excessive influx, on their own territories, of Algerian populations.[11]

So long as this and other concerns were defused in the negotiations, Defferre suggested, France should enter the negotiations by frankly stating that the integration of the OCTs would be a necessary condition.

As a final point, Defferre considered the crucial question of how to present this as an *offer* to the European partners. The impression that France used the OCTs to stall progress towards a common market needed to be avoided. As Defferre stated, France's negotiation delegation should 'instead make it appear that the offer made in this way by France is extremely constructive and that the accomplishment of a common enterprise in Africa is without doubt the most grandiose task that today may be proposed by a reassembled Europe'.[12]

Defferre was, at the same time, the key figure in the grand French attempt to reform the French Union, through the so-called 'Loi Cadre', which introduced a certain degree of autonomy and entailed a partial decentralization of power to locally elected assemblies in the overseas territories.[13] Defferre's crucial role in formulating the French position in the negotiations is verified by a memorandum from the French government dated 22 May and discussed the same day at the interministerial meeting. Between the first and second drafting, a footnote had been inserted that declared: '[T]he decision to include the overseas countries into the Common European Market is a political decision of primary importance [*au premier chef*], and the result of a Note from the Minister of France-Overseas.' Evidently, then, France's position was now decided: to enter negotiations on the Common Market with the Empire, or as the memorandum puts it: 'Granted all necessary

---

[11] Ibid., pp. 173–4.
[12] Defferre, 'Lettre à Guy Mollet', p. 177.
[13] For more on Defferre's reform of the French Union, see Rudolf von Albertini, *Decolonization: The Administration and Future of the Colonies, 1919–1960* (Garden City: Doubleday, 1971), pp. 425–42; Gérard Unger, *Gaston Defferre* (Paris: Fayard, 2011), pp. 139–71.

consultations and negotiations, the government of France holds that the overseas countries and territories should, in the same way as the metropolitan territories, be associated with the creation of a common European Market.'

The memorandum further states the two key principal conditions. First, the other member states would help to finance investments in France's African colonies. Second, as France supported development and production in its colonies by paying higher prices for products, an external protective tariff would be created by the Common Market, assuring that these products could continue to be imported into the market, despite prices being higher than world market prices. In addition, the French government argued that emerging industries should be subject to protection; and that labour migration between European countries and overseas countries should be 'subjected to particular dispositions that permits avoidance of repercussions ensuing from any too serious displacements of populations'.[14] These would then be the main lines along which negotiations would follow over the coming year.

'Great things': The Venice Conference

Great things are in the making, reported the news bulletin *Europe*, specializing in the coverage of the European Coal and Steel Community and European integration, on 26 May 1956. Under the headline 'On the Eve of Venice' the bulletin acknowledged that the forthcoming conference in Venice would consider the project for economic integration 'from an angle of greatest political importance: one that concerns the very boundaries of the new entity, which some would like to see extended to the overseas territories, and more precisely, to the African territories'. It added: 'This idea of an integrated Eurafrica

[14] HAEU, MAEF 31, 'Projet de Memorandum du Gouvernement Français sur l'établissement d'un Marché Commun (Deuxième rédaction)', 22 May 1956.

in fact corresponds to a bold vision, though some see it only as a way of eluding the political difficulties of the moment.[15]

On the morning of the first day of the Venice Conference, French foreign minister Christian Pineau set out by commenting on the Spaak Report. He then added the new item concerning the colonies, stating that from his government's point of view 'it is impossible not to foresee the inclusion into the common market of the overseas territories which the participating countries are responsible for.[16] Pineau proposed that a section of a future conference be devoted to the question. The five partners did not raise any objections or questions; on the contrary, as reported in *Le Monde*, 'The idea, for example, of linking Africa with Europe through the inclusion in the common market of the overseas countries and territories seemed to win over several of Mr Pineau's colleagues, most notably M. Spaak.[17] As Spaak summed up the discussion he returned to the French observation, and proposed that it be referred to a small group of experts.[18]

The conference, as *The New York Times* reported, ran unexpectedly smoothly and concluded at noon on 30 May,[19] upon which the delegates confirmed a press release in which they stated that, 'apart from the propositions contained in the [Spaak] report, the attention of the foreign ministers was particularly drawn to the question of the inclusion of the overseas territories and countries into the common market.[20] Explaining the outcome of the Venice Conference the next day, *Le Figaro* told its readers that 'the Eurafrican idea, long considered

[15] HAEU, CM 3/NEGO 92, *Europe: Bulletin quotidien*, Agence internationale de la presse, No. 919.

[16] HAEU, CM 3/NEGO 93, 'Procès-Verbal de la Conférence des Ministres des Affaires Etrangères des Etats membres de la C.E.C.A.', 29 and 30 May 1956, p. 5.

[17] 'Optimisme à Venise', *Le Monde*, 1 June 1956. Translation by CVCE, www.cvce.eu/obj/optimism_in_venice_from_le_monde_1june_1956-en-2bd68cad-967a-437a-a2a7-9e3c8cc9b14f

[18] HAEU, CM 3/NEGO 93, 'Procès-Verbal de la Conférence des Ministres des Affaires Etrangères des Etats membres de la C.E.C.A.', 29 and 30 May 1956, p. 17.

[19] '6 Nations accept atom pool report', *The New York Times*, 30 May 1956.

[20] HAEU, CM 3/NEGO 93, 'Procès-Verbal de la Conférence des Ministres des Affaires Etrangères des Etats membres de la C.E.C.A.', 29 and 30 May 1956, appendix IV.

to be a myth, will inscribe itself on African soil'.[21] This mirrored the attitude expressed by a subcommittee to the Comité Verret, or the interministerial committee of the French government, which had been tasked to investigate the French position on the Common Market's inclusion of the OCTs. In its first report, it predicted that, quite in line with the optimistic plans of Eirik Labonne, Louis Armand and others that we discussed in the previous chapter, such an inclusion would enable Africa's development and the establishment of a third power, providing Europe with a 'Frontier', as the USA had its Far West and the USSR its Siberia.[22]

This upbeat mood carried over into a commissioned report by the Central Bank of Belgian Congo and Rwanda-Urundi, released in September 1956. With explicit reference to the ongoing negotiations on the Common Market, the Central Bank piled up a wealth of statistical data to support the conclusion that both continents would benefit from the proposed integration. What Europe wanted to buy was produced by Africa; what Europe wanted to sell was needed in Africa. Or, as the document dryly puts it, 'Europe and Africa may find in this expansion a mutual advantage.'[23]

Associate the overseas: The French–Belgian argument

If Eurafrica's inclusion on the agenda was a tranquil affair at first, it would hit rough waters at the meeting of the heads of delegation in Brussels on 6 September. At this point, France's decree on the inclusion of the OCTs, proposed as an 'offer' to their partners, received a hostile response.[24] In order to amend the situation the French and Belgian

---

[21] 'L'Europe sans L'Afrique', *Le Figaro*, 31 May 1956.
[22] 'Conclusions du groupe de travail chargé d'étudier les problèmes posés par une eventuelle participation des pays d'outre-mer de l'ensemble français à un eventuel marché commun européen', quoted in Montarsolo, *L'Eurafrique*, pp. 206–7.
[23] 'Marché Commun Européen et Territoires d'Outre-Mer', *Bulletin de la Banque Centrale du Congo Belge et du Ruanda-Urundi*, Vol. 5, No. 9, 1956, p. 323.
[24] See Montarsolo, *L'Eurafrique*, p. 204; and Paul-Henri Spaak, *The Continuing Battle:*

delegations met a few weeks later, Spaak and the Belgians offering the French their assistance, and they produced a joint report that aimed to offset the cold reception. Finalized on 11 October, the French–Belgian report laid down the proper forms of the envisaged association of the colonial territories, specifying that 'the different economic structures' existing between the Six and the overseas territories did not permit any 'pure and simple inclusion' of these territories into the Common Market. That said, 'it remain[ed] necessary and desirable' for the OCTs to participate in the expansion entailed by the Common Market; the report thus went on to propose modes of 'association'.[25] 'Inclusion' was thus replaced by 'association', one of the alleged advantages of this change being that the question of political representation by Africans in the European community would then never be raised, as was the case in the EPC negotiations and which also played a part in the demise of the EPC.[26]

In this context, the report also asserted that 'it seems permitted, at a later stage, to envision the possibilities to establish a unique common market that unites the European countries and the Overseas ones'.[27] Having ascertained these principles, the report continued by outlining the modalities of association, which would be of two kinds: commercial exchange; and investment. Six principles of association were established: (1) OCTs would benefit in their relation with the European countries from the regime that these establish among themselves in the treaty; (2) in reciprocity to this regime, the OCTs would apply to every European member country the same regime they accorded to their 'own metropolitan centre' or mother country; (3) a period of transition would be decided, and the access and measures of economic integration as outlined in the two points above should be introduced in stages; (4) an investment fund would be set up, either as a special organism or as a branch of the European investment fund. The annual

Memoirs of a European 1936–1966 (London: Weidenfeld and Nicolson, English translation, 1971 [1969]), pp. 244–6.

[25] HAEU, CM 3/NEGO 252, 'Rapport Franco-Belge sur la participation des pays et territoires d'outre-mer en marché commun européen (établi le 11 Octobre 1956)', p. 1.

[26] Montarsolo, *L'Eurafrique*, p. 211.

[27] HAEU, CM 3/NEGO 252, 'Rapport Franco-Belge', p. 2.

needs would be set at US$1 billion. The fund would cover 'public investments demanded by the economic development of the overseas territories'; (5) studies would be made to investigate the possibility of setting up a common market between African countries of similar economic structures; and (6) studies would be made, at the end of the association process, of whether and by what means 'a single common market' encompassing the European countries and the OCTs should be established.[28]

Towards the end of October, Luc Durand-Réville, senator of Gabon and president of the section of Equatorial Africa in the French Central Committee for the Overseas, presented yet another report on the possible integration of the OCTs into the Common Market. Although an independent report, it is still interesting as it expressed the view of the French colonial administrators in Africa. It is filled with details and presented the same basic geopolitical arguments as so many previous studies, thus underscoring the familiar Eurafrican dictum of a colonial common market that offered Europe an opportunity to regain its geopolitical position vis-à-vis the USSR and the USA. There are slurs against the UN and the US, the latter being seen as pursuing 'a senseless anti-colonialism'. According to Durand-Réville, the 'French colonial professional circles' were in overall agreement on the opportunities offered by an integration of the colonies into the European Common Market, but there should be a period of transition and adaptation, and closer consideration should be given to the problem of having the other European states share in the investments.[29]

---

[28] Ibid., pp. 6–8.

[29] Luc Durand-Réville, in *La nouvelle revue française d'outre-mer*, No. 12, December 1956. (cvce: www.cvce.eu/obj/position_du_congres_interparlementaire_franco_belge_sur_l_association_des_ptom_au_marche_commun_liege_27_octobre_1956-fr-90fa073d-7cfc-4212-bc46-a7f16761e3a1.html).

Europe as revenge: The Suez Crisis

It is crucial to keep in mind that the Common Market negotiations in the summer and autumn of 1956 coincided with the escalation of the serious international crisis following President Gamal Abdel Nasser's decision, in July, to nationalize the Suez Canal. As such, the Suez Crisis would become a factor in the treaty negotiations. If the negotiations over the EDC had been deeply embroiled in the wider international cold war and colonial battles taking place in Indochina and Korea, the EEC negotiations thus had its counterpart in North Africa, and not just in Egypt but also – as we shall come back to – in Algeria, whose unexploited Saharan riches served as Eurafrica's promise and edifice.

For France and Britain, and also West Germany, the Suez debacle was utterly humiliating, and its Pan-Arabic implications came to serve as a grave warning of what would be in the offing should the Eurafrican Common Market fail to materialize (see Figure 4.1). As Spaak wrote to the British foreign secretary, Selwyn Lloyd, on 21 August 1956, calling 'for a policy of absolute firmness from the Western Powers': 'If Nasser's coup is allowed to go unpunished, the prestige of this new dictator will grow vastly, and so will his ambitions and audacity. The entire situation in North, and even in Central Africa, may be affected to our detriment.'[30] Spaak's position was perfectly in line with the inducements in Paris, for whom Suez in large part was synonymous with Algeria. At the meeting on Suez between France, Britain and the USA in the summer of 1956 (30 July–1 August) Foreign Minister Pineau thus stated that: 'If Egypt's action remained without a response, it would be useless to pursue the struggle in Algeria.' During the meeting he also informed US secretary of state John Foster Dulles that judging from 'the most reliable intelligence sources we have only a few weeks in which to save North Africa. Of course, the loss of North Africa would

---

[30] Spaak, *The Continuing Battle*, p. 126.

Figure 4.1 The Suez Crisis, caricature from federalist magazine *Le XXe Siècle*. Caption reads: 'Europe could make that balloon explode.' Source: *Le XX Siècle*, 1956. Historical Archives of the European Union.

then be followed by that of Black Africa, and the entire territory would rapidly escape European control and influence.'[31]

More generally, the Suez Crisis proffered a prime occasion for pro-European forces to rally in support of the integration cause. Jean Monnet, for instance, and his Action Committee for the United States of Europe – a group set up by Monnet on leaving his position as president of the ECSC's High Authority – would interpret the Suez Crisis as a powerful argument for the furtherance of European integration:

---

[31] Maurice Vaisse, 'France and the Suez Crisis', qouted in Wm. Roger Louis and Roger Owen (eds), *Suez 1956: The Crisis and its Consequences* (Oxford: Clarendon Press, 1989), p. 137.

The events of the summer [i.e. Nasser's nationalization of the Suez Canal] have revealed that only a United Europe can make its voice heard, and be respected, in the world of today. [...] In this respect, the Suez crisis is a grave warning. Even if, as we hope, it is solved by peaceful means, this fundamental lack of balance, with its threat to peace, will remain: namely, the weakness and growing dependence of Western Europe as regards its supplies of power.[32]

At its meeting in Stresa in September 1956, the Liberal International rallied around a 'United Europe', seeing it as the only potent antidote to figures such as Nasser. 'The efforts of Arab–Asian nationalists to oust Europeans', *The New York Times* reported, 'are seen by many liberals as the newest and most challenging reason for accelerating West European unity'. If Europe was united, the president of the Liberal International, Roger Motz,[33] asked rhetorically, 'Would Colonel Nasser have dared nationalize the Suez Canal, would the Algerian rebels have thought of gaining something by taking up arms?'[34] 'The Europeans' (or those in support of the integration cause), *The Economist* wrote around the same time,

> even fairly new ones like *Le Monde*, have gained points by claiming that Suez shows that European unity is more urgent than ever and that Britain should take steps towards it. [...] The French government has already endorsed the recent recommendation of M. Jean Monnet's action committee for a united states of Europe that the Six should establish European atomic power production targets in the light of Suez.[35]

As the Suez Crisis was appearing to reach a violent breaking point towards the end of October, so there was a simultaneous breakdown of the treaty negotiations in Paris (on 21 October). This is where the

---

[32] Quoted in Richard Mayne, *The Recovery of Europe: From Devastation to Unity* (London: Weidenfeld and Nicolson, 1970), pp. 239–40.

[33] Roger Motz was also president of the Belgian League for European Cooperation and former leader of the Liberal Party in Belgium.

[34] 'World liberals see a united Europe as the best answer to Nasser's moves', *The New York Times*, 14 September 1956.

[35] 'Black mood in Paris', *The Economist*, 29 September 1956.

French–Belgian report was presented and discussed and where the West German delegation refused to bow to French demands to have equal pay harmonization written into the treaty. The chief orchestrator of the West German refusal was Minister of Economy Ludwig Erhard, who generally disproved of the Common Market, referring to it as 'economic nonsense' and 'European incest'.[36] But as he returned to Bonn in triumph, Adenauer took him to task and subsequently, at a meeting on 31 October, Erhard was left with no choice but to accept Adenauer's vehement conviction that West Germany should compromise with France and return to the negotiation table. For Adenauer, this was directly related to Suez, which by this time, due to Soviet warnings, conjured up the threat of a nuclear World War III. A diehard champion of the Franco–British campaign against Egypt, equating – as so many European statesmen did – Nasser with Hitler, the Chancellor contended that Western Europeans, and especially the French and the Germans, had to stick together at this critical hour. Adenauer also justified his moral support for France's intervention in Egypt with reference to France's unconditional right to keep Algeria and to protect its soldiers against rebels who, according to Paris, were supported by Nasser. 'Algeria', Adenauer asserted in November 1956, 'is not a French colony, but a province of France since 1830 with 1.5 million white French men and women.'[37]

Adenauer's motivation for European integration was thus primarily political and geopolitical;[38] and it was a geopolitics to no little extent inspired by Coudenhove-Kalergi's interwar Pan-European movement.[39]

---

[36] Miriam Camps, *Britain and the European Community 1955–1963* (Princeton: Princeton University Press, 1964), p. 72.

[37] Quoted in Hans-Peter Schwartz, *Konrad Adenauer: A German Politician and Statesman in a Period of War, Revolution and Reconstruction*, Vol. 2: The Statesman, 1952–1967 (Oxford: Berghahn Books, 1997), pp. 240–2; 190.

[38] Paul M. Pitman, '"A General named Eisenhower": Atlantic crisis and the origins of the European Economic Community', in Marc Trachtenberg (ed.), *Between Empire and Alliance: America and Europe During the Cold War* (Lanham: Rowman & Littlefield, 2003), pp. 41, 51.

[39] Schwartz, *Konrad Adenauer*, pp. 237–8. Adenauer and Coudenhove-Kalergi were closely attached to one another and corresponded from 1928 onward. In 1958 Adenauer introduced Coudenhove-Kalergi to de Gaulle to hold discussions on European integration;

Not only did Adenauer believe in the 'superiority of Western civili-zation', but also he was equally convinced of the inherent racial inferiority of blacks, and it was therefore inconceivable, as he phrased it, 'that Africa, as a black continent, could be independent alongside the other continents'.[40] Such convictions were not, of course, unique to Adenauer. Spaak too, for instance, had little confidence in Africans' ability to govern themselves: 'What I have always found the greatest stumbling block in my relations with Africans has been my inability to get them to show any concern for the future. To govern is to foresee. While this tenet of political wisdom is universally accepted in the West, the Africans I have met seem to attach no importance to it.'[41]

Adenauer also firmly believed that '[t]he domination of the Mediterranean basin by the Soviet Russians would simply be the end for Europe'.[42] To prevent this from happening, he deemed it necessary for the West to embark on a massive economic development of the southern Mediterranean and the adjacent Middle East, so as to fully incorporate these regions into Western Europe's sphere of interests.[43] Thus, as events were seen as posing a challenge to Europe's influence in world affairs, it had become all the more important for Europe to stake out its common geopolitical interests in a more independent fashion. 'Then, just as Coudenhove-Kalergi had said in his time', Hans-Peter Schwartz notes, 'Adenauer spoke of the "appearance of non-white peoples on the political stage of world events". This, and its potentially detrimental effects on the future constitution of the UN, Adenauer found to be deeply disturbing.[44] Adenauer's advocacy for a strong European power, built on a solid French–German partnership and more independent from the USA, thus also solidified in tandem with France's decision to make the realization of the EEC hinge on Eurafrica.

---

see Paul Legoll, *Charles de Gaulle et Konrad Adenauer. La cordiale entente* (Paris: Harmattan, 2004), pp. 47, 60–1, 87–90, 103–4.

[40] Quoted in Schwartz, *Konrad Adenauer*, p. 191.

[41] Spaak, *The Continuing Battle*, p. 399.

[42] Schwartz, *Konrad Adenauer*, p. 190.

[43] Ibid., pp. 190–1, 373.

[44] Ibid., pp. 238, 254–5.

When Eisenhower on 6 November managed to generate enough (sterling) pressure on London to interrupt the French–British – and Israeli – onslaught in Egypt, which had begun the day before, this of course infuriated Adenauer. Incidentally, this coincided with a previously scheduled high-level meeting between France and Germany in Paris on 6 November, which had as its original purpose the sorting out of some of the obstacles that had stalled the treaty negotiations in October. Given the extreme situation in the hour of Adenauer's planned departure on the evening of 5 November – that is, a world apparently teetering on the brink of nuclear war due to the deeds of two colonial powers – the visit drew harsh criticism from many corners, the West German Social Democrats condemning it as a declaration of support for France's military attack on Egypt. But since Adenauer was in full agreement with France's actions, seeing it as an 'Akt europäischer Staatsräson',[45] such criticism could have no impact on his determination to go, which he did; indeed, as he was getting ready for bed, his train, on which Foreign Minister Heinrich von Brentano also was present, received the message about the Soviet threat of missile attacks on London and Paris should they fail to retreat promptly from Egypt.[46]

As Adenauer's train arrived at Paris' Gare de l'Est on the morning of the 6th, a large crowd was there to welcome him. He was given a ceremonial salute and national anthems were played.[47] The symbolic message to the world was unmistakable: for the sake of European unity and Europe's geopolitical interests, West Germany rallied to the support of France's campaign in Egypt. Later that day, as Mollet had hung up the phone with the British prime minister, Anthony Eden, having failed to persuade him to defy US pressure and prolong the Suez operation just a bit longer, Adenauer decided to comfort Mollet:

France and England will never be powers comparable to the United

---

[45] Quoted in Henning Köhler, *Adenauer: Eine politische Biographie* (Frankfurt am Main: Propyläen Verlag, 1994), p. 948.

[46] Schwartz, *Konrad Adenauer*, pp. 241, 243.

[47] Ibid., p. 242.

States and the Soviet Union. Nor Germany either. There remains to them only one way of playing a decisive role in the world; that is to unite to make Europe. England is not ripe for it but the affair of Suez will help to prepare her spirits for it. We have no time to waste: Europe will be your revenge.[48]

On his return from Paris, Adenauer issued new directives to the German delegation in Brussels, instructing the negotiators to repeal Germany's disapproval of the French requests that had stymied the negotiations in Paris a few weeks earlier.[49] Suez, for Adenauer, thus proved his point of a united 'third force' Europe as the only antidote to what he saw as the US and Soviet policy of carving up the world between them.[50] A subsequent Foreign Office memo argued along the same lines, claiming that, as a result of Suez, Europeans had 'discovered that there are many political problems that affect European nations in different ways than [...] the United States or the other NATO nations'.[51] According to Brentano, Suez had subjected Europe's world reputation to 'shame and humiliation'.[52]

However, such sentiments were not altogether new. As we shall return to later, since well before the Suez drama, Adenauer had expressed a growing unease over US priorities, seeing Washington's European loyalties compromised by President Eisenhower and Secretary of State John Foster Dulles' neglect of Europe's defence and their increasing attention to the Third World. Eisenhower's visit to Achmad Sukarno's Indonesia – one of the Bandung movement's most prominent leaders – in May 1956, for instance, had 'sent shivers through Bonn'. Not only had Eisenhower's visit been friendly, but also the president had publicly

---

[48] Christian Pineau recounts the episode in his memoirs: *1956/Suez* (Paris: Éditions Robert Laffont, 1976), p. 191; see also Gérard Bossuat, *L'Europe des français 1943-1959: La IVe république aux sources de l'Europe communautaire* (Paris: Publications de la Sorbonne, 1996), p. 335. Translation from Keith Kyle, *Suez: Britain's End of Empire in the Middle East* (London: I.B. Tauris, 2002, 2nd rev. edn), p. 467.

[49] Ronald J. Granieri, *The Ambivalent Alliance: Konrad Adenauer, the CDU/CSU, and the West, 1949-1966* (New York: Berghahn Books, 2003), p. 92.

[50] Ibid., Ch. 2; Schwartz, *Konrad Adenauer*, p. 243

[51] Quoted in Granieri, *The Ambivalent Alliance*, p. 92.

[52] Quoted in ibid., p. 92.

condoned the non-alignment, or neutrality, of some of the newly
independent countries – something that was anathema to Adenauer.[53]

The catastrophic ending of Suez, for which, according to Adenauer,
the USA first and foremost was to blame, thus vindicated Adenauer
even further and it convinced him of the need for the Federal
Republic of Germany to play a more active role in staking out Western
European policy, a course of action that, needless to say, could only
materialize by way of close partnership with France. This tallied with
the sentiment in Paris, which held that France's objectives, given
Britain's strong reliance on the US, would be better served through a
closer partnership with Germany.[54] With regard to the French position
in particular, Perry Anderson argues, it was the 'shock of the Suez
crisis' that really 'swung the balance' in favour of the Common Market
and the Treaty of Rome.[55] In specifically commenting on the impact
of Suez on the treaty negotiations, moreover, Robert Marjolin – vice-
president of the French delegation in the treaty negotiations – went so
far as to claim that the negotiations could be divided into 'two broad
phases': one before Suez, marked by hesitation and tardiness; the other
after Suez, characterized by greater purposefulness and vigour. Mollet,
Marjolin writes, 'felt that the only way to erase, or at least lessen, the
humiliation that France had just suffered from the Suez affair was to
conclude a European treaty quickly'.[56] 'The Suez fiasco', Miriam Camps
writes, 'had generated a new wave of "Europeanism" and had visibly
strengthened the feeling in France that only through European unity
could France regain a position of power and independence in the
world.'[57]

[53] Steven J. Brady, *Eisenhower and Adenauer: Alliance Maintenance Under Pressure,
1953–1960* (Lanham: Lexington Books, 2010), Ch.5.

[54] Ibid., Ch. 5; Pitman, '"A General Named Eisenhower"', p. 50.

[55] Perry Anderson, 'Under the sign of the interim', in Peter Gowan and Perry Anderson
(eds), *The Question of Europe* (London: Verso, 1997), p. 57; see also John W. Young, *Cold
War Europe 1945–1991: A Political History*, 2nd edn (London: Arnold, 1996), pp. 51,
132.

[56] Robert Marjolin, *Architect of European Unity: Memoirs 1911–1986* (London: Weidenfeld
and Nicolson, 1989), p. 297.

[57] Camps, *Britain and the European Community*, p. 77.

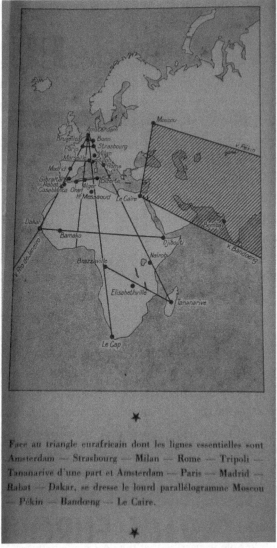

Face au triangle eurafricain dont les lignes essentielles sont Amsterdam — Strasbourg — Milan — Rome — Tripoli — Tananarive d'une part et Amsterdam — Paris — Madrid — Rabat — Dakar, se dresse le lourd parallélogramme Moscou — Pékin — Bandœng — Le Caire.

Figure 4.2 Cartographic representation of the geopolitical situation as envisioned by federalist magazine *Jeune Europe*. The caption reads: 'In face of the Eurafrican triangle, whose main lines are, on the one hand, Amsterdam, Strasbourg, Milan, Rome, Tripoli, Tananarive, and on the other hand, Amsterdam, Paris, Madrid, Rabat, Dakar, there rises the heavy parallelogram Moscow, Peking, Bandung, Cairo.' Source: *Jeune Europe*, No. 3, 1958. Historical Archives of the European Union.

For all the symbolic significance of Suez, however, one should be careful not to overemphasize its importance in the series of causes determining the process of postwar European integration in general, and of the Treaty of Rome negotiations in particular. Rather, Suez boosted integration efforts precisely because it was integral to the larger movement that was perceived as a challenge to Europe's global clout. From a European perspective Suez can be plotted in the sequence of other powerful challenges to European global and colonial power during the 1950s: to Indochina, Bandung and Algeria, then, Suez could now be added (see Figure 4.2). As the already-quoted sentence from *The New York Times* states, Suez was 'the newest and most challenging reason for accelerating West European unity'.

Moreover, as Paul Pitman argues in his illuminating account, Suez, by further aggravating *long-standing* German and French misgivings towards the USA and Britain, 'pushed public and parliamentary opinion in both Paris and Bonn toward European integration as an alternative to Atlantic cooperation'. In this sense, Suez should not be seen as a cause for Franco–German unity, but rather as marking the culmination of an extended development comprising several issues that all contributed to bring it about. As we will discuss more fully in the following sections, many of these revolved around Franco–German disagreements with the USA over NATO strategy and the integral questions of nuclear weapons and the role of EURATOM.

Before leaving Suez for now, though, it is important to point out that, while some of the voices cited earlier may give the impression to the contrary, Suez, although probably providing some lubrication, did not engender the magic bullet to finally unravel the mired negotiations on colonial association. And although both Paul Pitman and Irwin Wall do note in passing that the deal made between Mollet and Adenauer during their meeting in Paris at the height of the Suez Crisis included a German assent to France's demand for colonial association[58]

---

[58]   Pitman, "'A General named Eisenhower", p. 52; Irwin M. Wall, *France, the United States, and the Algerian War* (Berkeley: University of California Press, 2001), p. 65.

– a piece of information we have not come across anywhere else – this, if indeed it was the case, seems to have counted for little once negotiations on the issue were resumed.

For the equilibrium of the world: Stalled negotiations

Ten days after Eisenhower's intermediation had silenced the guns in Egypt, on 16 November, the French delegation formally added the matter of colonial association to the main negotiation agenda. Here, the French–Belgian report (see pages 155–56) was presented to the heads of delegation, accompanied by a declaration of the French delegation that Robert Marjolin was tasked with explaining. The declaration began by clarifying three reasons why France could not enter the Common Market without the overseas territories. First, this concern arose from the technical inconveniences that would result if France were to combine its participation in two customs unions. Second, it reflected France's desire to extend the advantages of the Common Market to the overseas territories, 'the destiny of which is bound to that of [France]'. Third, France intended to maintain the economic and commercial unity of the '*communauté française*'. However, since the overseas territories had such a variation of constitutional and political ties to France, a 'pure and simple' inclusion was out of the question; hence the formula of 'association' was proposed. This association might then lead to the 'establishment of a real common market unifying Europe and the Overseas'. The declaration then repeated the six principles of association spelled out in the French–Belgian report, but also highlighted the advantages of association offered to the other European members. The declaration listed these advantages, stressing, *inter alia*, that the large market and natural riches made available to the other members of the community would be bound to expand further because of the public investments that France had already made.[59]

---

[59] HAEU, CM 3/NEGO 252, 'Déclaration de la délégation française relative à l'inclusion des territoires d'outre-mer dans le marché commun', 22 November 1956, pp. 2–4.

This notwithstanding, the French initiative was confronted by a series of questions from the German and Dutch delegations, questions that were elaborated further a few days later (22 November), where all delegations, although recognizing the political importance of the posed problem, were still not convinced that association should be negotiated and settled at this stage. In sum, they proposed to postpone any settlement on the association and to move ahead with a common market of the Six – a move that sent the negotiations into a new crisis.

At this point, in this seven-hour-long meeting, Marjolin made a forceful intervention. 'The French thesis', he insisted,

> has already been indicated during the previous debate: the French government will refuse to enter the Common Market if the OCTs are not associated. On the other hand, it is not conceivable from the French point of view that the OCTs are opened to European imports without there being in place a European participation in the fundamental investments in these territories. Finally, [...] these fundamental investments can only be realized with public funds.[60]

Marjolin was seconded by the head of the Belgian delegation, Baron Snoy, who added the general argument that: 'Our industrial economies of Western Europe have the greatest interest possible in the association of the Overseas.' France's Pierre Uri, for his part, also weighed in, criticizing the other countries for presenting 'byzantine' and narrow-minded objections. Uri – who would become the drafter of the treaties and thus seen as one of *the* chief architects of both the EEC and EURATOM – was keen to remind the meeting of the principles at stake. The Common Market ought to be *'une grande oeuvre politique'*: 'we must attach the OCTs to the European ensemble; this is a capital point for the equilibrium of the world.' Uri also mentioned 'the role of the OCTs as furnishers of raw materials: oil, minerals, etc.', which were 'vital products for Western Europe'.[61]

---

[60] HAEU, SGCICEE 3109, 'Resumé des deliberations. Réunion du Comité des Chefs de délégation du 22 novembre 1956', 23 November 1956.
[61] Ibid.

Outside the negotiation rooms, meanwhile, the OEEC's economic counsellor and former chief of the IMF's European Division, Raymond Bertrand, lent his support to the French position. As Bertrand put it in the November issue of the prominent journal *International Organization*:

> Many farsighted people in France, in the overseas territories themselves, and in other European countries, have come to the view that a bold new policy is needed to prevent other French African territories from following Tunisia and Morocco into secession, and Algeria into rebellion. It is also essential that Tunisia and Morocco should be discouraged from drifting into Nasser-like habits of blackmail. Other parts of Africa would follow such a trend if it developed, and many countries besides France are deeply concerned to avoid these dangers. If the need for a new policy were accepted, association of the overseas territories with the common market could be a major part of such a policy, because of the economic advantages which it could secure fairly quickly for the overseas territories – and the even greater promise which it would hold for the future.[62]

Given the serious and fast-moving developments taking place in Africa at that moment, Bertrand went on to say that Europe could not afford to get bogged down in details, bickering about such things as 'import concessions on bicycles in the Cameroons against Italian purchases of cocoa'. By this, he was not denying that overseas association could involve certain minor economic sacrifices on the part of the European countries in the short term. Rather, it served to get the message across that any such potential losses resulting from association 'would be a small price to pay if it succeeded in convincing Africans that partnership with Europe and with the west is the best way to freedom and prosperity'. Therefore, Bertrand concluded, 'the Brussels Conference' must 'now recognize the whole breadth of the problem

---

[62] Raymond Bertrand, 'The European Common Market Proposal', *International Organization*, Vol. 10, No. 4, 1956, p. 570.

and show the same imagination as it has displayed in tackling the purely European questions'.[63]

With such 'imagination' failing to be forthcoming in Brussels and with the negotiations approaching a deadlock, Mollet can be seen as becoming increasingly public with France's agenda and vision for Europe. On 25 November, for instance, he addressed a reunion of members of the Socialist Party in Moulins, pressing the exact same point that Adenauer had conveyed to him on the eve of the Suez Crisis:

> The American and Soviet reactions to the aftermath of Suez have made evident the necessity, for the mid-ranking nations [*nations moyennes*], to group together in order to attain the authority they need. Not even Great Britain with its Commonwealth has the weight any more that is needed to discuss with the two big ones. Should we allow them to divide the world between themselves, or enter into war, a war in which we would be the first victims? Whatever your opinion has been in the past, today you can only be in favour of Europe, or otherwise accept to become a satellite.[64]

As negotiations resumed in Brussels at the end of November, further quarrels ensued. Why, the Dutch delegation asked, should the other Five be forced to shoulder colonial responsibilities that they did not desire, and pay for investments the benefits of which they could not enjoy? To facilitate the negotiations an intergovernmental Ad-Hoc Overseas Territories Group was set up, comprising two members of each delegation and scheduling its first meeting within a few days, thus underscoring the urgency of the matter. In addition, each of the Italian, Dutch, German and Luxembourg delegations was called on to prepare a note containing their views on the issue of association.[65]

Shortly thereafter, Jean-Michel de Lattre, unofficial spokesperson for the Labonne Committee and Louis Armand's Bureau for the Industrialization of Africa (BIA), was invited by *Le Monde* (2 December)

---

[63] Ibid., pp. 570–1.
[64] HAEU, EN 2734, *Les Cahiers du Propagandiste Socialiste*, supplement to *Documentation Socialiste*, No. 25, 17 November 1956.
[65] HAEU, CM 3/NEGO 252, 'Extrait P. V. réunion chefs de délégation 29 novembre 1956'.

to repeat the main lines of his argument for a rapid industrialization of Africa through a co-European effort. Apparently, the EEC negotiations had given his message renewed urgency: 'It is in Africa that Europe will be made.'[66]

German convictions: Brentano to Adenauer

While it is certainly correct to say that the negotiations over colonial association had basically ground to a halt by early December 1956, it is crucial not to lose sight – as the literature often does – of what the procrastination and irritation stemmed from, namely, at least for the most part, financial detail and pure petulance. Let us illustrate this point by juxtaposing two broad tendencies in the West German position.

On the one hand, the German delegation persisted in sifting the details. So, sticking to our chronology, on 6 December in Brussels the German delegation presented a list of new questions to the Ad-Hoc Overseas Territories Group. It was a set of extremely detailed – and insidious – questions on investments and infrastructure, ending tellingly on the following snide query: 'Once created, who will be the owner of the infrastructure [created by common European funds]?'[67]

On the other hand, though, and just two days later, Foreign Minister Heinrich von Brentano wrote to inform Adenauer about the specific problems posed by the negotiations on the association of the colonial territories. He explained that the 'centrepiece' ('Kernstück') of the French–Belgian proposal for colonial association was the 'investment fund for economic infrastructure [in the colonial territories] that should be furnished with one billion dollars annually. Precisely this

---

[66] Jean-Michel de Lattre, 'Les grands ensembles eurafricains', *Le Monde*, 2 December 1956.
[67] HAEU, CM 3/NEGO 255, 'Note de la délégation allemande sur l'association des PTOM au Marché Commun', 6 December 1956. A long list of additional questions was submitted on December 10 (HAEU, CM 3/NEGO 255, 'Questions de la délégation allemande [complémentaires aux questions sur les investissements]', 10 December 1956).

proposal has encountered loud criticism on our part.' But, Brentano stated, this criticism was really 'beside the point'. So what would be the point? In fact, that West Germany wanted to see France's and Belgium's African colonies enter the Common Market. Here we need to quote at length from Brentano's letter:

> In principle, the demand for inclusion [*Einbeziehung*] of the overseas territories should be welcomed. For many years and in numerous European organizations, as in the Council of Europe and the OEEC, plans have been worked out which have had as their aim the joint exploitation [*Erschließung*] of the overseas territories by the European states. Until now the realization of this has failed [...]. Within the frame of the Schuman Plan it also did not succeed in pushing through the inclusion of the overseas territories in the European Coal and Steel Community. However, in all these negotiations no doubts were ever expressed, from the perspective of the majority of the European states, and especially from the perspective of the Federal Republic, that the joint [*gemeinschaftliche*] inclusion of the overseas territories is desirable. Precisely from the German side it has been repeatedly complained that the Schuman Plan did not provide for the inclusion of the overseas territories. The significance of this persistent demand of the European states and especially also of the Federal Republic has in no way been diminished by the most recent events in world politics. There can remain no doubt that a conflict is emerging over the overseas territories, especially the African territories, between on the one hand the communist states and on the other hand the Western community of states. The outcome of this conflict will have a great, if not decisive importance as concerns the future constellation of power in the worldwide context. It follows from all this, that the demand for an inclusion of the overseas territories must not just be accepted, but welcomed.[68]

This letter shows that although West Germany fought France in the negotiations on the financial details of the investment fund,

---

[68] Letter by Heinrich von Brentano to Konrad Adenauer, 8 December 1956. Politischen Archivs des Auswärtigen Amts, PA AA. B 10 Abteilung II, Politische Abteilung, Bd. 915, Brüsseler Integrationskonferenz.

it enthusiastically embraced France's demand, and the inclusion of
the colonies, as a geopolitical and geo-economic imperative of the
highest order. The position was underlined around the same time by
Franz Blücher, Adenauer's vice-chancellor: 'The attitude of the Federal
Republic toward Africa is clear – German trade and German industry
look upon it as target no. 1.'[69]

This point is also backed up by a remarkable document dating from
two years earlier, in which France's ambassador and high commissioner in Germany, André François-Poncet, reported to Prime Minister
Mendès France on West German initiatives to re-establish or expand in
Africa. The pretext is an article in the French newspaper *L'Information*
(7 August 1954) in which journalist Daniel Mayer accused the Germans
– and specifically the banking interests behind the old president of the
Reichsbank, Hjalmar Schacht – of using the European integration
process (particularly the EDC on which a decision was forthcoming) to
recuperate colonial influence. The ambassador assured Mendès France
that such warnings about Germans sneaking into Africa via the back
door of European integration were both confused and misguided. It
was not that the Germans lacked such ambition but that, in fact, they
had always been knocking at the front door. 'The attempts toward
German expansion in French Africa have never been done in secret.
The Germans have from the beginning demanded admittance to
participate in the development of our African territories.'[70] François-
Poncet subsequently listed the grounds on which West Germany had
based its demands: the Schuman Declaration's clause about Africa as
a common European task; the OEEC's stated aims to assist Africa; the
Point Four programme launched by Truman in 1949 to aid 'underdeveloped' areas; the Labonne Committee's proposals for joint European
investments in African industrial zones; and the proposal by France's
State Secretary of the Air Force to transfer Europe's aeronautic industry

---

[69] Quoted in Jakov Etinger, *Bonn greift nach Afrika* (Berlin: Dietz Verlag, 1961), p. 7.
[70] HAEU, MAEF 82, Letter from André François-Poncet to Pierre Mendès France, 'D'un
article de M. Daniel Mayer sur les projets d'expansion allemande', Haut Commissariat de
la République Française en Allemagne, 10 August 1954, pp. 2–3.

to North Africa. Proceeding to an analysis of the West German contexts in which the issue of European collaboration in Africa had been raised, François-Poncet stressed the importance of Anton Zischka's publications, Johannes Semler's implicit authorship of the Council of Europe's Strasbourg Plan, Schacht's lobbying in conservative circles for the revival of German colonialism, the Institute of Economic Research in Munich, and a number of additional associations, initiatives and communities of interest. While admitting that the Eurafrican fervour had diminished somewhat since 1950, the ambassador reached an unequivocal conclusion: 'There is thus in Germany, undoubtedly, a broad movement of interest in the exploitation and development of Africa.'[71]

It is precisely this 'broad movement of interest' that Brentano refers to in his letter and that always held the upper hand in the negotiations in late 1956 and early 1957, a fact ignored in scholarship. Indeed, most commentators dealing with the treaty negotiations have failed to distinguish that disagreement over the investment fund did not mean disagreement on the principles of association as such.[72] As already indicated, the Treaty of Rome negotiations on Eurafrican colonial association were replete with precisely this consensus dictum. Indeed, in Paris on 10 December the Italian delegation presented its list of outstanding questions to the Ad-Hoc Overseas Territories Group. But in doing so the Italians emphasized that their questions concerned only certain technical aspects and in no way prejudged the 'definitive attitude of the Italian delegation on the matter'.[73] As we mentioned in the previous chapter, for political and demographic reasons Italy strongly supported the Eurafrican project, which would rehabilitate

---

[71] Ibid., p. 15.

[72] In the entire body of scholarship, Guia Migani is the only one who explicitly and, against the received idea, correctly points out that 'the criticisms [of West Germany, Italy, the Netherlands and Luxembourg against the French-Belgian association proposal] all concerned the modalities of association; nobody explicitly contested the principle that the African territories would participate in the Common Market'. Guia Migani, *La France et l'Afrique sub-saharienne, 1957–1963: Histoire d'une décolonisation entre idéaux eurafricains et politique de puissance* (Brussels: Peter Lang, 2008), p. 54.

[73] HAEU, CM 3/NEGO 254, 'Questions posées par la délégation italienne'.

the already-existing Italian settler presence in North Africa and reopen access to resources and trade routes lost in World War II. As stated in *The Economist* around the same time: 'In principle it has been agreed that they should come in; this African market of 37 million people and the other smaller territories, will after all, be a welcome commercial acquisition to German [...] exporters.'[74] France's 'five partners concur', *The Economist* continued a few weeks later, 'that investment and development in Africa is in their interests too. But there has not been time to work out the sort of detailed conditions for investment under the fund which will satisfy them.'[75]

The only negotiating party that came close to a principled misgiving was the Netherlands. The Dutch government feared high costs, held divergent views on trade policy and, at times, expressed a political wariness of becoming involved in France's and Belgium's colonial projects and problems.[76] This came to the fore in Brussels on 13 December as the Ad-Hoc Overseas Territories Group presented its first draft of responses to the French–Belgian report. Crucially, this draft focuses on Dutch objections, according to which a separation needed to be made between the establishment of a trade zone on the one hand, and the assumption of responsibilities for development of the OCTs, which translated into the investment fund, on the other. The Dutch delegation had no objection to the first, but proposed that the second aspect should be resolved at a later stage. The Dutch feared they would otherwise be drawn into *political* issues – that is, 'all the problems relative to the development of the overseas territories, among which one cannot dissociate the economic problems from the political ones'.[77]

---

[74] 'Challenge in Europe', *The Economist*, 15 December 1956.

[75] 'The Common Market takes shape', *The Economist*, 19 January 1957.

[76] Pierre-Henri Laurent, 'The diplomacy of the Rome Treaty, 1956–57', *Journal of Contemporary History*, Vol. 7, No. 3–4, 1972, p. 214; Frances M. B. Lynch, *France and the International Economy: From Vichy to the Treaty of Rome* (London: Routledge, 1997), p. 204; Anjo G. Harryvan and Jan van der Harst, 'A bumpy road to Lomé: The Netherlands, association, and the Yaounde Treaties, 1956–1969', in Marie-Thérèse Bitsch and Gérard Bossuat (eds), *L'Europe unie et l'Afrique: De l'idée d'Eurafrique à la convention de Lomé I* (Brussels: Bruylant, 2005).

[77] HAEU, CM 3/NEGO 253, 'Groupe Ad hoc territoires d'outre-mer, Document de travail relatif à l'association des territoires d'outre-mer au marché commun', 13 December 1956.

However, the Dutch never came close to an all-out rejection of colonial association and on other occasions gave expression to a principled consent. It should also be remembered that on the key issue of Algeria, the Netherlands was one of the staunchest supporters of French policy, opposing Algerian independence, for instance, on grounds that it would jeopardize NATO, its foreign minister, Joseph Luns, describing the Algerian leadership as 'murderous cutthroats with whom it was impossible to deal'.[78]

Shortly after the following Brussels meeting, held on 18 December, the Ad-Hoc Group circulated a draft of a preamble to its final report to the heads of delegation. Being the result of the joint work by an equal number of representatives from each country, the document confirmed the overarching consensus on all general geopolitical, political and economic issues involved. The Ad-Hoc Group's chairman, Belgian diplomat Albert Hupperts, presented it as a first balance sheet of the advantages of the association of the overseas territories:

> Economically speaking, the European member states of the common market have an essential need for the cooperation and support that the overseas territories – particularly the African ones – are able to offer in order to establish long-term balance of the European economy. The sources of raw material, diverse and abundant, which the overseas territories possess are likely to ensure for the entirety of the European economy of the common market the indispensable foundation for an expanding economy and present the additional advantage of being situated in countries whose orientation may be influenced by the European countries themselves. In addition to the mineral riches of all kinds and the agricultural and exotic products of the overseas countries, it is fair to mention as a concrete incentive, the results of very recent prospections in the petroliferous area carried out in connection with the systematic exploration of the immense African reserves of metals, phosphates, hydraulic energy, etc.[79]

---

[78] Wall, *France, the United States, and the Algerian War*, p. 131.
[79] HAEU, CM 3/NEGO 252, 'Groupe Ad hoc territoires d'outre-mer, Projet de préambule (établi par le Président)', 18 December 1956.

Further down the preamble, comparison with the Marshall Plan for Europe was made with the assertion that the association of the overseas territories should be undertaken in the same spirit. The preamble concludes:

> The proposed enterprise entails consequences of major importance for the future of Europe. [...] In aiding Africa and supporting itself on her, the community of the six is able to furnish Europe with its equilibrium and a new youth. It is in this perspective that all other elements of information assembled in the present report should be understood.[80]

Integrating Sahara, winning Algeria: French arguments

Despite this general consensus, however, the report and efforts of the Ad-Hoc Group did not amount to a green light for agreement. Instead, more bickering ensued and there were still scores of details to be ironed out. Before continuing our account of the negotiations though, we need to take a moment to examine the coinciding developments in France concerning the Sahara region in general, and Algeria in particular, which together formed an integral part of France's push for colonial association with the Common Market.

On 27 December, a week after the Ad-Hoc Group had presented its final report, the French National Assembly debated a government proposition to institute the 'Organisation Commune des Régions Sahariennes' (OCRS), which was formally established in January 1957.[81] The proposition was presented in parliament by Félix Houphouët-Boigny – a member of Mollet's government as the first-ever West

---

[80] Ibid.
[81] For an in-depth account of the OCRS, see Berny Sèbe, 'In the shadow of the Algerian War: The United States and the Common Organisation of Saharan Regions (OCRS), 1957–62', *The Journal of Imperial and Commonwealth History*, Vol. 38, No. 2, 2010, pp. 303–22.

African delegated minister, and later the first president of Côte d'Ivoire – who had been in charge of developing this plan since the formation of the Mollet government. Partly resulting from the studies and efforts undertaken by Eirik Labonne's ZOIA Committee and Louis Armand's tireless lobbying for African industrialization, the OCRS amounted to a grand organization with three objectives: development (*mise en valeur*) of the Sahara region; economic expansion; and promotion of social development of the African territories. Primarily, it would be an economic organization, but with significant military strategic, social and political consequences. At its head, there would be a director (named by the government) with far-reaching executive powers and in charge of an executive body modelled on the above-mentioned Bureau d'Industrialisation Africaine (BIA) headed by Armand. Interestingly, too, this authority would coordinate 'migration'. In his concluding remarks to the Assembly, Houphouët-Boigny delivered a passionate plea:

> Ladies and Gentlemen, dangers appear that threaten our national patrimony, and from different directions. Recently, we have bitterly experienced to what extent our independence itself was threatened. We have, at the centre of the French Republic a land until now impossible to exploit, but which the ingenuity of our scientists and the labour of our workers may valorize so well that we would be able to turn it not just into a point of support, but perhaps into the very foundation of our economic independence. This does not only concern the self-sufficiency in energy that the exploitation of Sahara's hydrocarbons would guarantee, but also the rich deposits of minerals and metals that are necessary for the Metropole, and for the supply of which it is dependent on foreigners. [...] According to all experts, Sahara, if it would remain as it is, fragmented, divided between several territories, would tomorrow continue to be dominated by drought, famine and death. It is therefore of the highest importance that the territories bordering it prove their solidarity by relinquishing parts of their economic rights in the hands of the Common Organization of the Saharan Regions.

He concluded by answering the rhetorical question: 'What will we encounter?'

> We will perceive in front of us a beautiful avenue, broad and straight, lined with flowers, in which all of us together may henceforth engage ourselves. It will lead us to the new city, to the city of our dreams, to the city of our wishes, the great fraternal French–African community. If you adopt the text proposed to you, if you thus permit our researchers, our technicians, our workers to organize the rational exploitation of this immense Sahara, you will have given to France and the French Union, on the threshold of this new year, a new hope and a unique chance. But you will have done more, you will have affirmed your will to contribute to a new world, you will thus have forged a link with the overseas territories, but what a link! The most precious link of the great chain of human fraternity toward which the entire world aspires.[82]

The next day, Mollet endorsed and presented the proposition in the Senate. No longer 'a barrier', Sahara should evolve into 'a bond', offering 'a lasting solution within the bounds of French Africa'. 'In fact', Mollet continued, 'the Saharan economy harmoniously integrates itself into the French-African economic whole'. For Algeria's industrialization in particular, Sahara offered great prospects. Like Houphouët-Boigny, Mollet spoke of the exploitation of Sahara as an epoch-defining event. 'What should evolve around French Sahara is a mystique belonging to grand projects of continental proportions.'[83]

Mollet also paid homage to the 'pioneers, who have been determined, since ten years back, to furnish the demonstration of the immense riches contained in the desert's subsoil, and to prove also that the exploitation of them is technically possible and economically profitable'. He was referring above all to Labonne, Armand and de Lattre. Mollet emphasized the need for investments, but did not

---

[82] Journal Officiel de la République Française, Débats parlementaires, Assemblée nationale, séance du jeudi 27 Décembre 1956, pp. 2895–98.
[83] HAEU, EN 2735, 'Déclaration prononcé par M. Guy Mollet, Président du Conseil, au cours du débat sur le Projet de loi instituant une Organisation Commune des Régions Sahariennes'.

mention – he was speaking in the French Parliament – the possibility of foreign sources. Neither did he mention the secret meeting that had taken place in Cologne the year before between French and German industrialists and where both Armand and Labonne had been present. As reported by the British *Tribune Magazine* on 25 March 1955, the meeting, held two weeks earlier, had broached a 'revolutionary scheme' – namely, the establishment of an armaments complex in the Sahara. At the meeting, Armand and Labonne expressed confidence that new technology was now available for the exploitation of 'the hidden industrial wealth of the desert', particularly in the southern parts of Algeria. However, as with the Eurafrican project in general, the French delegation also let it be known that since France was unable to shoulder the financing part alone, the dormant Saharan wealth needed German capital for its realization. In an attempt to persuade its German partner about the lucrative investment opportunity on offer, Armand is quoted as having told the Germans that '[t]he H-bomb has made the Ruhr out of date as an armaments centre. The Sahara is much more immune to attack by Russian bombers'.[84] At the time of this meeting, Armand was also in the process of being appointed by the French government – for a period of three years – as head of a 'central committee of Eurafrican vocation', which would 'define a policy of foreign investments in French Africa', 'direct and oversee negotiations with interested foreign governments and establishments', and facilitate political decisions in France pertaining to such investments. The main rationale behind this decision, as it can be traced in preparatory notes, was the need to encourage prospecting and fund infrastructural projects in the Sahara region so as to 'associate the Germans, the Italians and, eventually, other European and foreign countries to important achievements in Africa'.[85]

As we saw in the previous chapter, the notion of a Saharan 'desert Ruhr' was not new; it dated back at least a decade to precisely the work conducted by Labonne, Armand and other 'visionaries', to use *The New*

[84] 'Desert Ruhr', *Tribune Magazine*, 25 March 1955.
[85] HAEU, MAEF 63, 'Note des investissements étrangers en Afrique Française', 3 March 1955.

York Times' term.[86] As a headline for a full-page Associated Press article in the *Pittsburgh Post-Gazette* from 1952 had it: 'French hope to find new Ruhr under Sahara.'[87] But high-level negotiations between France and West Germany over North Africa were not new either. In 1954, for instance, as *The New York Times* reported, 'The West German Chancellor and his fifty-man delegation arrived in Paris enthusiastic about the prospects of a French–German rapprochement that would interlock the industrial capacities of the two countries in Europe and North Africa.' Ruhr industrialists, the report continued, were particularly enthusiastic. France's invitation to them as future partners in North Africa's great industrial leap not only matched perfectly with their immediate interest in gaining access to North Africa's natural wealth but also conformed with the Ruhr's more general outlook, 'according to which Europe's prosperity could be assured if the highly industrialized states would concentrate on the exploitation of the underdeveloped areas.'[88]

The Economist also took a great deal of interest in the Sahara scheme. 'Four years of intensive geological research have shown', it wrote as the proposal to create the OCRS was being prepared for the French Assembly, 'that the Sahara may rival Canada as a source of raw materials.' Iron ore 'on the scale of Lorraine and of almost Swedish quality' has been found, as have copper, tungsten, zinc, lead, manganese, natural gas and coal. Most important of all, *The Economist* highlighted, '[t]here is the smell of oil in the Sahara.' But as is commonly known, in order to exploit these immense riches France needed the aid of foreign investment. Hence, the report noted, 'there has been talk of Eurafrica, with Germany as an active partner.'[89] As W. N. R. Maxwell of the British Consulate in Dakar commented on Eurafrica in January 1957: '[I]t sounds a bit like the continuation of French colonialism supported by German funds.'[90]

---

[86] 'French to exploit Sahara resources', *The New York Times*, 24 October 1953.

[87] 'French hope to find new Ruhr under Sahara', *Pittsburgh Post-Gazette*, 3 June 1952.

[88] 'Adenauer's hopes suffer a setback', *The New York Times*, 20 October 1954.

[89] 'Investing in the desert', *The Economist*, 25 August 1956.

[90] Quoted in Gordon Martel, 'Decolonisation after Suez: Retreat or rationalisation?', *Australian Journal of Politics and History*, Vol. 46, No. 3, 2000, pp. 408–9.

In the course of the 1950s, then, Sahara emerged, in Houphouët-Boigny's words, as 'the centre of the French Republic', 'the foundation of its economic independence', or, to use *The New York Times*' depiction, as 'rapidly becoming a new frontier' that if 'true to its promise [...] may have a powerful effect on the industrial and economic renaissance of France'.[91]

The OCRS was voted into law at the height of the negotiations concerning another economic integration project, the EEC. There, one of the main questions turned out to be that of the investment fund for social and economic infrastructure development in France's and Belgium's African colonies. At the same time, by way of preparing itself to pool and manage European investments, France reorganized its economic authority in most of French Africa and instituted a whole new governmental organization to coordinate it. In a subsequent speech by Mollet, the OCRS, Eurafrica, the EEC and settlement of Algeria were presented as the pride and cornerstones of French foreign policy. The rhetoric surrounding the Sahara organization was as grand and utopian as the one surrounding the European Common Market. The OCRS, as Martin Evans puts it, was one of Mollet's 'big ideas: the symbol of his "Eurafrican" future'.[92] Obviously, the Sahara plan contributed with economic reality and momentum to the Eurafrican association plans.

But there were more signs of consolidation of the French power elite in support of the EEC–Eurafrica nexus during this time. In January 1957, Robert Schuman weighed in on the treaty negotiations with a forceful plea for Eurafrican integration that partly echoed the report of the Ad-Hoc Overseas Territories Group. 'Eurafrica', he asserted, 'does not just signify the creation of a system of assistance; but the constitution of an economic whole, of a true association, in the interior of which a reciprocity of advantages and a communal politics of development will be put to work.'[93] In words alluding to the Suez

---

[91] 'French to exploit Sahara resources', *The New York Times*, 24 October 1953.

[92] Martin Evans, *Algeria: France's Undeclared War* (Oxford: Oxford University Press, 2012), p. 303.

[93] Robert Schuman, 'Unité européenne et Eurafrique: Politique révolutionnaire – Aperçu d'ensemble', *Union française et Parlement*, January 1957, pp. 1–3.

Crisis, Schuman added Eurafrica's by now much rehearsed geopolitical rationale, arguing that since the Soviet quest for world hegemony had now set its eyes on Africa, 'we should respond through the institution of a true community between the peoples of Europe and of Africa, the notion of which is at the basis of the Eurafrican idea'.[94]

For Mollet's Socialist-led government, such staunch support from the opposition was of course welcomed. As noted in the previous chapter, it reflected what Tony Smith referred to as the 'colonial consensus' that characterized the Fourth Republic, basically encompassing all the political parties with the exception of the Communists. Absolutely central here, of course, was the conviction that Algeria had to remain French.[95] And since French Algeria was fundamental to the wider Eurafrican cause, much of the Paris international propaganda drive to seek support for its new Algerian policy operated *precisely* by linking it to the ongoing negotiation on the Common Market's Eurafrican integration scheme. As Evans elucidates, during the Mollet government's tenure 'two interconnected themes were given a new urgency': on the one hand, European integration; on the other hand, reforms in Algeria that would also decentralize authority in French Africa and embed Algeria in a new geopolitical context. These two themes, according to Evans, were 'seen as absolute priorities in the international field' and they 'were summed up in the concept of "Eurafrica".'[96]

According to the strategy of Mollet's socialist government, then, Eurafrica was seen as a formation allowing for reforms towards increased autonomy and political rights for Algeria and French Africa, while simultaneously integrating them on more equal terms with Western Europe. Algeria would here demonstrate both the necessity of France's European commitment and the possibility for 'dependent peoples' to pass over the stage of *national* and *political* independence by entering into a larger community. Only such a larger Eurafrican

[94] Robert Schuman, *France-Forum*, February 1957, p. 21.
[95] Tony Smith, 'The French colonial consensus and people's war, 1946–58', *Journal of Contemporary History*, Vol. 9, No. 4, 1974, pp. 217–47.
[96] Evans, *Algeria*, p. 194.

community would be compatible with the new and commanding stage of *interdependence* that the world had entered. The efforts and resources of each of the community's participating parties would complement each other towards the *social* and *economic* sustainability of the whole.[97]

A good example of France's strategy was Mollet's statement on France's position concerning the Algerian situation, issued to the UN General Assembly on 9 January 1957. Mollet ended his note on Algeria with reference to Eurafrica:

> France is negotiating at this time with her European partners for the organization of a vast common market, to which the Overseas Territories will be associated. All of Europe will be called upon to help in the development of Africa, and tomorrow Eurafrica may become one of the principal factors in world politics. Isolated nations can no longer keep pace with the world. What would Algeria amount to by itself? On the other hand, what future might it not have, as one of the foundations of the Eurafrican community now taking shape? [...] Independence would result in inevitable economic and social regression as well as political regression toward dictatorship or the quasi-feudal regime of certain Arab States – would this be progress? [...] interdependence among nations is becoming the rule.[98]

In the statement Mollet also made sure he clarified the fact that 'France [would] never abandon Algeria'.[99]

Major support for this outlook also came from Raymond Aron, one of France's foremost intellectuals at the time. Warning against 'propagandist slogans' – 'as though liberty were always incarnate in the nationalists and slavery in the Europeans' – Aron argued that Algerians had everything to gain by remaining with France: 'Without the European minority the Algerian masses would know a still worse

---

[97] Guy Mollet, *Bilan et perspectives socialistes* (Paris: Plon, 1958), pp. 45–6; see also, Talbot C. Imlay, 'International socialism and decolonization during the 1950s: Competing rights and the postcolonial order', *The American Historical Review*, Vol. 118, No. 4, 2013, pp. 1119–20.

[98] HAEU, EN 2736, 'Text of the French Government's Statement on Algeria', 9 January 1957.

[99] Ibid.

fate, because the fragile structure of modern economy would collapse.' But there was no hiding the reciprocity of it all, because, as Aron also made sure to point out, 'Algeria is the indispensable southern base of the defense of Western Europe; it is the access to the oil in the Sahara.'[100] Moreover, as the reference to 'Western Europe' indicates, in order for this reciprocity to materialize it could not stop short with a French–Algerian equation; rather it had to transcend the national logic on both sides of the Mediterranean and so had to involve a Eurafrican constellation:

> Neither alone nor with Africa, which is for the time being a liability rather than an asset, can France attain first magnitude on a world scale. Committed to Europe, and Europe's agent in Africa, she might well claim a higher mission. [...] [I]f she continues to arrogate to herself alone a role which can be assigned only to Europe, if she tries to keep for herself the advantages of both an independent diplomacy and European solidarity, she is once again running the risk of losing on both counts [...].[101]

Thus, Aron projected, 'if peace is restored in Algeria, the task of economic development with Eurafrica as a final result, which France cannot accomplish alone, could be considered a common European responsibility.'[102]

As Evans underscores, and as we shall illustrate further later, 'in the run-up to the signing of the Treaty of Rome [...], no theme was more insistent than "Eurafrica" in justifying government action in Algeria.'[103] In contrast, however, Mollet's statement earlier refers only in passing to the new Common Organization of the Sahara Regions, although it is alluded to: 'The large-scale support given by Metropolitan France makes it possible at the same time to continue a major program of

---

[100] Raymond Aron, *France Steadfast and Changing: The Fourth to the Fifth Republic* (Cambridge: Harvard University Press, 1960), pp. 157, 89, 134. Originally published as *Immuable et changeante. De la IVe à la Ve République* (Paris: Calman-Lévy, 1959).

[101] Ibid., p. 168.

[102] Ibid., p. 167.

[103] Evans, *Algeria*, p. 195.

public investments, aimed particularly at irrigating the land and industrializing the country.' Whatever this 'program' was, it was either identical to the OCRS or would be linked up with it.

The day after Mollet's statement, though, Sahara was made very explicit in Maurice Faure's, head of the French delegation, discussion with Walter Hallstein, West Germany's State Secretary for Foreign Affairs. During their meeting in Bonn, which was an attempt to break the deadlock on the association question, Faure told Hallstein that 'the future will carry brilliant possibilities' and 'the discoveries in Sahara are the evidence of this'. Hence, 'there is no need to underline the collective interest of the European powers in maintaining their positions in Africa, which, if they disappeared, would risk exposing them to very great dangers'.[104]

A few days later, the Mollet government tried to further boost domestic support for its negotiation platform. Although important figures from the opposition, such as Schuman, had already endorsed the government's association stance in the treaty negotiations, Mollet aimed for an even broader national consensus by calling for an extended debate on the matter in Parliament. In the debate, which lasted from 15 to 22 January, Mollet spoke about 'the creation of the great European space, the creation of the Eurafrican ensemble', adding that '[t]he natural consequence of our politics of expansion is the European Common Market. It is by inserting itself into an economic space of the size of the United States and the USSR that France can ensure, with the least difficulties, the development of its trade, which is a condition and corollary for the development of its production.'[105]

Another prominent French politician from the opposition to speak in favour of the government's association bid was Pierre-Henri Teitgen. Like Schuman, Teitgen – as we mentioned in the preceding chapter – was a Christian Democrat of the *Mouvement républicain populaire* (MRP) and a leading figure within the European Movement who also,

---

[104] Quoted in Montarsolo, *L'Eurafrique*, p. 231. Fondation Jean Monnet pour l'Europe, ARM 16/9/11, 'Entretien Faure-Hallstein du 10 janvier 1957 de 10 à 13 heures à Bonn'.
[105] HAEU, EN 2735, 'Discours prononcé par M. Guy Mollet', 22 January 1957, p. 3.

in the early 1950s, became Minister for Overseas France. Addressing Parliament on 15 January, Teitgen alerted the European partners to the fact that the National Assembly might not ratify the Common Market treaty should the OCTs be excluded. 'Eurafrica appears as indispensable to Europe as it is to Africa, the historical task of a generation, the only chance for a better destiny for our territories, the only chance for France to continue its mission, and the only chance for peace in the world.'[106]

As for the debate in general, the Suez affair constituted a crucial theme, proffering wide agreement on the position that 'only by joining together could the countries of Europe hope to arrest, and then to reverse, the decline in their influence on world events'.[107] Indeed, one pro-European voice went as far as to extend his ironic gratitude to Nasser and Bulganin for making Western Europeans alive to the importance of standing together.[108] Commenting on the Assembly debate, *The Economist* reported that 'since the Suez adventure, integration schemes, far from being suspected as "American plots," have a third force halo.'[109] This, of course, reverberated in the more specific debate on association. As Mollet argued:

> The Association of the overseas territories with Europe, the constitution of a Eurafrican entity are political decisions of such an importance that they justify a negotiation at the highest level. Is there any better chance for Europe than this entente with Africa! The authority of Europe in world affairs already surpasses that of the sum of countries of which it is composed – and just think then of the association of Europe and Africa! On the political level as on the economic level as on the strategic level, the union of the two continents will be a significant factor in the global relations of forces, and a factor favouring peace and understanding between peoples. Does France have a reason to worry about the association of the overseas territories to the European

---

[106] Journal Officiel de la République Française, Débats parlementaires, Assemblée nationale, séance du mardi 15 janvier 1957, p. 14.
[107] Camps, *Britain and the European Community*, pp. 79–80.
[108] Pitman, '"A General named Eisenhower"', p. 33.
[109] 'M. Mollet pleads for Europe', *The Economist*, 26 January 1957.

economic ensemble? No. It is by opening to our overseas populations the abundant perspectives of a union with Europe, it is by permitting them to enter this vast entity through our intermediary that we will best perpetuate our influence. We do not create the French–African community that is under construction today through egotistical aims. It is founded on the mutual trust between the French and African peoples. Is there any better pledge to this trust than to give Africa a chance to benefit from the chances of Europe.[110]

Mollet then referred back to the recent great debate in the Assembly – namely, the one concerning the creation of the 'Common Organization of the Sahara Regions' – stating that the EEC and the Association were of the same importance and kind:

Some weeks ago, by voting into effect the law that organizes the Sahara regions, you ensured the realization of a grandiose project that will remain an honour to this legislature. The vote on the Common Market will also be a historical event. The development [*mise en valeur*] of Sahara, the European Common Market, the one like the other, offers our youth, and that of our overseas territories, immense perspectives, new fields of activity, and a response to their wish to construct. It is of this youth that you will think in a little while, at the moment you make your decision.[111]

In the speech, Mollet also admitted that the determination to form the Common Market was sealed with Adenauer in November 'last year'.[112] Intervening in the assembly debate, former French member of government, parliamentarian, poet, co-initiator of the Négritude conception and future president of Senegal, Léopold Sedar Senghor, criticized the government for having conceded too much to its five partners. Ironically, he remarked that he understood that the other Five were not that willing to share with France 'the White Man's Burden'. Senghor also asserted that African representatives had been kept outside in the process – 'one has given us very little enlightenment'

---

[110] HAEU, EN 2735, 'Discours prononcé par M. Guy Mollet', 22 January 1957, pp. 11–12.
[111] Ibid., p. 13.
[112] Ibid., p. 6.

– which is why his intervention, he stated, should be seen as an interrogation. Senghor continued to interrogate especially the dangers of the association to emergent industries in Africa along with the dangers of immigration into Africa of 'petit blancs' (a white underclass).[113] In the debates about the European Political Community (EPC), Senghor, we should recall, had argued for a Eurafrican conception that would allow Africans fair representation in the emerging political framework, and he was concerned that the new EEC association would not entail the parity between Africans and Europeans which, for him, was the entire purpose of the Eurafrican idea.

On the whole the Mollet government received the parliamentary support it had asked for, the Assembly endorsing its negotiation platform by 322 votes to 207, and in a motion adopted by the Assembly during the debate, the government was requested, and thus encouraged, to stand firm on its demand on overseas association in the treaty negotiations.[114]

Meanwhile, as the parliamentary debate in Paris was winding down, Félix Houphouët-Boigny took the stand at the heads of delegation meeting in Brussels (19–22 January) and delivered a strong plea for the Eurafrican cause. Forming part of Mollet's innermost circle, Houphouët-Boigny emphasized the political necessities of associating the overseas territories with the Common Market,[115] and there could be no mistaking that Mollet had called on him for the precise purpose of pretending that Eurafrica had a strong *African* backing. On the final day of the French parliamentary debate (22 January), Mollet referred to Houphouët-Boigny's splendid appearance in Brussels the day before. The weight assigned to Houphouët-Boigny's intervention in the treaty negotiations was also underscored in *Le Monde* (January 23) and by the French ambassador in Belgium,

---

[113] Journal Officiel de la République Française, Débats parlementaires, Assemblée nationale, séance du 18 janvier 1957, p. 167. For more on Senghor's conception of Eurafrica, see John Chipman, *French Power in Africa* (Oxford: Basil Blackwell, 1989), pp. 79–81.

[114] Camps, *Britain and the European Community*, p. 79.

[115] HAEU, CM 3/NEGO 252, 'Procès verbal, réunion des chefs de délégation' 19–20 January 1957.

Raymond Bousquet, as a few days later (25 January) he reported to Foreign Minister Christian Pineau about the progress made in the negotiations.[116] According to Bousquet, Houphouët-Boigny seemed to have 'made an excellent impression' at the Brussels meeting of the heads of delegations:

He [Houphouët-Boigny] put emphasis on the danger to the French–Belgian ensemble represented by the attraction of the powers of Bandung (Afro-Asians). In his view, the politics of Great Britain in Africa, which assures independence to its old black colonies, but without taking measures concerning the level of life and social and economic improvement of its populations, *is extremely dangerous to the French–Belgian ensemble*. It will result from this that, if the Six do not associate the overseas territories to their exchanges and investments, the Afro-Asian bloc, 'spearhead of communism', will implant itself on these territories. Already, the Afro-Asians and the communists begin to exercise their harmful activities in Britain's old African colonies. However, neither of them is able to make anything but ideological propaganda, and without bringing anything tangible to the native populations. Europe has its opportunity, if she is wise enough to seize it, to victoriously combat this double influence, in assuring, through her actions on the financial, economic and social level, to black Africa an increasing standard of living. From an egotistical point of view, Europe has the greatest interest in this, since, without black Africa, her 150 million inhabitants will be cramped within their borders. If the Europe of the Six, through a truly efficient financial and investment policy, succeeds in making the black populations feel that the Eurafrican Association is capable of producing practical results, the French–Belgian territories of this part of the continent will not just reject the attempt of the Bandung group and the communists, but the French–Belgian territories will also constitute a symbol of prosperity to its neighbouring colonies. It is then likely that Britain's old African colonies will demand their own association to the Eurafrican Common Market on the same

---

[116] For more on Houphouët-Boigny's intervention see Lynch, *France and the International Economy*, pp. 204–5.

conditions that Great Britain will do, at the right moment in the future European Market.[117]

At the Brussels meeting the delegations also discussed the very first draft of the treaty articles on association as later adopted. Two articles were confirmed, one of them stipulating that association should be in accord with the United Nations Charter (Articles 73 and 76) concerning territories that were not autonomous and under tutelage.[118] This followed from a previous German proposal, aiming to assuage Dutch scepticism by putting association in accord with and support of the United Nations Charter on aid to insufficiently developed zones.[119] Although anticipating events, it should be mentioned here that it is precisely to these, what we may term, African (e.g. Houphouët-Boigny, as seen earlier) and UN alibis that France was clinging when the EEC's association regime came under criticism in the UN subsequent to the Treaty of Rome's ratification. In response to criticism, launched in 1958 by a group of mainly non-aligned countries (e.g. India, Ghana, Indonesia, Yugoslavia), pointing to possible adverse effects of EEC-association for the 'Non-Self-Governing-Territories' concerned, and for a protracted failure to supply information to the UN on the types of measures planned to be enacted as part of the association scheme, France thus invoked two conditions, or alibis. First, it claimed that 'the principles underlying the establishment of the "European Common Market" were quite in accord with the United Nations Charter'. Second, it (falsely) asserted that '[i]t was only at the express request of representatives from Overseas Territories that France had urged the other EEC members to accept the association of the Territories with the Community. The future would show that the EEC would mean progress not only for Europe but also for the Territories concerned.'[120]

---

[117] HAEU, SGCICEE 3109, Raymond Bousquet to Christian Pineau, 'Territoires d'Outre-Mer', 25 January 1957, Ambassade de France en Belgique, letter no. 184.
[118] Ibid.
[119] HAEU, CM 3/NEGO 253, 'Note concernant l'association des pays et territoires d'outre-mer au marché commun', 20 January. 1957.
[120] 'Question concerning Non-Self-Governing Territories and the international trusteeship system', *Yearbook of the United Nations*, Part 1, Sec. 3, Ch. 1, 1958, pp. 305–6. See also

Figure 4.3 Europe – personified by Marianne (France) and Germania (Germany) – showers its gifts and blessings on the African continent. Source: *Le XX Siècle*, 1956. Historical Archives of the European Union.

There was yet another crucial parallel between the Brussels meeting on 19–22 January 1957 and the French defence of the EEC association in the UN a year later. As intimated in the UN exchange, this concerned the vision of the 'future' or, better, the anticipated time frame in which

'Trusteeship and Non-Self-Governing Territories', *International Organization*, Vol. 12, No. 1, 1958, pp. 100–2, 107.

Figure 4.4 Caricature from the German press by Hans Erich Köhler, 1957. The caption reads: 'Get going, Michael! Close your eyes and think of Europe.' Source: Hanns Erich Köhler, *Pardon wird nicht gegeben: Karikaturen unserer Zeit* (Hannover: Fackelträger-Verlag-Schmidt-Küster, 1957).

the EEC was to be in charge of the development and 'progress' of the associated colonies, or the 'Non-Self-Governing-Territories'. At the Brussels meeting on 19–22 January the German proposal under consideration included the idea that the EEC's Council of Ministers should decide, *after twenty years*, whether the states of the Common Market should continue to contribute to the social development of the overseas territories.[121] We can only speculate about whether this proposal also contained a tacit assumption that twenty years on, EEC association would still encompass overseas territories as in colonies or 'Non-Self-Governing-Territories'. But given the prevailing Eurafrican conception, as seen for instance in Mollet's statement earlier – and as we will discuss further later – that '[i]solated nations can no longer keep pace with the world', that Algeria certainly had no future 'by itself', or in Adenauer's firm rejection of the notion 'that Africa, as a black continent, could be independent alongside the other continents', it is not far-fetched to suppose that the German proposal indeed operated under the assumption that colonial relations with ('Non-Self-Governing-Territories' in) Africa would be sustained for at least another twenty years.

Shortly after the Brussels meeting, Mollet continued his public appeal for the Eurafrican cause. Addressing the Republican Circle, he spoke of Eurafrica as the solution to Europe's, France's, Africa's and the world's problems. Without Eurafrica, Europe would, in effect, be lost:

> The future of Africa is at issue. The European nations that assume particular responsibilities on this continent should today create their response to the profound desire for emancipation among the peoples of the old colonies. The destiny of Africa is tied to this response, but above all that of Europe, which, cut off from Africa, would remain isolated at the extremity of an immense continent dominated by communism.[122]

Yet, no agreement on association was reached at the conference of foreign ministers on 26–28 January. The president of the conference, Spaak, addressed the situation in a critical note of 30 January, and proposed how the outstanding problems could be resolved. He first

---

[121] HAEU, CM 3/NEGO 252, 'Association des pays et territoires d'outre-mer au marché commun, Document de travail établi par la délégation allemande', 23 January 1957.

[122] HAEU, EN 2735, 'Allocution prononcé par M. Guy Mollet, Président du Conseil, à l'issue du déjeuner offert en son honneur par le Cercle Républicain et Société des Etudes Economiques', 22 January 1957.

stated that 'the obstacles to overcome are economic, political and even psychological'. He therefore found it necessary to repeat the principal arguments. 'If the problem is posed clearly', he began, 'it will perhaps be possible to resolve it'. He then went on to state the economic dilemma that France was in, as it is tied to its overseas areas for exports and imports. To these are then added 'political arguments of exceptional importance. The effort made by France answers a political imperative which is paramount not only for it, but for Europe.' According to Spaak, the political considerations were of three kinds: first, development; second, the scale of Europe's sphere of support and influence; and, third, the global balance of power:

> The politics of aid to underdeveloped countries is now, at least in principle, recognized and proclaimed by all states. Should it not be applied so as to essentially direct it toward the territories ready to associate their destiny with that of Europe? From the perspective of the development of production in the world, what would be the situation of Europe if it would find itself cut off from the essential sources of raw materials, and deprived of riches whose extent is now beginning to reveal itself? The political view on the liaison with the overseas countries and territories is modified when a complete rupture of the relations between them and the motherland actually implies not a true independence, but transition into a dependence of another kind. Europe in its entirety ought to preoccupy itself with these under-developed countries which, in the actual division of the world, will make the power balance tip over.[123]

Having discussed these political issues, Spaak concluded that everyone agreed on them. What caused disagreement were the economic questions about the real costs and benefits of the association. What were the Five asked to contribute? And what would they receive in return, especially concerning the investments demanded by France? This was

---

[123] HAEU, CM 3/NEGO 252, 'Conférence des Ministres des affaires étrangères, Note du Président sur les pays et territoires d'outre-mer', 30 January 1957.

the source of disagreement.[124] Yet again, we are faced with the fact that, regarding political arguments for Eurafrica, there was agreement all along. Spaak was thus correct and uncontroversial in emphasizing this point. Also, there was no disagreement regarding France's justification for wanting to include or associate the OCTs. Finally, all agreed on the geopolitical, strategic and historical motivations behind the association and the creation of Eurafrica. What alienated the partners was that they were unexpectedly asked to pay for investments in what they saw as France's territories. Hence, some were not convinced about the extent to which, and how freely, they would be able to reap their fair share of the profits stemming from the joint investment in French Africa.

Saving the West: The Cold War context

Such uncertainty and suspicion partly explains why France, as already noted, throughout the negotiations was adamant about framing Eurafrica as a 'collective' enterprise, foremost intent on serving the general European interest as it claimed to be anchored in a realism of 'interdependence' between countries. As such, it was also a historical opportunity and a French 'offer' not only to its European partners, but also to the Africans. As a subscriber to this view, Jean Farran of *Paris Match* had a hard time understanding why France's generous association offer to Europe was still disputed in the negotiations. 'It was a remarkable and significant scene', Farran wrote on 9 February, 'as France and Belgium placed their empires on the table before their partners, who responded by being choosy.'[125] A week earlier, Mollet had reiterated the French 'offer' in a statement issued to the Swedish daily *Aftonbladet*, claiming, among other things, that 'France itself, accepts to limit her sovereignty' for the sake of a European community that invited 'the peoples of black Africa and Algeria to integrate themselves

---

[124] Ibid.
[125] Jean Farran, 'La marmite de l'Europe', *Paris Match*, 9 February 1957.

into a great Eurafrican entity, in which, and with the collective assistance of the most developed nations, they will attain democracy and a
true independence'.[126]

It is crucial to note too that France's concurrent military activity in
Algeria and Cameroon was persistently articulated in this very same
collectivist and post-nationalist idiom. The warfare in Algeria, as Edgar
Furniss delineated the French position in *International Organization* at
the time, was not primarily a struggle for French national interests, 'on
behalf of outmoded, nineteenth century colonialism or even for herself
alone, but for the West, for the free world, in combating an extension
of the general [anti-colonialist] nationalist offensive which so troubles
Britain and the United States in the near east'.[127] Soon after the Algerian
rebellion had commenced in 1954, Gaullist hardliner Michel Debré (as
described in Chapter 3) – later the first prime minister to serve under
de Gaulle and the Fifth Republic – announced that the French task in
Algeria was 'above all to be the guardian of the free world'.[128] Algeria,
Debré contended with much approval two years later in a debate in the
French Senate, constituted a 'battlefield of world conflict' and so was
fundamental to the West[129] – an opinion that, as Martin Thomas and
Raoul Girardet underscore, he shared with a massive majority of the
French political establishment at the time.[130]

This is also the central argument used by France in order to justify
its massive transfer of French NATO troops from Europe to Algeria. By
1955, France had made clear to its NATO partners that, if necessary,
it might very well send all its European NATO forces to Algeria, since
'the defence of North Africa is essential to the defence of Europe and

---

[126] HAEU, EN 2735, 'Déclaration faite par M. Guy Mollet, Président du Conseil, à M. Jack
Miller, Correspondent du journal suédois *Aftenbladet* [sic!]', 2 February 1957.

[127] Edgar S. Furniss, Jr., 'France, NATO, and European security', *International Organization*,
Vol. 10, No. 4, 1956, p. 554.

[128] Quoted in Stephen Tyre, 'The Gaullist, the French Army and Algeria before 1958:
Common cause or marriage of convenience?', *Journal of Strategic Studies*, Vol. 25, No. 2,
2002, p. 103.

[129] Quoted in Martin Thomas, *The French North African Crisis: Colonial Breakdown and
Anglo–French Relations, 1945–62* (Houndmills: Macmillan, 2000), p. 139.

[130] Ibid., p. 139. Raoul Girardet, *L'idée coloniale en France de 1871–1962* (2nd edn, Paris:
Hachette, 2009), pp. 335–6.

the free world'. Similarly, the French commander-in-chief in Algeria, General Jacques Allard, stated in 1957 that his mission was 'to defend the free world', and 'the rear line of defence, the last one, runs through Algeria'.[131] France thus wanted other NATO members to acknowledge that from now on its primary role within NATO would be committed to the West's defence of North Africa, the western Mediterranean and Central Africa, since, in French eyes, this was equivalent to a defence of Europe.[132] What this amounted to was nothing less than a French attempt to have NATO function as a Eurafrican defence alliance, and it is as befitting as it is logical that this endeavour was unfolding in tandem with the negotiations over the Eurafrican Common Market and EURATOM. The correlation is further substantiated when adding in the fact that France, from 1956 onwards, petitioned to have NATO also assume an economic and social role in Africa, with a particular focus on North Africa. Referring to Mollet's and Pineau's insistence that NATO 'should be economic as well as military', *The New York Times* reported that according to this view 'it would be logical for the [NATO] Council to consider North Africa and its capital needs since its economic health, like that of the Middle East, is regarded as having strategic importance for the Western World'.[133]

From the perspective of several non-Western governments, France's actions were soon seen as indeed implying a (Eurafrican) trans-formation of NATO. By September 1955 the head of India's UN delegation, Krishna Menon, among others, criticized France's NATO troop transfers in the UN, claiming this now meant that 'all the allies' of NATO were implicated in France's Algerian conflict.[134] Less than a year later, eight Arab governments harshly condemned NATO's involvement in Algeria, alleging that NATO's function had been 'deformed' by countenancing the deployment of French NATO troops in Algeria. As a consequence, the statement went on, NATO had grown

---

[131] Quoted in Girardet, *L'idée coloniale en France*, p. 343.
[132] 'French may shift European forces to North Africa', *The New York Times*, 7 August 1955.
[133] 'The question of Algeria', *The New York Times*, 1 April 1956.
[134] 'Algeria barred by U.N. as issue', *The New York Times*, 23 September 1955.

into a 'direct means to support colonialism',[135] which, in essence, was exactly the role France wanted NATO to assume.

Inside NATO, meanwhile, the French troop transfers gained firm support from West Germany, Belgium and the Netherlands. But the bleeding of NATO's continental strength also caused concern among several others of the partners. The Americans (who supplied most of the weapons to France), and subsequently the British too, were alarmed and soon outright hostile to the continuous French troop diversion, which by 1957 had basically emptied Europe of French NATO forces.[136] Likewise, the Supreme Allied Commander in Europe, General Alfred Gruenther, complained repeatedly, warning that Algeria was depleting the Rhine command of French troops.[137]

Despite increasing misgivings, the NATO Council and the USA nonetheless had to submit since France could claim it had the North Atlantic Treaty on its side. NATO's Algerian, or Eurafrican, outfit, which, as we discussed in Chapter 3, had been added as a French *sine qua non* in 1949 and much to the disapproval of the Americans, was now paying great dividends to the French. When France contemplated further troop transfers in the summer of 1955, the NATO commanders, although with great reluctance, thus conceded that the defence of French Algeria was vital to European security.[138] Similarly, when Mollet notified the NATO Council of yet another troop transfer in the spring of 1956, designating the Algerian insurgency as jeopardizing the security of Europe, the Council again had little choice but to stand by France, acknowledging Algeria as being within the purview of the NATO treaty as well as recognizing 'the importance of the North African region to the security of Europe'.[139] Given the publicly little-known fact, until this point, concerning Algeria's status within NATO,

[135] 'U.S. get warning from Arab lands on Algeria issue', *The New York Times*, 16 June 1956.
[136] Thomas, *The French North African Crisis*, pp. 136–8; Wall, *France, the United States, and the Algerian War*, pp. 20–2. For Britain's negative post-Suez attitude towards France's war in Algeria and NATO designs, see Martin Thomas, 'The British Government and the end of French Algeria, 1958–62', *Journal of Strategic Studies*, Vol. 25, No. 2, 2002, pp. 172–98.
[137] Thomas, *The French North African Crisis*, p. 137.
[138] Ibid., p. 137.
[139] Wall, *France, the United States, and the Algerian War*, p. 21.

the press made sure it was brought to the world's attention time and again from the mid-1950s onwards.

Of course, since the French government had not justified Algeria's incorporation into NATO as a precautionary measure in anticipation of a future large-scale war in Algeria when negotiating the NATO treaty in 1949 – although there were some who suspected something approaching this to be the hidden motive[140] – such dividends were not hailed as resulting from some prophetic propensities on the part of the French government at the time. But what many within France's political, military and intellectual elites indeed could claim to have had corroborated was the accuracy of the wider Eurafrican rationale for insisting on Algeria's NATO incorporation in 1949. We should mention that this rationale was also behind NATO's second Eurafrican enlargement in February of 1952 when the NATO Council decided to incorporate Morocco and Tunisia into the organization through a provision of association that deemed the defence of these French protectorates part of the defence of Western Europe. Again, the decision resulted from a French demand, which in turn, as reported in *The New York Times*, emerged from a massive parliamentary majority, save for the communists, who having endorsed Greece's and Turkey's NATO membership received Foreign Minister Schuman's promise that the government would make sure it convinced NATO to make the common defence also apply to Morocco and Tunisia.[141]

As with the Eurafrican association platform in the Common Market negotiations, the Mollet government's assertion that France was fighting for Europe and the West in Algeria now resonated very well with the military and Gaullists' long-standing preoccupation with North Africa as a key strategic area from which the defence of Western Europe could be upheld in the event of a Soviet attack, much in the same way as North Africa eventually had come to function in the fight

---

[140] See Escott Reid, *Time of Fear and Hope: The Making of the North Atlantic Treaty 1947–1949* (Toronto: McClelland and Stewart, 1977), p. 218.
[141] 'NATO African role is sought in Paris', *The New York Times*, 25 January 1952.

against Germany during World War II.[142] In the 1950s, after Nasser had come to power in Egypt, Algeria of course also emerged as the prime strategic bastion against Soviet incursion and Pan-Arabic infiltration in North Africa, which aimed to strengthen Moscow's position vis-à-vis both continental Europe and Europe's African colonies. As Stephen Tyre shows – drawing among others from exchanges between the French military and Ministry of Defence in the autumn of 1956 – the strategic position assigned to Algeria thus 'fitted perfectly into the development of a Eurafrican conception of permanent and mutually beneficial links between Europe and Africa, not to mention its role in providing air and sea bases to NATO and guarding those installed further South, notably at Dakar'.[143]

Writing in *Foreign Affairs* in 1953, the decorated French General Joseph de Monsabert[144] did his utmost to affirm North Africa's immeasurable strategic value to Europe. Monsabert, who on retirement from his military duties became a Gaullist parliamentarian, reporting, among other things, for the same parliamentary Defence Committee that in 1952 had firmly recommended Morocco's and Tunisia's incorporation into NATO's common defence, maintained that 'North Africa and Europe form one and the same body, and the Mediterranean is its circulatory system'. In a nutshell: 'Without North Africa, Europe cannot breathe and cannot act.' According to Monsabert, then, '[t]he real frontier of Europe' follows 'the ancient Roman *limes*, bordering the Sahara. From Casablanca to Berlin, from Kiel to Gabès, everything interlocks.' In spelling out the fundamentals of what ought to be a 'modern strategy' for Europe and the West, Monsabert went on to

---

[142] See Claude d'Abzac-Epezy and Philippe Vial, 'In search of a European consciousness: French military elites and the idea of Europe, 1947–54', in Ann Deighton (ed.), *Building Postwar Europe: National Decision-Makers and European Institutions, 1948–63* (Houndmills: Palgrave Macmillan, 1995); Martin Thomas, 'Defending a lost cause? France and the United States vision of imperial rule in French North Africa, 1945–1956', *Diplomatic History*, Vol. 26, No. 2, 2002, pp. 227, 234.

[143] Tyre, 'The Gaullist, the French Army and Algeria before 1958', p. 107.

[144] General de Monsabert was, among other things, a commander in the allied fighting in both North Africa and Italy – leading, *inter alia*, the Corps Francs d'Afrique and the 3rd Algerian Infantry Division – and then went on to become the first chief commander of France's occupation forces in Germany.

assert that 'there no longer are three separate and distinct continents – Europe, Asia and Africa. *There are only Eurasia and Eurafrica*.'[145]

In line with what we accounted for earlier regarding France's plans for Sahara's industrialization and the concerns regarding the Ruhr's vulnerability to a Soviet attack, Monsabert also highlighted the geopolitical aspects and advantages of North Africa's industrial potential. In his view, the industrialization of North Africa spelled the ultimate solution to Europe's perilously situated industrial heartland. 'In developing a heavy industry there', he wrote, 'we would be following the example of the Russians, creating a "Urals" in the Atlas Mountains of Morocco and a "Siberia" in Central Africa.'[146] Within the Fourth Republic of the 1950s, Wall notes, French geopolitical concerns thus looked less and less to the Rhine and Elbe and more to the Mediterranean, Algeria and Africa at large; or as he quotes François Mitterrand's statement from 1957: 'The Mediterranean, not the Rhine, is the axis of our security and our foreign policy'.[147]

But although France, in the spring of 1956, publicly praised the NATO Council's sanctioning of French troop transfers as a sign of NATO support and unity, the crisis within NATO was already well under way. The Council's consensus rested on very precarious ground, with the USA and some other NATO members being increasingly at odds with French NATO manoeuvring. And this was certainly no public secret. 'France', wrote *The New York Times*' C. L. Sulzberger in his comment on the NATO Council meeting, 'has consigned the best part of its Rhineland Army to the sub-Mediterranean deserts. Every French division allotted to Gruenther in Europe has been stripped

[145] General de Monsabert, 'North Africa in Atlantic Strategy', *Foreign Affairs*, Vol. 31, No. 3, 1953, pp. 423, 419, 425, italics in original.

[146] Ibid., pp. 424–5.

[147] Wall, *France, the United States, and the Algerian War*, pp. 21, 271 n30. As Alfred Grosser put it in *International Organization* in 1963: 'French national security was no longer menaced on the Rhine, nor to any substantial extent on the Elbe. The line of defence of French national security, however, extended from the Paris-Algiers-Brazzaville axis. This conception was not limited to military and rightist political elements. Both national defence and defence of the West seemed to justify military action in Algeria.' 'France and Germany in the Atlantic Community', *International Organization*, Vol. 17, No. 3, 1963, p. 558.

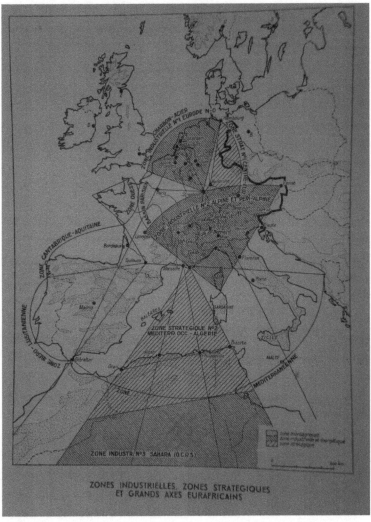

Figure 4.5 Map depicting projected 'industrial and strategic zones and the major axes of Eurafrica'. Source: *Jeune Europe*, No. 3, 1958. Historical Archives of the European Union.

of infantry to fight Arab nationalists.' In Sulzberger's opinion – one shared by many – the situation in the spring of 1956 was on the brink, a fact compelling him to ask: 'What is to be done about NATO's relations with the Arabs? The alliance's oil, the alliance's economy, the alliance's air strategy all depend upon the answer.'[148] At the same time as Algeria, in particular, and Eurafrica, in general, were influencing the conception and construction of a common market in the making, so they proved to be impacting tremendously also upon the workings and debate on the future of NATO.

If relations within the Atlantic alliance were already strained in the spring of 1956, then the American handling of the Suez Crisis had them spiralling into a full-blown crisis, setting off a French barrage of verbal attacks against the USA, with the French government going so far as threatening to leave both NATO and the UN.[149] Suez, then, boosted even further the geopolitical cogency of Paris' 'Eurafrican mission'.[150] Equally important, as noted earlier, by further corroborating established German suspicions of American and Britain intentions, Suez also vindicated Bonn and Paris in their pursuit of European integration as an alternative to Atlantic cooperation. Thus, as we also pointed out earlier, and as the crisis over France's continuous transfer of NATO troops to Algeria confirms too, Suez was not the primary cause for Franco–German unity over European integration, but rather marked a crucial milestone on a protracted journey of disagreements between France and Germany, on the one side, and the US and, to a lesser extent, Britain, on the other. The core element in these disagreements revolved around the wider NATO strategy in Europe; and since this became integral also to the wider Eurafrican strategy and so had a fundamental bearing on the treaty negotiations, it is important here to delve a bit further into the nexus of the EEC, NATO and Eurafrica.

---

[148] 'The two invisible members of NATO', *The New York Times*, 7 May 1956.
[149] Wall, *France, the United States, and the Algerian War*.
[150] Tyre, 'The Gaullist, the French Army and Algeria before 1958', pp. 106–7, 112.

The Southern flank: Military strategy

As discussed earlier, prior to the controversy over Suez and France's NATO troop transfers to Algeria, both France and West Germany were becoming increasingly apprehensive about the American and British readiness to defend the continent against a Soviet attack. Instead of abiding by what was still the official NATO policy of blocking the Soviets at the West German border – so-called 'forward defence' – Paris and Bonn feared that the US and Britain were now opting for a 'peripheral strategy', whereby a NATO counter-offensive, employing nuclear weapons, would not be launched until after the Soviets first had, in effect, been permitted to conquer most of continental Europe.[151] The suspicion was thus that nuclear weapons would compensate for the reduction of NATO's already insufficient conventional arsenal. When news leaked to *The New York Times* in July 1956 indicated that the chairman of the American Joint Chiefs of Staff, Admiral Arthur Radford, was indeed planning along these lines – proposing to cut the armed forces by 800,000 men in three years – this served to confirm what Paris and Bonn had feared all along, and immediately produced a serious crisis. 'Any war', *The New York Times* summarized Admiral Radford's view, 'most likely would be a general one, short, violent, and involving nuclear weapons. Consequently Army forces overseas [...] would be reduced, as one source said, to "small token forces that would wave the flag" [...] and would have atomic weapons.'[152]

The so-called Radford Plan was particularly reviled by the Germans. For Adenauer, it confirmed his long-standing fear of a world divided between, and totally dominated by, the USA and the Soviet Union.[153] And such a world, where nuclear weapons would make conventional wars redundant, would also, Adenauer railed, condemn Germany to

---

[151] Pitman, 'A General named Eisenhower', p. 43.
[152] 'Radford seeking 800,000-man cut', *The New York Times*, 13 July 1956.
[153] See e.g. Hubert Zimmermann, *Money and Security: Troops, Monetary Policy, and West-Germany's Relations with the United States and Britain, 1950–1971* (Cambridge: Cambridge University Press, 2002), pp. 90–5.

become a nuclear combat zone.[154] 'They are dividing world supremacy between themselves', Adenauer asserted when deliberating on the Radford Plan with his cabinet, 'and all the other countries do not matter any longer.'[155] At the cabinet meeting immediately after the story of the Radford Plan had broken, Vice-Chancellor Franz Blücher opined that the only way to amend this grave situation was to build a 'unified Europe': 'Only then will Europe stand a real chance of preserving her position of power between the USA and the Soviet Union.' At the same meeting, Minister for Atomic Energy Franz Josef Strauß made the claim that: 'At present, a nation that cannot produce atomic weapons is déclassé.' His statement came in response to Adenauer's comment that due to the fundamentally changed circumstances regarding the relationship between conventional and nuclear armaments that were suddenly unfolding, West Germany now had the right – as part of the '*clausula rebus sic stantibus*' – to revoke the ban on nuclear weapons possession that it had agreed to as part of the accession to the Western European Union in the Paris Treaties in 1954 and NATO in 1955.[156]

In the face of the unacceptable scenario at hand, France and West Germany settled on the building of a 'Eurafrican bloc', to use Pitman's term, as an alternative strategy for the continent's defence. Such a bloc was to obtain its own nuclear deterrent, independent from Washington, at the same time as it benefitted from the vast resources and geopolitical clout contained within France's African colonies. For France, the development of a nuclear deterrent – which was necessary to arrive at a position of strength both vis-à-vis the Atlantic powers and anyone doubting its ability to defend its position in Africa – would thus be much facilitated by means of German technical and financial

---

[154] Pitman, 'A General named Eisenhower', p. 46; see also Mark Cioc, *Pax Atomica: The Nuclear Defense Debate in West Germany During the Adenauer Era* (New York: Columbia University Press, 1988), pp. 33–4; Granieri, *The Ambivalent Alliance*, pp. 86–90.

[155] Köhler, *Adenauer*, p. 949.

[156] 'Gespräche über Rüstungsbeschränkungen in den USA und England', Kabinettssitzung, 20 July 1956, *Die Kabinettsprotokolle der Bundesregierung*, Vol. 9, 1956 (Munich: R. Oldenbourg Verlag, 1998), pp. 488, 487, 486.

assistance, which France had been denied by the USA and Britain.[157] In actuality, France had been contemplating nuclear weapons cooperation with Germany ever since 1954, and in the spring of 1955 Paris had sent its first feeler to Bonn. Since Germany chose not to answer at this point in time, France turned to other potential partners from within the ECSC, a pursuit that Paris would subsequently continue within the negotiations for EURATOM that ran parallel to the EEC negotiations. EURATOM would thus become a means whereby France sought a joint, and thus financially less demanding, production of weapons-grade uranium.[158]

As already intimated, however, with Bonn's extremely hostile reception of the Radford Plan in the summer of 1956, things took a sharp turn in favour of the long-standing French wish of obtaining Germany's support for the building of an independent European nuclear deterrent.[159] The Franco–German rapport was put on display at a NATO Standing Group special meeting, held at the end of July. Here, as Pitman reveals, France had seen to it that General Adolf Heusinger, a leading German representative, was given room to elaborate Bonn's negative opinion on the Radford Plan. While Heusinger emphasized the serious consequences of American and British troop withdrawals on the continent, he also communicated his government's support for France's military conduct in Algeria. In addition, Pitman shows, Heusinger 'referred to the importance of holding North Africa as NATO's southern flank'.

Needless to say, the French representative to the Standing Group, General Jean Valluy, was extremely supportive of Heusinger's remarks. In connection with the meeting, and in the company of several high-ranking military personnel from both countries, the two generals took the opportunity to further explicate the strategic accord between Bonn and Paris, emphasizing, *inter alia*, the importance of marking their

---

[157] Pitman, 'A General named Eisenhower', p. 43.
[158] Ibid., pp. 45–6. See also Wall, *France, the United States, and the Algerian War*, pp. 76, 64.
[159] For further elaboration, see also Catherine McArdle Kelleher, *Germany and the Politics of Nuclear Weapons* (New York: Columbia University Press, 1975), pp. 123–55.

distance from Atlantist designs by joint action in both the conventional and nuclear fields, as well as drawing attention to North Africa's crucial role for the security of the continental powers.[160]

As the Common Market negotiations were about to enter a critical phase with many unresolved questions on the table, Pitman's penetrating work thus shows that this took place in tandem with 'French and German strategists [...] discovering that they shared not only reasonable fears regarding Anglo–American tendencies to revert to a peripheral strategy, but also an interest in establishing a Eurafrican defense bloc with atomic capabilities.'[161]

Such convergence of French and German strategic interests would, of course, be instrumental in facilitating the Common Market negotiations, as well as making sure that these became interlinked with an agreement on EURATOM.[162] As Pitman also shows, in September 1956, Maurice Faure, the head of the French negotiation delegation, met with German foreign minister Brentano to inform him that EURATOM could very well be utilized for nuclear weapons purposes and that France had no intention of blocking Germany's attainment of tactical nuclear weapons. In submitting that the realization of Germany's desire to acquire the bomb would be expedited through French cooperation, Faure also 'linked progress in European integration to Franco-German armaments collaboration'.[163] Just a few weeks later, Adenauer could confirm that he was more than willing to answer the call. As Pitman quotes from the Cabinet Protocols, Adenauer made it very clear to his government that 'he wanted to use EURATOM as the quickest way to gain the option to produce nuclear weapons'. In December, the Chancellor reiterated his firm stance, asserting to his cabinet that 'Europe will have a longer life than NATO. It is now necessary to push ahead with the unification of Europe and to produce atomic weapons

---

[160] Pitman, 'A General named Eisenhower', pp. 46–7.
[161] Ibid., pp. 47–8.
[162] Wall, *France, the United States, and the Algerian War*, p. 64.
[163] Pitman, 'A General named Eisenhower', p. 50.

in the Federal Republic.'[164] As Wall evinces, in January 1957, at France's missile site in Algeria, France and West Germany signed a protocol on extensive military cooperation, which was followed, a month later, by Mollet and Adenauer meeting to talk about nuclear weapons research. This process, hidden from the Americans, would soon include Italy too. Before de Gaulle terminated it in 1958, it was to culminate in a tripartite agreement, in November 1957, to produce nuclear weapons, the first step, agreed on in April 1958, being the joint financing of an isotope separation plant, with France and Germany shouldering 45 per cent of the cost, respectively, and Italy the remaining 10 per cent.[165] As with the Eurafrican Common Market, then, it was French chutzpah and German financing that would cut the mustard and divide the world into an equilibrious three.

Countering Bandung: The United Nations

We have strayed from the immediate negotiations over the Common Market. But in doing so, we have been able to situate them in their proper and wider context. What went on in Brussels concerning the question of colonial association formed part of a much larger geopolitical and geo-strategic scheme and struggle in which Eurafrica and its Algerian linchpin took centre stage. Our straying has also enabled us to clarify and substantiate better that Eurafrica cannot be reduced to a purely French scheme, with Germany's role reduced to a more or less passive financer and interested taker of spoils. Rather, and as the 'Eurafrican defence bloc' illustrates, there was quite a bit of German agency involved too. In addition, by touching on the developments pertaining to NATO we have been able to further underscore the multiplicity of organizational and institutional settings in which Eurafrica made up an important issue. Before reconnecting with

[164] Ibid., pp. 52, 51.
[165] Wall, *France, the United States, and the Algerian War*, p. 78; see also Zimmermann, *Money and Security*, pp. 60–1, 95.

what became the final stage of the Common Market negotiations, it is necessary to take a brief look at yet another such setting where the Eurafrican argument was pursued, namely the UN.

We have referred to the UN on a number of occasions, pointing to its partial transformation into an anti-colonial arena and the bitterness and frustration that this caused in Western capitals. A defining moment in this development that we have not mentioned yet, however, and which carries Eurafrican implications, concerns the French walkout of the UN General Assembly over Algeria on 30 September 1955. France's ending up on the losing side over a motion to reject the Assembly bureau's advice to bar Algeria from the UN agenda triggered the walkout. As Martin Thomas describes it, the attempt to exclude Algeria from the agenda 'occasioned the strongest attacks hitherto from Afro–Asian bloc delegates against French colonial oppression and human rights abuses'.[166] Once the motion to dismiss the Assembly bureau's recommendation had been passed (by a margin of one vote), thus allowing for the Algeria question's inclusion on the agenda, the French delegation protested by walking out of the General Assembly, claiming that the motion was in apparent violation of the UN Charter's prohibition of interventions in member states' internal affairs. Reports that Paris contemplated withdrawing from the UN altogether immediately hit the news wires, and when asked about such prospects Foreign Minister Antoine Pinay chose not to deny the rumours, while France's UN ambassador Hervé Alphand's answer was: 'We might.'[167]

Since the UN crisis erupted just some three months after the Messina Conference and thus in the midst of the work on the Spaak Report, it is of interest to note that the official who emerged as the staunchest supporter, indeed spokesperson, for France's stance in the UN was none less than Paul-Henri Spaak himself. During the Assembly debate preceding the vote on the motion, in turn preceded by his long discussion with Pinay, Spaak rose to the defence of France not once but twice in what *The*

[166] Thomas, *The French North African Crisis*, p. 140.
[167] 'Algerian debate voted by the U.N.; French quit hall', *The New York Times*, 1 October 1955.

New York Times chose to characterize as the Belgian foreign minister's 'dramatic reappearance' on the General Assembly floor, after seven years on the sidelines. The motion to include the Algerian conflict on the UN agenda, Spaak was quoted as saying, had 'profoundly shocked' him. Backing to the full the French claim that the UN had no business meddling in France's Algerian matters, he, according to the *Times*, 'argued that France's present policy had nothing in common with nineteenth-century colonialism and should be permitted to work unhampered toward a solution of the problems in Algeria.' In the debate, Spaak also remarked that the time period since his last intervention in the UN Assembly in 1948 'had been marked by "far reaching and serious changes" in the United Nations', prompting his warning 'that "international demagogy" would spell the doom of the United Nations'.[168]

Such anxiety over the course on which the UN seemed to have entered in the mid-1950s reconnects neatly with Mark Mazower's unveiling of the imperial roots of the UN, the fact that many of its architects wanted the UN to serve the interests of the colonial powers rather than, as it would turn out – and much to the horror of Spaak, Mollet, Adenauer, Bevin and the like – a platform for the struggle against it.[169] In describing Dag Hammarskjöld as 'not always being entirely fair with Europe and the white race in general' in the UN, Spaak epitomized the sentiment of those who deeply resented the UN's anti-colonial turn.[170] In a long letter to President Kennedy, just prior to resigning his post as NATO Secretary General in February of 1961, Spaak vented this sentiment in more elaborate terms. In it he depicted a dystopic future scenario: 'If we are encircled in twenty-five years' time

---

[168] Ibid. In the meantime, as he was resigning as president of the Parliamentary (or Consultative) Assembly of the Council of Europe in 1951, Spaak – in a speech in the Belgian Parliament – had also lambasted the Council of Europe, accusing the Assembly for 'being hesitant' and for showing a 'lack of urgency' concerning Europe's standing in the world: 'The Europe of which we are speaking is a Europe which we have allowed to be grossly mutilated. [...] It is a Europe against which Asia and Africa have risen in revolt.' Spaak, *The Continuing Battle*, p. 223.

[169] Mark Mazower, *No Enchanted Palace: The End of Empire and the Ideological Origins of the United Nations* (Princeton: Princeton University Press, 2009).

[170] Spaak, *The Continuing Battle*, p. 136.

and reduced to the position of a small minority surrounded by vast masses of humanity indifferent towards or even hostile towards us, the fate of our civilization will rapidly be sealed at our adversary's time of choosing.' Spaak obviously felt that such a grim outlook warranted a blunt question to the American president, one where he made no effort to spare Kennedy of the European sense of American betrayal that had been building over the years:

> [D]oes the United States attach more importance to the UN than NATO? In other words, is it ready, in order to win the support or the friendship of the non-aligned countries, to go so far as to sacrifice the interests or to hurt the feelings of its NATO allies? This did in fact occur in connection with the Suez affair and Algeria. More recently, the same thing happened in connection with the Congo and the Portuguese territories in Africa.[171]

A few months later, on 13 November 1961, Spaak made a speech before the UN Security Council, defending the position of Belgium in the ongoing conflict in the Congo. In his memoir reflections he recalled the feeling of entering the Security Council with 'several trump cards': 'I had been present in San Francisco when the Charter was drawn up and signed. I had been President of the [first] Assembly [in 1946] and, during its early years, had played an important part in it.' In attacking the Congo resolution on the Security Council's table, Spaak stated that,

> what all this amounts to in fact is a bid to hunt down the white man. The white man is to be left defenceless, he is to be deprived of a chance to plead his cause, he is to be left helpless. We would never accept such a situation in a civilized country, and what we cannot tolerate from a civilized country we can tolerate even less from the world's most important organization.[172]

In his characteristic self-congratulatory manner Spaak continues in his memoirs by recalling: '[A] good many people came up to me to say that

[171] Ibid., pp. 347–8, 350.
[172] Ibid., pp. 366–7.

they had not heard a European speak out so clearly and vigorously for a long time against the accusations – which had become a sort of ritual exercise – levelled against the former colonial Powers.'[173]

For many Western European statesmen in the 1950s the prospects of having the UN serve as a viable arena for the defence and propagation of Europe's global role and interests were becoming slimmer by the day. Or as Britain's colonial secretary phrased it in 1957, 'the path of compromise on colonial issues in the United Nations is a primrose path'.[174]

Indeed, just a few days after the French walkout, *The New York Times* ran the headline: 'Colonialism foes win again in U.N. on agenda issue'. Up for grabs this time were the remains of the Dutch Empire, over which, as the *Times* put it, 'The anti-colonial powers scored another victory in the United Nations today when the General Assembly placed the question of West New Guinea on its agenda.'[175] One should note that the description of the world as divided not only between East and West but also along the fault line between 'colonial powers' and 'anti-colonial powers' was commonplace in *The New York Times*' reporting during this period. Just as his French counterpart, the Dutch foreign minister, Joseph Luns, responded by rejecting the notion that, as he is quoted as saying, 'the United Nations should endeavor to lend assistance to the effort of one country [Indonesia] to obtain part of the territory of another'.[176] Even more worrisome to the Europeans, of course, was that this time round, and in contrast to the voting on the Algerian agenda issue where the USA had voted with France (albeit reluctantly), the USA did not side with the Dutch and the other colonial powers, deciding instead to abstain. Given that continental countries, unlike Britain's 'special relationship', felt they were at cross purposes with Washington regarding the precise issue that, to a large extent, defined their world role – namely, their vindication of colonial

---

[173] Ibid., pp. 366–7.
[174] Quoted in Martel, 'Decolonisation after Suez', p. 402.
[175] 'Colonialism foes win again in U.N. on agenda issue', *The New York Times*, 4 October 1955.
[176] Ibid.

rule in Africa – this made the UN all the more ineffectual, or, worse, outright counterproductive, showcasing, as it did, a divided West and purportedly facilitating a report between the USA and the non-aligned anti-colonialists.

White Europe, to paraphrase Spaak, was facing isolation on the world scene; it was hounded by a degenerating world organization that failed to live up to civilized standards and it had been betrayed by its most important ally in Suez and Algeria. Not only that, if nothing was done before long it would soon run the risk of being delimited on its southern flank by hordes of people teeming with misguided animosities towards Europe.

From our account so far, we already know that such views were commonplace among European integration's chief proponents and architects. Yet, when focusing on their indignant projection onto the UN, in general, and to the corrosive influence that this organization was said to have on Europe's chief ally, in particular, this lends important clues and additional context to the Eurafrican pursuit in the latter part of the 1950s. It signals the sense of urgency to close the Eurafrican deal, which walked in tandem with the sense of international isolation on the issue of colonial sovereignty. With the UN, USA and thus also NATO and the UK seen as a forlorn hope, there was just one type of international organization and cooperation left for the continental powers to sustain Europe's global greatness, and that was the EEC, or 'Little Europe' as it was commonly referred to at the time. 'Although the present crisis presents dangers for both the United Nations and NATO', Spaak argued in *Foreign Affairs* in January 1957, 'it may well be beneficial for the cause of European unity. Ever since the nationalization of the Suez Canal there has been a strong current of opinion in that direction. Colonel Nasser's bold move showed what a definite lack of esteem for the great European nations exists in certain quarters. And the failure of the United States to support the Anglo-French cause has underlined the same theme.'[177]

---

[177] Paul-Henri Spaak, 'The West in disarray', *Foreign Affairs*, Vol. 35, No. 2, p. 189.

As it turned out, of course, France's walkout did not amount to a walkover in the ensuing UN battles over Algeria and colonialism. Instead, on 4 February 1957, it was France that brought both issues on the agenda for the UN General Assembly's Political Committee. This time though, and clearly in anticipation of a successful conclusion of the Treaty of Rome negotiations, Europe and Eurafrica had replaced France as history's prime movers. 'Europe in its entirety', French foreign minister Christian Pineau argued, 'bringing to Africa its capital and its techniques, should enable the immense African continent to become an essential factor in world politics'. Linking Eurafrica to the Algerian crisis, Pineau cautioned that an estranged Algeria would be 'pledged to fanaticism and by its very poverty, open to communism'. By contrast, 'its participation in Eurafrica would mean for Algeria comfort, riches – in other words, the true condition of independence'.[178] Pineau's address struck a chord with *The New York Times*, whose subsequent editorial went all out to endorse his message:

> The voice of the civilizing France of long history was heard in the United Nations on Monday. Foreign Minister Pineau's presentation of France's Algerian case was a reminder that the world as a whole owes much to the French and that in these tormented days of political and nationalistic strife there are perennial values in the ideals of France, Britain and the West in general (we would like to include our own American mission) that should not be beaten down in the current rage against so-called colonialism. [...] The oversimplification of the case by the Arab–Asian bloc, supported by the Soviet group, has impressed and fooled many millions of well-meaning people around the world. [...] What was especially challenging and hopeful in M. Pineau's presentation to the General Assembly was his vision of a broader European–African community, based on common cultural, economic and strategic interests. [...] 'Europe in its entirety', said M. Pineau, 'bringing to Africa its capital and its techniques, should enable the immense African continent to become an essential factor in world

[178] Quoted in 'France proposes new plan to link Africa to Europe', *The New York Times*, 5 February 1957.

politics.' So it should; so it should. 'Eurafrica,' as he called it, can only
be a dream today, but it is the sort of dream that other Frenchmen,
like Jean Monnet, have envisaged for Europe herself and have done
much to foster. It is the sort of dream that can become reality and
that, perhaps, must become reality if the world is to avoid another and
greater holocaust.[179]

A Eurafrican Common Market: Agreement reached

In resuming our account of the treaty negotiations, it is apposite to start
with a status summary of the negotiations issued by Pineau's foreign
ministry on the day after his speech in the UN (5 February). The
summary began by noting that 'Spaak seems to desire an association of
the Overseas countries to the Common Market, which is predestined
to provide the unified Europe with an extension of Eurafrica'. It then
described a more or less general readiness to come to an agreement
on the issue of colonial association. Germany, for instance, 'sincerely
wishes to arrive at a compromise', and while the Netherlands remained
sceptical 'it may align itself with the Germans as long as it does not
mean excessive financial charges'.[180]

A few days later, on 15 February, Adenauer added substance to the
French picture when he tried to convince the minority in his cabinet
to embrace Eurafrica and thus endorse colonial association as part of
the Common Market treaty. Adenauer's stance was spelled out in the
cabinet protocols: 'The Chancellor [...] is of the opinion that in the
long term France offers much better economic prospects than Britain.
France possesses a latent wealth, just think of the Sahara with its oil
and uranium deposits. Equatorial Africa also constitutes a significant
reserve. In comparison, Britain's development points to a substantial
decline.'[181] For Adenauer, a Eurafrican Common Market was thus the

---

[179] 'Europe and Africa' (editorial), *The New York Times*, 6 February 1957.
[180] HAEU, MAEF 3, 'NOTE, Territoires d'Outre-Mer et Marché Commun', 5 February 1957.
[181] 'Assoziierung der überseeischen Gebiete', Kabinettssitzung, 15 February 1957, *Die*

obvious and, by far, more beneficial choice for West Germany than the
simple European free trade area advocated by his Minister of Economy
Ludwig Erhard and which London had brought to the table in what
was seen by many as a hostile attempt to saw division among the Six.

Adenauer's accentuation of Saharan oil partly resulted from France's
discovery in 1956 of huge oil and gas reserves in the Algerian Sahara,
soon leading Paris to envisage self-sufficiency in oil within a few
decades.[182] As reported in *The New York Times* a few days prior to the
German cabinet debate, the managing director of the Algerian Oil
Research and Exploration Company, Armand Colot, 'predicted that
in fifteen years the Sahara would be providing France with all her
petroleum needs', thus 'freeing France from dependence on Middle
Eastern oil'.[183] Adenauer might also have been influenced by an article
published the very same month in the German Journal *Die politische
Meinung*, where Waldemar Lentz analysed the Eurafrican enterprise as
basically boiling down to the French colonial resources in general and
Algerian oil in particular. Indeed, as Lentz asserted, 'the Sahara stands
at the centre of the Eurafrican problematic'[184] (see Figures 4.6 and 4.7).

At the same time, progress was being made in the heads of delegation
negotiations on the issue of colonial association. The negotiations
were based on a detailed report produced by the Ad-Hoc Overseas
Territories Group, which summed up the agreements and disagreements between the partners and specified outstanding issues. It was
also the first document in which the negotiating partners explicated
which territories to associate and, as such, it coveys an imperial atmosphere. The future of foreign peoples and territories were being decided
in the Val Duchesse palace in Brussels:

Kabinettsprotokolle der Bundesregierung, Vol. 10, 1957 (Munich: R. Oldenbourg Verlag,
2000), p. 144.
[182] Sèbe, 'In the shadow of the Algerian War', p. 306; Matthew Connelly, *A Diplomatic
Revolution: Algeria's Fight for Independence and the Origins of the Post-Cold War Era*
(New York: Oxford University Press, 2002), p. 203.
[183] 'Wider oil search set for Algeria', *The New York Times*, 7 February 1957.
[184] Waldemar Lentz, 'Eurafrika – Fata Morgana oder Ernst?', *Die politische Meinung:
Monatshefte für Fragen der Zeit*, Vol. 2, No. 9, 1957, pp. 33–8. On the wider repercussions of France's oil discovery in Algeria, see Sèbe, 'In the shadow of the Algerian War'.

Figure 4.6 Drilling through the Sahara. Advertisement for Compagnie Française des Pétroles (Total), 1960. Source: *Cahiers économiques et de liaison des Comités Eurafrique*, Nos 5–7, 1960. Bibliothèque nationale de France.

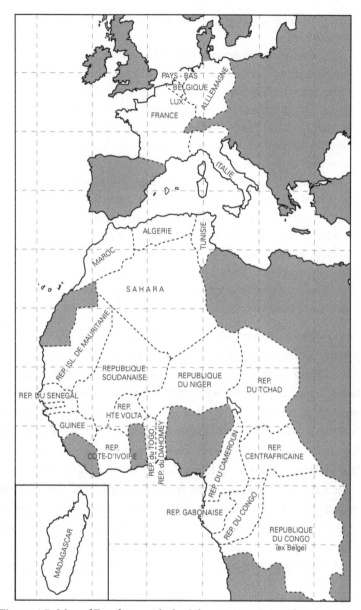

Figure 4.7 Map of Eurafrica, with the Sahara region inserted at its centre, as perceived from a French–Algerian perspective. Source: *Cahiers économiques et de liaison des Comités Eurafrique*, Nos 5–7, 1960. Bibliothèque nationale de France.

– Belgium demands the association of the Belgian Congo, of Rwanda, and of Urundi.

– Italy demands the association of Somalia, and envisions to demand that Libya, like Morocco and Tunisia, should be invited to associate.

– The Netherlands demands the association of New Guinea, provided the association regime to be established is acceptable to it. Concerning Surinam and the Dutch Antilles, the Dutch government does not have the competence to make on its own a decision requiring the agreement of the local authorities. [...]

– For France, the overseas territories, Togo and Cameroon should be part of the association. Algeria and the overseas French departments (Réunion, Guadeloupe, Martinique and Guiana) are comprised within the Common Market as they are integrated parts of the national territory. As for the independent countries of the Franc Zone (Morocco and Tunisia), France proposes that the states of the community invite them through a declaration of intent to associate themselves to the Common Market.[185]

We should note that this was the first time Algeria officially figured as an issue and France stated its intention to incorporate it into the EEC.

In order to come to an agreement, and as a sign that this might be close at hand, negotiations were now referred to a foreign ministers' meeting which took place in Paris on 18 February. Here, the matter concerning association was the only question on the agenda, in addition to the related one of fixing the common exterior tariffs affecting importations of certain products – mainly agricultural ones – that were in competition with those imported from the overseas territories of the member states. This revealed that the association of the OCTs was, at this stage, the issue on which the success or failure of the EEC hinged. In fact, all other outstanding questions initially included on the agenda – agriculture, labour mobility, atomic research,

[185] HAEU, CM 3/NEGO 254, 'Groupe de travail des territoires d'outre-mer, Rapport aux chefs de délégation', 17 February 1957. Concerning France, the 'overseas territories' here referred to French West and Equatorial Africa, Madagascar and French Somaliland. For a more detailed account concerning the African territories that were associated with the EEC in 1957/1958, see Tom Soper, 'The EEC and aid to Africa', *International Affairs*, Vol. 41, No. 3, 1965, pp. 463–77.

state monopolies – were excluded and referred to the Committee of the heads of delegation. As *The New York Times* reported on the eve of the meeting, '[t]he question of overseas territories is the principal remaining hurdle for the six to pass before agreeing on a treaty'. The *Times* also let it be known that West Germany was busy garnering support for an eleventh-hour proposal that would satisfy French demands and so smooth the process to a speedy agreement.

Most important, the *Times* had gained access to a French memorandum that had been circulated to the Five and which contained crucial information concerning the long-term perception of overseas association. In it, the *Times* conveyed, France had announced that 'their ultimate objective was to bring all the overseas territories completely into the common market'. Thus, after the five-year start-up period, during which trade and investments pertaining to the OCTs would be attuned and developed, the overseas territories, as the *Times* paraphrased the memorandum, 'should enter fully into the common market at the end of the provisional period for that market (twelve to seventeen years)'.[186] The 'twelve to seventeen years' refers to the timetable for the gradual establishment of the EEC's customs union, which was to be adopted in the Treaty of Rome.[187] If this yet again points to a tacit assumption that the African overseas territories, or colonies, would remain as overseas territories for the foreseeable future – rather than transforming into formally independent states – it also serves as a tangible illustration of the fact that what had been brought to the negotiating table was not a European common market, but rather a Eurafrican common market.

Spaak, foreign minister of Belgium and president of the Intergovernmental Conference of Foreign Ministers, opened the foreign ministers' meeting on 18 February. He observed that no agreement had yet been reached, and went on to propose a compromise in order to

---

[186] 'Bonn backs Paris on wider market', *The New York Times*, 18 February 1957.

[187] As specified in the treaty's Article 8: 'The common market shall be progressively established during a transitional period of twelve years.' Treaty Establishing the European Economic Community, 25 March 1957, Art. 8, p. 17.

break the impasse. The difficulty pertained mainly to the balancing of two issues: the size of the contributions of the Five to the investment fund that would mainly benefit French territories; and under which conditions France would be ready to reciprocate by allowing the five other member states to trade freely with, invest in and export to these overseas territories. A third but less serious issue was the exact level at which the external tariff for certain agricultural products should be fixed in order to give the associated overseas territories competitive advantage over similar products from other countries and territories; this amounted to an extension of France's customs protection of products from the franc zone.

Negotiations began with the German foreign minister, Brentano, proposing a Marshall Plan for the French OCTs, to last for five years, through which Germany would tap funds into French Africa. Pineau rejected this proposal, and this way of stating the problem, by countering that France would then offer Germany a Marshall Plan, helping Germany to export its products into French Africa.[188] The real discussion, though, centred on the difficulties in agreeing on a formula concerning the member states' contributions to the investment fund, and what the investments should cover. France wanted the Five to contribute more, in return for allowing them access to the new export markets for their products. Germany for its part wanted to see a stronger French commitment to abolishing all trade barriers for such exports to the overseas areas. Spaak proposed a compromise that would make the rules agreed on span a first period of five years, during which the investment fund should be built up in return for France's scrapping of all barriers to invest in and trade with the overseas territories. The size of the fund should be US$100 million annually (one-tenth of the billion dollars that France had initially suggested). Spaak also suggested that the fund should cover investments in the overseas territories of other member states.

[188] HAEU, SGCICEE 3109, Bousquet to Pineau, 'Conférence des Ministres des Affaires Etrangères du 18 février 1957. Problème de l'Association des Territoires d'Outre-Mer au Marché Commun', Brussels 21 February 1957, letter no. 401.

In the ensuing discussion the foreign ministers approached a consensus on the principles of Spaak's compromise. However, Luxemburg's Joseph Bech maintained that the amount each member state would contribute to the fund should be fixed beforehand, whereas Brentano reasserted that the investment fund was not meant to replace, but should rather add to, the investments that the mother countries had already allocated to their respective overseas territories. The German foreign minister also reaffirmed his position that reciprocity must prevail in all areas – that is, the same rules must apply for metropolitan exports to overseas territories as for overseas exports to metropolitan Europe. Hence, there should be no preferential trade treatment for the respective mother countries. In addition to this, Brentano suggested that the initial association agreement should span twelve years instead of the five recommended by Spaak; this because the overseas territories needed a longer-term commitment – an outlook once more signalling that these territories, in the minds of the negotiators, would not become independent in the foreseeable future. In response, Pineau and Faure reiterated their right to decide on exports to the overseas territories because sensitive sectors of the overseas economies may need protection from competition. For France, the resolution of this problem would be contingent on the other member states' willingness to contribute to the investment fund in order to build up the necessary infrastructure of the overseas territories.

An exchange then followed between Brentano and Faure where Faure reserved France's right to defer trade benefits to the Five in French overseas territories, if these did not after five years continue to contribute to the overseas development. Brentano retorted that it would be hard to imagine that the Five others would continue to contribute if they did not continue to enjoy open markets. Thereafter, Italy's foreign minster, Gaetano Martino, submitted that Italy was currently so burdened by developing its southern part that the country would not initially be able to contribute its share in five years, but rather would need a period of eight years. Spaak then intervened to break off the discussion, stating that since they had not reached an agreement the problems should be referred to the next day's conference of the Heads of Government.[189]

To add a bit more context we could also mention that, in his report to Pineau, Bousquet remarked that this last part of the foreign ministers' meeting, which took place around midnight, was not without comical intermezzos, such as Martino complaining about the terrible quality of the coffee imported from the French colonies, which would now flood the Italian market as a result of the overseas association. This, he claimed, would not make Italians favourably inclined towards the EEC, as it would force upon them a product they would not appreciate.[190]

During the following two days, 19–20 February, the Heads of Government, under the chairmanship of Guy Mollet, met in Paris' Hôtel Matignon to resolve the final and most difficult problem in the Common Market negotiations. And on the second day agreement on overseas or colonial association was finally reached. The agreement, which was to be codified in the Treaty's Part IV (Articles 131–6), included the following items:

1. The treaty would incorporate articles expressing the will to associate the OCTs in order to invest in them and further their development.
2. A period of five years was stipulated during which the application of these principles would be applied and a convention would be made to direct the application.
3. The convention would decide contributions of various member states to social and economic investments as well as the regime of exchange between the members and the overseas.
4. The contribution, totalling US$581.25 million for the initial five years of the member states, would be divided as follows: Germany US$200 million; France US$200 million; Belgium US$70 million;

189   HAEU, CM 3/NEGO 97, 'Projet de Procès-Verbal de la Conférence des Ministres des Affaires Etrangères des Etats membres de la C.E.C.A. (Paris 18 February 1957)', 6 March 1957.
190   HAEU, SGCICEE–3109, Bousquet to Pineau, 'Conférence des Ministres des Affaires Etrangères du 18 février 1957. Problème de l'Association des Territoires d'Outre-Mer au Marché Commun', 21 February 1957, letter no. 401.

Netherlands US$70 million; Italy US$40 million; Luxemburg US$1.25 million. Of these sums, US$511.25 million would be for French territories, including Algeria; US$30 million for Belgian, US$35 million for Dutch, and US$5 million for Italian.[191]

At the conclusion of the meeting a Communiqué de Presse was drawn up and issued after the conference. Crucially, it stated that work was sufficiently far ahead for the results to go into the treaty, which would shortly be signed in Rome.[192] Two announcements were thus made: one declaring the association of the overseas territories; the other the establishment of the Common Market and EURATOM as marking a decisive phase of European integration. As such, agreement on association came across as indispensable and as a precondition for the successful completion of the negotiations on European integration. This perception was also commonplace in the press reporting on the agreement. 'First step toward Eurafrica', blazoned *Le Monde* the day after the conference, remarking that the agreement had a distinct French colouring, primarily because of the association of French Africa, the investment fund and the inclusion of Algeria.[193] The next day's editorial was wholly devoted to the association of the OCTs enabled by the EEC, *Le Monde* now unequivocally asserting that the 'Eurafrica' that had just been established by the Six 'is not incompatible with the maintenance of the French Union. On the contrary, it may provide a last chance for it to evolve in a better climate.'[194] *The New York Times* opened its extensive

---

[191] HAEU, CM 3/NEGO 97, 'Projet de Procès-verbal de la Conférence des Chefs du Gouvernement et des Ministres des Affaires Etrangères des Etats membres de la C.E.C.A tenue à Paris, en l'Hôtel Matignon, les 19 et 20 février 1957', 26 February 1957. The US$581 million over five years that were finally agreed amounted to far less than France had suggested initially. Nonetheless, 'By African standards', listening to Cosgrove, 'this sum was large, as in 1956 French aid in public investment of a social and economic nature in West and Equatorial Africa totalled $200 million.' Carol Ann Cosgrove, 'The Common Market and its colonial heritage', *Journal of Contemporary History*, Vol. 4, No. 1, 1969, p. 79.

[192] HAEU, CM 3/NEGO 254, 'Communiqué de Presse', 20 February 1957.

[193] 'Première étape vers l'Eurafrique: Accord des Six sur l'association des territoires d'outre-mer au marché commun', *Le Monde*, 21 February 1957.

[194] 'Bulletin de l'étranger: Un point de départ?', *Le Monde*, 22 February 1957.

report in lofty terms: 'What may prove to be the greatest step so far toward the economic and, eventually, the political union of Europe was taken in Paris today.' It went on to mention the two treaties agreed upon – one being the EURATOM and the other the Common Market, where the latter 'would introduce gradually, over a period of twelve to seventeen years, a single or common market without tariffs or other barriers covering both the European and the overseas territories of the six nations'.[195] Similarly, the *Times*' editorial mentioned as its first point that: 'One of the agreements entered into at Paris calls for the organization of a common market among the six participating countries and the overseas territories of four of them.' But, as was added further down, 'this is not to be achieved overnight. It will be somewhere between twelve and seventeen years before the common market without tariffs and other barriers will spread over the six signatory countries and their overseas territories.' Again, it was not a European, but rather a Eurafrican, Common Market that had been adopted in Paris; and yet again, too, it was an undertaking in which colonial overseas territories were set to remain integrated for the long term. According to the *Times*' editorial, EURATOM would also need time to develop before it could make nuclear power a major source of energy in Europe. But then again, 'Egyptian President Nasser is of course doing his best at the moment to make home-grown atomic power popular in Western Europe.'[196]

Included, yet excluded: Algeria's place in the EEC

The Paris agreement was also significant in that it contained a special application for Algeria.[197] Being an integral part of metropolitan France, the agreement established that Algeria would, for most

---

[195] '6 European premiers join for a tariff-free market and atom resources pool', *The New York Times*, 21 February 1957.

[196] 'Toward European unity', *The New York Times*, 22 February 1957.

[197] In the Treaty of Rome, the status of Algeria was stipulated in Part VI (Article 227).

purposes, form an integral part of the EEC. However, in some respects Algeria was also to be treated in a similar way to overseas territories. Crucially, for instance, it was decided that the investment fund could be used in Algeria. This meant some tricky terminological innovations. The territory of the Common Market was now of two kinds: (1) a European territory of the member states of the European Economic Community; and (2) a non-European territory of the European Economic Community (i.e. Algeria, but also, as would be specified in the Treaty of Rome, the French overseas departments of Guadeloupe, French Guiana, Martinique and Réunion).[198]

Immediately following the Paris agreement, Bousquet, in a report designated as 'top-secret', summarized the negotiations on the status of Algeria to Pineau. During the intergovernmental conference, France did not raise the question of Algeria. Initially, at the time of the French–Belgian report, it was France's intention to include Algeria in the OCTs. This was in order to have Algeria benefit from the investment fund to be reserved for the French overseas, which was proposed at US$210 million per year, of a total of US$1 billion dollars in five years. Having realized that the European partners were not willing to contribute as much, and having heeded Minister of Overseas France Gaston Defferre's argument concerning the large investment needs in the African territories, France revised its position. On 17 February, France stated its intention to include Algeria into the Common Market as such, rather than having it associated and thus grouped together with the OCTs. According to Bousquet,

> this provoked a great stir among our partners, mainly in the Italian delegation, which was little disposed to see Algerian agricultural products, direct competitors with Italian agricultural products, benefit from the same advantages as those of Italy on the metropolitan markets of the Six. The Italian delegation was no less terrified by the risk implied, for the workers of the peninsula, by the application to

---

[198] HAEU, CM 3/NEGO 97, 'Projet de Procès-verbal de la Conférence des Chefs du Gouvernement et des Ministres des Affaires Etrangères … les 19 et 20 février 1957'.

Algerian emigrants of the chapter of the Treaty on the free movement of workers in the Common Market which is of particular interest precisely to Italy. Finally, the funds of the Investment Bank, which Italy desires to see used to as large extent as possible for the benefit of the poor regions of the peninsula, would now risk, given the situation of our Algerian departments, to be equally used to the benefit of the under-developed regions of Algeria.[199]

France's response to this was that the parties had to come to an acceptable agreement on Algeria, since otherwise the treaty would be rejected in France. France suggested that it should obtain agreement *in principle* on insertion of Algeria into the Common Market, and it would then be content to have Algeria excluded or exempted from certain chapters of the treaty, while leaving pending those chapters pertaining to the free movement of workers and the Investment Bank. It was agreed, at the meeting of the heads of delegation on 17 February, that Algeria would be included, in principle, into the EEC, but with the proviso that the application of certain parts of the treaty to Algeria would be determined at a later date.

This agreement gained approval at the subsequent conference of the Heads of Government (19–20 February), which was charged with deciding the Algerian issue. This meant that once the treaty had been ratified, the clauses concerning customs union (free movement of goods), minimum price for agricultural products, liberation of services, rules on competition and the institutions should all apply to Algeria and the other French overseas departments.[200] With regard to other treaty areas – including, for Italy, the most politically sensitive issue of freedom of movement for Algerian workers with French nationality – the status of Algeria and the other French departments was set be 'determined', as stipulated in the treaty, 'within two years of

---

[199] HAEU, SGCICEE 3109, Bousquet to Pineau, 'Conférence des Premiers Ministres et des Ministres des Affaires Etrangères – Application du Traité de Marché Commun à l'Algérie', Brussels 21 February 1957, letter no. 402.

[200] This would correspond to the treaty's Article 227; Treaty Establishing the European Economic Community, p. 153.

the entry into force of this Treaty, by decisions of the Council, acting unanimously on a proposal from the Commission'.[201]

In principle, however, and despite such prospects, the treaty drafters had no intention of turning them into reality. Italy thus had the backing of the partners in wanting to bar Algerians from the freedom of movement provisions.[202] But if this was the case, one may ask, why did the treaty not do the seemingly obvious and explicitly exclude Algeria from the freedom of movement for workers? According to Goedings, this was because such an explicit exclusion would have necessitated what France refused – namely, to have the treaty establish an equally explicit differentiation between French citizens in the metropole and those residing in Algeria.[203] If undertaken candidly, a discriminatory differentiation of this type would have been in obvious contradiction with French colonial myth and ideology. And it would have been particularly contradictory, we may add, at a time when the French government claimed to be doing its utmost not to exclude or discriminate but rather to include and ensure the full equality of the 'Muslim French citizens from Algeria', which was a new legal category created in 1956 specifically for the alleged purpose of rectifying the inequalities faced by Algeria's Muslims, who, formally speaking, were all French citizens or nationals.[204]

---

[201] HAEU, SGCICEE 3109, Bousquet to Pineau, 'Conférence des Premiers Ministres et des Ministres des Affaires Etrangères – Application du Traité de Marché Commun à l'Algérie', Brussels 21 February 1957, letter no. 402. Treaty Establishing the European Economic Community, Part VI, Art. 227, p. 154.

[202] S. A. W. Goedings, *Labor Migration in an Integrating Europe: National Migration Policies and the Free Movement of Workers, 1950-1968* (The Hague: Sdu Uitgevers, 2005), pp. 134–5.

[203] Ibid., p. 133.

[204] As established by the French constitution of 1946 (the Fourth Republic), all Algerians were French citizens. Given that 'Muslim', or non-European, Algerians were formally excluded from several political rights, not to speak of the many forms of harsh racist discrimination and social deprivation that they were subjected to, such formal French citizenship was of course marred by numerous inequalities. Nonetheless, as Todd Shepard has shown convincingly, this did not make it formally meaningless or practically inconsequential. See further Todd Shepard, *The Invention of Decolonization: The Algerian War and the Remaking of France* (Ithaca: Cornell University Press, 2006). Here, as our account indicates, we may see the French nationality question's impact on the EEC negotiations as a case in point.

In order to avoid a potentially devastating crisis over this contentious matter, the whole thing was resolved by subtracting the question
of nationality from the draft chapter on free movement, a manoeuvre
that also meant the working group on migration was relieved of the
nationality question. Instead, the issue was referred to the Ad-Hoc
Overseas Territories Group, where, as mentioned earlier, it was decided
that the application of the free movement provisions to Algeria and the
French overseas departments was to be decided within two years of the
treaty's ratification.

Once this was accomplished, however, the nationality question
was not referred back to the working group on migration. As a result,
nationality in relation to free movement dropped out of the treaty.[205]
As Goedings understands it, there is really no way of knowing whether
this was deliberate or not. But given the fact that all parties were on
the same page as far as the intention to exclude Algerian workers from
free movement was concerned, Goedings does not find it far-fetched
to assume that they were also quite content with the solution arrived
at. After all, to reintroduce the nationality question on the agenda
would have opened Pandora's box and thus risked a potentially lethal
eleventh-hour crisis.[206] According to Meriam Chatty, however, there
is enough evidence to establish that the ejection of the nationality
question was, in fact, a deliberate decision. As Chatty demonstrates, it
was not until the final draft that the free movement chapter's ultimate
formulation 'workers of the Member States' replaced a formulation
that would have specified free movement for 'national workers'; this
must obviously have been a deliberate substitution, performed in order
to enable member states to exclude certain 'national workers' such as
Algerians with French nationality from the member states without this
being in breach of the treaty. As Chatty puts it: 'The Treaty then created
a space where it was possible for member states to legally distinguish
between the nationals of the member states *sensu lato* and nationals

---

[205] Goedings, *Labor Migration in an Integrating Europe*, pp. 133–4.
[206] Ibid., p. 134.

[to be synonymous with the treaty's 'workers'] for Community laws purposes.'[207] In this sense, the differentiation that France refused to make explicit in the treaty was, through the substitution of 'workers' for 'nationals', devolved to the member states' discretion.

That this substitution was premeditated seems to be borne out too by the sequel to the Paris agreement, where divergences appeared within the group in charge of translating the decisions made by the Heads of Government in Paris into treaty text. With a treaty signature anticipated within the month of March, these last remaining hurdles were set to be cleared in Brussels between 28 February and 3 March. The divergences included German complaints over tariffs on bananas and bickering over possible trade discrimination against German bicycles (vis-à-vis French ones) for export to the overseas. Apart from these technical issues, more fundamental ones were also broached, such as what would happen after the first five-year period of the overseas association. Here it was agreed that the Council of Ministers must decide, unanimously, and before the termination of the five years, whether to impose a new regime of association. There was no talk at all about letting the overseas territories themselves have a say in this matter.[208]

As seen in the negotiations reports from Bousquet to Pineau, the crucial issue of Algeria and the French overseas departments also loomed into the foreground. The two questions to be sorted out dealt with the extent to which the treaty would apply to them with regard to agriculture and free movement of workers.[209] After some deliberation, Germany pulled back its reservation on agriculture, thus allowing for agricultural products from Algeria and the Antilles and

---

[207] Meriam Chatty, forthcoming Doctoral Dissertation (Örebro University).

[208] HAEU, SGCICEE 3109, Bousquet to Pineau, 'Comité des chefs de délégation des 28 février–3 mars 1957 – Problème de l'Association des Territoires d'Outre-Mer au Marché Commun', 4 March 1957, letter no. 450; and Bousquet to Pineau, 'Comité des chefs de délégation des 28 février–3 mars 1957. Chapitre de Traité relative à l'Association des TOM à la Communauté économique européenne', 4 March 1957, letter no. 451.

[209] HAEU, SGCICEE 3109, Bousquet to Pineau, 'Comité des chefs de délégation des 28 février–3 mars 1957. Application à l'Algérie et aux Départements français d'outre-mer du Traité instituant le Marché Commun. Débat au Groupe du Marché Commun', 4 March 1957, letter no. 456.

French Guiana to be traded on much the same terms as other goods. Furthermore, it was agreed that no mention would be made in the treaty concerning workers of French citizenship from Algeria and the overseas departments. Technically speaking, this meant that they would be included in the treaty – that is, they would not, as the Italians had first called for, be explicitly excluded – yet, at the same time, Bousquet noted,

> It has been understood that the national administrations of the member states may, in this respect, apply protective measures demanded by all our partners. This formula evidently contains inconveniences in the sense that French citizens of Algeria and of the overseas French departments who have reason to complain against such protective measures are likely to contest these before the Court of Justice of the Common Market.[210]

In line with what had previously been decided regarding free movement and Algeria and the French overseas departments as something to be determined within two years of the treaty's ratification, it was agreed that the European Commission would work out common rules in these matters.[211]

Given the emphasis on and awareness of the matters at stake in this deliberation, it seems safe to suggest that neither the treaty's omission of the nationality question nor its substitution of 'workers of the Member States' for 'national workers' could have been the results of decisions or non-decisions taken haphazardly. Rather, they were taken with the intent of excluding non-European Algerians from free movement while at the same time ensuring that such exclusion did not contradict French colonial rhetoric on citizenship as a universal category. We should add Chatty's remark, too, that despite the decision that the free movement provisions' application to Algeria and the French overseas

---

[210] HAEU, SGCICEE 3109, Bousquet to Pineau, 'Comité des chefs de délégation des 28 février–3 mars 1957. Application à l'Algérie et aux Départements français d'outre-mer du Traité instituant le Marché Commun. Décisions des chefs de délégation, 6 March 1957, letter no. 457.

[211] Ibid.

departments were to be determined within two years of the treaty's ratification, this was not done until 1968, after Algeria's independence and subsequent exit from the EEC. Although not entirely true in letter, *The New York Times'* assertion concerning the Paris agreement was certainly true in spirit: 'While the other French territories will enter the common market step by step, as European investments in them grow, Algeria will enter the market on much the same basis as France. But Algerian labor will not share the freedom of movement of other labor in the six nations, nor will it receive wages or social insurance at European rates.'[212]

After the settlement of the Algerian matter, there were, as it turns out, just a few problems left to be ironed out, the only potentially major one being the mounting domestic criticism in Belgium, claiming that Spaak had sold out the Congo and Belgium's colonial and national interests to foreign interests. The main complaint was that the Belgian Congo received too little from the investment fund, whereas French Africa, in many ways in competition with the Congo for investments and development, received much more. In Bousquet's report to Pineau, the ambassador concluded that the Belgian opinion was troubling; perhaps it would even cause the Belgian Parliament to reject the treaty. Bousquet ended his report on a more comforting note, however, as he referred to a speech given by Spaak on 5 March at a dinner organized by Vlaams Economisch Verbond: 'Mr Spaak, with his eloquence, simplicity and usual common sense victoriously refuted, in the name of Europe and Eurafrica, the argument of the newspapers [...]. His words were greeted by enthusiastic applause and a true ovation on the part of the numerous Flemish industrial and business representatives present.'[213]

A few days later, on 9 March, Bousquet was able to inform Pineau that negotiations were finally complete. As always, the association was

---

[212] '6 European premiers join for a tariff-free market and atom resources pool', *The New York Times*, 21 February 1957.

[213] HAEU, SGCICEE 3109, Bousquet to Pineau, 'L'opinion belge et Val Duchesse', 5 March 1957, letter no. 462.

the trickiest issue to resolve for the partners at Val Duchesse: 'It was not until the end of the conference's debates, between midnight and two o'clock in the morning that, in conditions that may appear satisfactory, the problem of Association of the OCTs to the European Economic Community was finally settled.'[214]

A statue to Nasser: Triumphant Eurafricanism

While the last remaining details of colonial association were finally put to rest on 9 March, it was the Paris agreement of heads of state on 19–20 February that marked the decisive moment of the EEC's colonial settlement. But as we have seen earlier, the Paris agreement was also the agreement that delivered the EEC as such. Thus, without colonial agreement, there would be no European integration agreement; and, vice versa, in order to achieve colonial agreement this presupposed a European accord on integration. This brings us back to Coudenhove-Kalergi's dictum: 'To save Africa for Europe, is to save Europe by way of Africa.' And conversely: 'Africa cannot be made available, if Europe does not unite.'[215] Some three decades and a European world war later, key elements of this Eurafrican geo-economic and geopolitical design had emerged as one of the platforms upon which the European Economic Community was set to be built.

In the immediate aftermath of the Paris agreement this was reflected in the statements made by some of the most key figures at the forefront of the EEC negotiations. Arguing for 'der Vision von Eurafrika' before his cabinet on the day after the Paris accord (February 21), Adenauer admitted that no grand geopolitical blueprint for the world was without risk. But, he added, 'the free Europe must be prepared to confront this risk, in order not to be crushed, in the foreseeable future,

---

[214] HAEU, SGCICEE 3109, Bousquet to Pineau, 'Comité des chefs de délégation des 7 et 8 mars', 9 March 1957, letter no. 502.

[215] Richard Coudenhove-Kalergi, 'Afrika', *Paneuropa*, Vol. 5, No. 2, pp. 3–5.

between the peoples of Asia and Africa should these peoples assume a hostile attitude towards Europe.'[216]

'The most important event in the history of Europe since the French Revolution.' Those were the words of Paul-Henri Spaak, as he summarized the intergovernmental negotiations and outlined the aims behind the overseas association before business and army circles in Brussels on 25 March. Explaining the importance of the new EEC organization, Spaak dwelled on the relation of scale to community. The rapid development of the USA and the Soviet Union 'proves that economic and social expansion is enabled by large human communities', he stated. He went on to argue that the world-historical importance of the EEC consisted of the creation of a community of the same size and scale as these 'empires'. Spaak thus emphasized that the scale of the EEC extended beyond the European landmass. A 'great historical decision' had been made in Paris on 20 February – namely, to 'admit into the Common Market, on certain terms, the overseas territories'. By adding the African territories, the market would include more than 200 million inhabitants and Europe would have access to the raw materials necessary for its sustainability, Spaak told his audience. For this Belgian foreign minister and chieftain of European integration, the constitution of a community incorporating Europe and Africa was thus the boldest part of the Treaty of Rome: 'Would it not be a success, if we could realize the dream of Eurafrica, which, after the reunion in Paris, seems able to become reality?'[217]

The same day, Spaak was also interviewed by Albert Housieaux, socialist parliamentarian and editor of the newspaper *Le Peuple*. According to Bousquet's report, the interview was largely devoted to the overseas association. Bousquet quotes Spaak: 'I consider what has been done in Paris concerning the African territories to be of an absolutely exceptional importance: 1. A new market of more than fifty million inhabitants is thus opened for the European countries. 2. The Treaty

---

[216] 'Außenpolitische Lage', Kabinettssitzung, 21 February 1957, *Die Kabinettsprotokolle der Bundesregierung*, Vol. 10, p. 155.

[217] Spaak gave his lecture on 25 February 1957 to military and business circles in Brussels and it was subsequently published in *Mars et Mercure*, No. 3 (March), 1957.

surpasses its purely commercial and economic character, because it is the introduction of a common policy of the countries of Europe in Africa.'[218]

Simultaneously, on 25 February, Guy Mollet for his part began an official visit to the USA. As he put it in his first address, fresh off the plane in New York: 'In a very cordial and frank talk with your great President I would like to stress among others, the following points: Build Europe, link it closely to Africa.'[219] Later the same day, Mollet arrived in Washington where he gave another talk, once again laying emphasis on the Eurafrican settlement: 'I would like to insist upon the unity of Europe: it is now a fact. A few days ago we jumped over the last hurdles that were on its way, and now an even broader unity is being born: EURAFRICA, a close association in which we will work together to promote progress, happiness and democracy in Africa.'[220] Two days later Mollet spoke about French foreign policy to an audience of journalists in Washington. He began by commenting on the most recent developments:

> Eight days ago [...] we settled the last difficulties concerning the Euratom Treaty and that of the Common European Market. We took also a capital decision: to associate Europe with the territories of Black Africa which today are linked with Belgium and France. [...] In associating the Overseas Territories of our countries with this market, the road is open to the union of Europe and Africa, to what we are beginning to call Eurafrica.[221]

'This is not a hazy dream. I am firmly convinced that EURAFRICA will be the reality of tomorrow', Mollet asserted before the US Senate on the same day. In this speech, Eurafrica was presented as the keystone of the Treaty of Rome and as the key to a better world; as such, Mollet

[218] HAEU, SGCICEE 3109, Bousquet to Pineau, 'Interview de M. SPAAK au sujet de la Conférence de Paris', 25 February 1957, letter no. 417.
[219] HAEU, EN 2735, 'Statement given by Premier Guy Mollet on his arrival in New York', 25 February 1957, p. 25.
[220] HAEU, EN 2735, 'Statement given by Premier Guy Mollet on his arrival at the Washington Airport'.
[221] HAEU, EN 2735, 'Speech to be delivered by Mr Guy Mollet, President of the Council of Ministers, at the luncheon of the National Press Club', 27 February 1957; published as Guy Mollet, 'The Euratom Treaty: The Common European Market', *Vital Speeches of the Day*, Vol. 23, No. 11, 15 March 1957, pp. 349–52.

also emphasized, it was in perfect line with the interests of the USA and of the wider NATO.[222] Similarly, going on to address the House of Representatives later on, Mollet confirmed that 'This new Europe also aims at associating African territories with the making of a more prosperous economic entity. It is now our task, hand in hand with our European partners, to put our industrial resources at the disposal of Africa; thus EURAFRICA will come into existence.'[223]

Mollet ended his North American tour in Canada, where he addressed the Canadian Parliament on 4 March. With regard to Africa, he declared that 'we are moving ahead with quasi-revolutionary transformations in the overseas territories'. He also stated that France, through the EEC, was opening the doors to Europe for the peoples of the African territories. (No metaphor could be less correct, of course.) Mollet ended his long speech by asking about the 'exalting tasks' that the French were about to shoulder, to which he responded: '*l'Europe à construir, le Sahara à mettre en valeur, l'Eurafrique à édifier*' ('to construct Europe, to develop Sahara, to build Eurafrica'). Here, again, is the holy trinity of Mollet's foreign policy, and the three are firmly connected in a geopolitical logic that, through the Eurafrican EEC, is also said to entail the resolution of the conflicts in Algeria and Suez.[224]

In addition, we should mention that some of this is also alluded to in the ceremonial speeches given at the formal signing procedure for the Treaties of Rome, which took place on 25 March at the Palazzo dei Conservatori, on Capitoline Hill in Rome. Whereas Pineau made reference to the Cold War context and argued that the EEC was a necessary balancing power,[225] Adenauer stated: 'It is with resolve and confidence we will approach our tasks. We know in this respect the

---

[222] HAEU, EN 2735, 'Address by Guy Mollet before the Senate of the United States', 27 February 1957.

[223] HAEU, EN 2735, 'Address by Guy Mollet before the House of Representatives', 27 February 1957.

[224] HAEU, EN 2735, 'Declaration prononcée par M. Guy Mollet, président du conceil des ministres de France, devant le parlement canadien', 4 March 1957.

[225] HAEU, CM 3/NEGO 98, 'Discours prononcé par S.E. M. Pineau, Ministre des Affaires Etrangères de la France, à l'occasion de la signature des Traités instituant la Communauté Economique Européenne et la Communauté Européenne de l'Energie Atomique'.

seriousness of our situation, to which only the unification of Europe permits a remedy. We know, also, that our plans are not egoistic, but that they are destined to promote the well being of the entire world.'[226] The most direct reference to the colonial ambitions of the EEC, however, was given by the Dutch foreign minister, Joseph Luns: 'It is our firm conviction that these treaties, in eliminating the barriers that separate our countries, [...] assure the conditions of an increasing prosperity to our old continent and permits the continuation of her grand and global civilizing mission [sa grande mission civilisatrice mondiale].'[227]

Finally, the celebrations in Palazzo dei Conservatori could not have been complete without a reference being made to Nasser, or so it seemed. Nasser's shocking refusal to play according to the European colonial rules had earned him many names from the likes of Adenauer, Mollet and Spaak – a Hitler, a Mussolini, a Moscow puppet, a Napoleon of the Arabs. In Palazzo dei Conservatori he was given yet another one. But this time there was actually some truth to go around as Louis Armand, now the first president of EURATOM, jested: 'We ought to erect a statue to Nasser. To the federator of Europe.'[228]

---

[226] HAEU, CM 3/NEGO 98, 'Discours prononcé par S.E. M. Adenauer ..., Chancelier de la République Fédérale d'Allemagne ...'.

[227] HAEU, CM 3/NEGO98, 'Discours prononcé par S.E. M. Luns, Ministre des Affaires Etrangères des Pays-Bas ...'.

[228] Quoted in Merry Bromberger and Serge Bromberger, *Jean Monnet and the United States of Europe* (New York: Coward-McCann, 1969), p. 176. See also Jean Monnet, *Memoirs*, trans. Richard Mayne (Garden City, NY: Doubleday, 1978), p. 422.

5

Conclusion: Ending Colonialism by Securing its Continuation

The inventors and entrepreneurs of Eurafrica – from Richard Coudenhove-Kalergi, Paolo d'Agostini Orsini di Camerota, Eugène Guernier, Albert Sarraut and Joseph Caillaux to Robert Schuman, Anton Zischka, Eirik Labonne, Paul-Henri Spaak and Guy Mollet – all hailed the European Economic Community as a realization of their once pioneering designs. Guernier, writing in early 1958, was thrilled: 'After decades of engagement, the nuptials of Europe and Africa has finally been celebrated.'[1] Coudenhove-Kalergi, for his part, described the Treaty of Rome as a partial fulfilment of the Pan-European programme and emphasized that Adenauer, Monnet, Spaak and other architects of the EEC were all leading members of the Pan-European organization.[2] After many failed attempts to turn the colonial management of Africa into a common European issue and responsibility, the promoters of Eurafrica had thus prevailed, establishing precise arrangements and institutions for the purpose of incorporating Algeria and associating the colonies of the six founding members with the Common Market.

---

[1] Eugène Guernier, *France-Outre Mer*, 29 January 1958.

[2] Richard Coudenhove-Kalergi, *Eine Idee erobert Europa: Meine Lebenserinnerungen* (Vienna: Verlag Kurt Desch, 1958), pp. 329–44. As for D'Agostini Orsini di Camerota, he described the creation of the EEC and its association of African countries as a realization of Eurafrica and the first step toward creating 'the largest ensemble, the largest space, the largest mass in material, human and economic terms, which will become the greatest economic power in the world' (*I problemi economici dell'Africa e l'Europa*, Rome: Edizioni Cinque Lune, 1961, p. 424). As for Sarraut's continued belief in Eurafrica, and in the EEC as its realization, see his letter of support in *Cahiers Économiques et de liaison des Comités Eurafrique*, special issue 'Regards sur l'Afrique', Nos 5–6–7, 1960, p. 14.

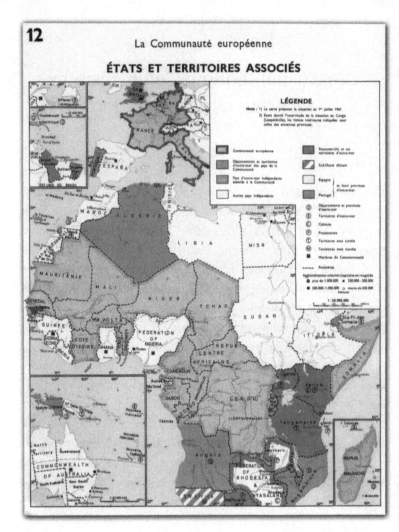

Figure 5.1 Official EEC map showing the six Member States and the associated Overseas Countries and Territories (OCTs) as at 1 July 1961. Source: La Communauté européenne – Cartes. Luxembourg-Bruxelles: Service de presse et d'information des Communautés européennes, Avril 1962. Copyright: © Communautés européennes.

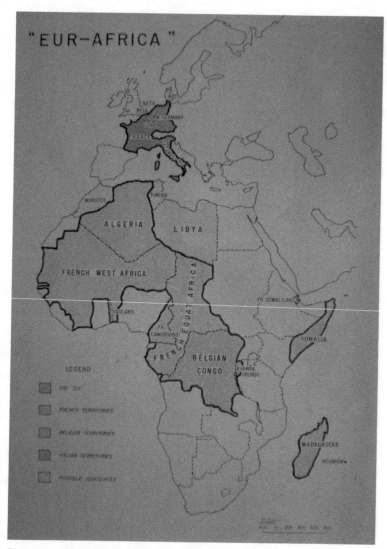

Figure 5.2 Map of 'Eur-Africa', as perceived from a British perspective.
Source: James Hunt, *Europe and Africa – Can it be Partnership?*
(London: Federal Union, without date [1958?]). Kenya National
Archives, Nairobi.

Figure 5.3 Cover of special issue of *Cahiers économiques et de liaison des Comités Eurafrique*, Nos 8–9, 1960. Bibliothèque nationale de France.

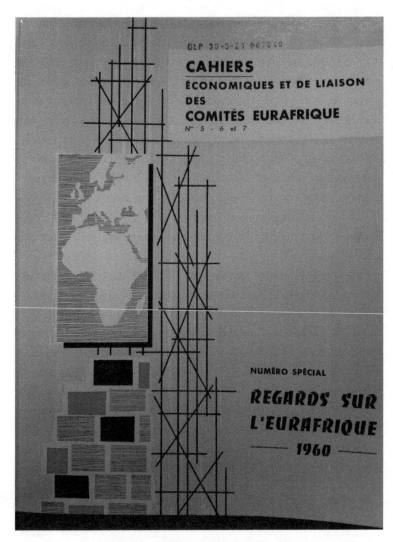

Figure 5.4 Cover of special issue – 'Regards sur l'Eurafrique' – of *Cahiers économiques et de liaison des Comités Eurafrique*, Nos 5–7, 1960. Bibliothèque nationale de France.

We have, throughout this book, drilled deeply especially into the years 1955–7. Our findings provide an empirical demonstration of what Eurafrica was about and help explain how it was established through the EEC's association of the overseas territories. As for the preceding interwar and postwar periods, we have relied on a more eclectic set of documents, ranging from archival sources and reports in news media of the period to memoirs and research material from a broad range of disciplines. Through this material, we are able to assert that the Eurafrican association realized with the EEC was but the final and successful effort to rationalize the colonial management of Africa by turning it into a shared concern and a shared possibility for the six founding member states and, potentially, for Europe as a whole.

Thus, in the view of the founders of the EEC, their community was far more than a nascent customs union encompassing six metropolitan European states. Covering a territorial sphere stretching from the Baltic to the Congo, the EEC was equally conceived in terms of geopolitical strategy, one that would ensure Western Europe's security, economic sustainability and relative political autonomy between the two superpowers. A year after the Treaty of Rome was signed, Guy Mollet confessed that this was 'probably the finest source of pride of my government. Not only did the European Community attain a solid foundation, but the first supports for an association of Europe and Africa were fixed. The Eurafrican community began to take shape.'[3] In April 1958, with the offices of the European Commission set up in Brussels, the Directorate General for the overseas territories – or the DG VIII – began its work under the commissioner Robert Lemaignen (see Figure 5.5). He structured the EEC's Eurafrican activities into four areas, based on the Commission's interpretation of the Treaty of Rome: research and programme activities; cultural and social questions; trade matters; and financing of development through the

---

[3] Guy Mollet, *Bilan et Perspectives Socialistes* (Paris: Plon, 1958), p. 34.

Figure 5.5 'Africa: A European Necessity'. Issue of *L'Européen. Revue des Marchés et des Affaires autour du Marché Commun* (September/October 1958), featuring a statement by commissioner Robert Lemaignen on Eurafrica and the association of the African colonies.

investment fund.[4] Initiatives in each area ensued from Lemaignen's policy statement that 'the European community was a common good of all its participants including all the African peoples'. In 1964 the Commissioner summarized the first five years at the DG VIII, concluding that 'a broad foundation had been laid for the Eurafrican economic symbiosis', adding that this was 'an essential element of the world of tomorrow'.[5]

What this book has shown, in short, is that Africa was of paramount importance in most, if not all, efforts at European integration from the launching of the Pan-European Union in 1923 to the foundation of the EEC in 1957; that Africa was one of the biggest stakes in the Treaty of Rome negotiations; and, finally, that Eurafrica initially formed an integral part of the EEC's policy vocabulary. In this way, we have corroborated and explained what we noted in our introductory chapter – namely the surprisingly strong correlation between the historical discourses that, from the aftermath of World War I to the late 1950s, dealt with European integration and those that dealt with Africa and Europe's allegedly 'civilizing missions' in the 'dark continent'.

Much remains to be said about the Eurafrican project. First, we have indicated that the EEC's association of the African colonies staked out the future direction of the French and Belgian colonies in Africa that became independent around 1960. Through its Eurafrican arrangement, the EEC exercised a profound influence on the decolonization process and its terminus in the various arrangements of dependence, clientelism and in the perpetuation of Africa's function as a raw materials reservoir. Second, the EEC's association of the colonies and, subsequently, formally independent African states also had a wider resonance in international relations of the period, which may be traced in other international organizations, institutions and fora, such as the UN, the World Bank, the IMF and GATT. These two areas will be covered in another book, in which we also provide more archival

[4]   Robert Lemaignen, *L'Europe au Berceau: Souvenirs d'un Technocrate* (Paris: Plon, 1964), p. 119.
[5]   Lemaignen, *L'Europe au Berceau*, pp. 123, 160.

documentation to back up our claim concerning the intrinsic relation between European integration and European colonialism.[6]

Anti-independence and yet non-colonial: Eurafrica institutionalized

Already at this stage, though, it is clear that the forgotten historical relation that we recover implies several crucial conclusions concerning the history of European integration, colonialism and the decolonization process in Africa, as well as postwar European and world history more generally. Here we could start from the observation that as we enter the 1960s and the formal decolonization drive in Africa, Eurafrica would rapidly disappear from the political agenda and wider public discussion. This is probably why, even if they could conceive of its importance at the time, many scholars tacitly dismiss Eurafrica as nothing but a grand vision with little political substance or historical significance.

As early as June 1960, an article in the German daily *Die Welt* carried the anxious headline 'Läuft Afrika der EWG davon?' ('Is Africa running away from the EEC'?). The article asserted that at the time when the Treaty of Rome was drafted, 'the fact that Europe would be faced by independent States in Africa within only a few years could scarcely have been anticipated'. Such independence, the author warned, risked upsetting the EEC's entire edifice of African association. Lest a new EEC strategy towards Africa was promptly launched, the article concluded, the situation could soon prove 'dangerous for Europe and hence for the West in its entirety'.[7] When, in 1963, eighteen independent African states decided to retain multilateral EEC association under the

---

[6] For an original account of the EEC's Third World relations in the post-independence era, starting in the late 1950s, see Giuliano Garavini, *After Empires: European Integration, Decolonization, and the Challenge from the Global South, 1957–1986* (Oxford: Oxford University Press, 2012).

[7] Ferdinand Himpele, 'Läuft Afrika der EWG davon?', *Die Welt*, 2 June 1960. CVCE, www.ena.lu/africa-running-away-eec-die-welt-june-1960-020200670.html (accessed 11 October 2013).

negotiators

Yaoundé Convention, any such fears were, of course, put to rest; by the mid-1970s most African states had opted for EEC association through Yaoundé's successor, the Lomé Convention (1975–2000, later replaced by the Cotonou Agreement, 2000–).

Such precipitate apprehensions aside, *Die Welt* was certainly right in its judgement that the Treaty of Rome was negotiated under the assumption that most African territories had a long way to go before they would attain formal statehood. As Uwe Kitzinger noted in 1962 when commenting on the Rome Treaty's colonial association provisions: 'They were based on a largely static conception of the political relations between the African countries and the metropolitan Member States. In the past three years that relationship has evolved *beyond all expectations*. Since the Treaty was signed, most of the Associates have become politically independent of any Member State.'[8] Writing a few years later, Carol Ann Cosgrove also stressed this crucial point:

> The treaty was drafted at a time when rapid decolonization was discounted by the European metropoles, with the result that no reference was made to the possible attainment of sovereign independence by the associate except in the case of Somaliland. Despite rumblings in North Africa and the imminence of independence in the Gold Coast [Ghana], it seemed likely that the colonial regimes would continue to be the recipients of any benefits yielded by association.[9]

The dismal outlook on the EEC–Africa relations expressed by *Die Welt* in 1960 thus starkly contrasted with the Eurafrican buoyancy at the time for the Treaty of Rome signing in 1957. Indeed, if *Die Welt* agonized over the prospect of 'Africa running away from the EEC' on 2 June 1960, on 26 March 1957 – the day after the Rome Treaty's signing ceremony – *The New York Times* took note of Europe's latest move in its run – or should we say *Drang* – to the South: 'Germans go to Africa: Bonn mission to study ways to develop resources'. As reported,

---

[8] Uwe Kitzinger, *The Challenge of the Common Market* (Oxford: Basil Blackwell, 1962), p. 98, our emphasis.

[9] Carol Ann Cosgrove, 'The Common Market and its colonial heritage', *Journal of Contemporary History*, Vol. 4, No. 1, 1969, pp. 77–8.

a German delegation was heading for 'France's African colonies to survey the joint development of industrial raw materials required by West Europe'. It was also related that this formed part of the EEC accord, 'signed today in Rome', and its objective to secure 'the joint financing of the economic development of France's African colonies'.[10]

Another headline in *The New York Times* in 1957 ran as follows: 'Europe may get new oil source: Common Economic Market could mean shift from Mideast to Africa: Resources big factor'. Again, we are reminded of the self-evident stability and durability with which the EEC's ownership of Africa was perceived in 1957. Here, in the wake of the agreement on the EEC, *The New York Times* recounts the upbeat mood concerning the great economic prospects proffered by the new European community's joint development of Algeria and its members' 'overseas possessions'. In as little time as five or six years, the article states, the EEC may very well, thanks to the recently discovered oil reserves in Algeria, 'bring about a most important and perhaps permanent change in the European oil picture and a partial solution to a tough foreign exchange problem'. As also noted, the EEC's 'ultimate goal appears to be a self-sufficiency in oil and some other raw materials available from the overseas possessions, mostly in Africa'.[11]

But while the American newspaper spoke about 'colonies' and 'overseas possessions' in relation to the EEC–Africa relations, such a designation was also a cause of concern in Europe. To be sure, Eurafrica had no place for national independence, as illustrated with utmost clarity in the case of the Algerian emergency. At the same time, Eurafrican advocates also, not least in the UN, fought an uphill struggle to distance the project from an increasingly ill-reputed and outmoded colonialism. After agreement on the EEC's overseas association scheme had been reached in late February 1957, for instance, journalists in Bonn immediately criticized their government, asking whether West Germany was not in fact now harnessed to France's and Belgium's

---

[10] 'Germans go to Africa: Bonn mission to study ways to develop resources', *The New York Times*, 26 March 1957.

[11] 'Europe may get new oil source', *The New York Times*, 7 October 1957.

colonialism and the war in Algeria. Foreign Secretary Brentano flatly denied this, stating that the aid intended within the frame of the EEC's investment fund 'has nothing to do with the colonial administration'.[12] Adenauer, too, underlined that 'the association of the overseas territories has nothing in common with colonialism'.[13] In their rhetoric, Eurafrica rather entailed the dawn of an international order guided by the United Nations Declaration of Human Rights, thus serving 'the general interest and above all favouring the indigenous populations', as Brentano put it.[14]

Meanwhile, in Algeria and elsewhere, the Eurafrican community was hailed as a warrant for the perpetuation of the colonial system. Octave Meynier, a high-ranking military officer and publishing editor of *Eurafrique* (an influential organ in French colonial circles in North Africa), portrayed the association of Algeria and French Africa to the EEC as following in the tracks of the 'Great Discoveries' and the 'Great Conquests'. Meynier admitted that these periods now belonged to the past and that 'a page must be turned'; but, he continued, 'it must none the less be understood that colonization allowed us to encounter and bring up the under-developed peoples. The time has now come to bring them up to our level. The Era of PROMOTION of the African peoples and of their UNION with Europe has begun. In this way, EURAFRICA has been constructed in love, in an act of trust and generosity'.[15] For Meynier, the Eurafrican association turned a page in the colonial story. This change was necessary – not in order to abolish European rule in Africa but to secure a future for it: 'The maintenance of French sovereignty in Algeria, supported by the creation of Eurafrica, is the only remedy able to prevent the tragic consequences of a situation that the Western world cannot allow to deteriorate any further.'[16]

[12] 'M. von Brentano: les résultats des entretiens de Paris sont entièrement satisfaisants pour l'Allemagne de l'Ouest', *Le Monde*, 23 February 1957, p. 6.
[13] 'Le Chancelier Adenauer: l'association des territoires d'outre-mer n'a rien de commun avec le colonialisme', *Le Monde*, 24 February 1957, p. 3.
[14] 'M. von Brentano', *Le Monde*, 23 February 1957, p. 6.
[15] Anonymous [Octave Meynier], 'L'Eurafrique est crée, L'Eurafrique vit …', *Eurafrique: Revue d'action africaine et méditerranéenne*, No. 9, January 1957, p. 15.
[16] Octave Meynier, 'L'Eurafrique – Tache urgente', *Eurafrique: Revue d'action africaine et méditerranéenne*, No. 11, July 1957, p. 2.

As institutionalized by the EEC, then, Eurafrica was perceived both as the end of colonialism and as authorizing its continuation; or, if you like, as anti-independence yet non-colonial. Since Eurafrica and initial EEC–Africa relations ruled out formal African statehood, this may explain *Die Welt* and others' trepidation towards African independence in 1960. More important, it could also be taken to explain the rapid decline of Eurafrica as a political concept, rallying call and overall enterprise as we enter the 1960s. In short, with its backbone of deferred independence broken, Eurafrica had ceased to be a viable project.

But as we shall come back to later, this explanation has very little to say about the fact that Africa, with a few exceptions, did *not* run away from the EEC after formal independence had been reached. On the contrary, the EEC's African association was continued through the signing of the Yaoundé Convention in 1963, although this time with nominally independent states on the African side. Equally importantly, it offers no clues as to why Eurafrica also disappeared from the radar of scholars and intellectuals, a predicament that has left the vast field of EU studies practically void of any serious investigations into a matter of paramount importance in all efforts at European integration.[17] So

---

[17] In early EU studies, it was generally recognized that parts of Africa and the Common Market were bound together in one imperial polity, and social scientists saw the association agreement as one of the central features of the EEC. For instance, in the very first issue of the *Journal of Common Market Studies*, since then the major organ of its field, Thomas Balogh dealt comprehensively with 'Africa and the Common Market' (*Journal of Common Market Studies*, Vol. 1, No. 1, 1962, pp. 79–112). Similarly, the earlier cited article by Carol Ann Cosgrove from 1969, 'The Common Market and its colonial heritage' (*Journal of Contemporary History*, Vol. 4, No. 1, 1969), sets out from what was self-evident at the time: 'That the EEC was endowed with a colonial heritage is not in dispute' (p. 73). Erling Bjøl, in his monumental dissertation *La France devant l'Europe: La politique européenne de la IVe République* (Copenhagen: Munkgsgaard, 1966), states that the colonial question in Africa was one of three major motivations behind France's support of European integration (pp. 262–72, 295–6). In another major work, Mario Andreis reaffirmed the central importance of Eurafrica: *L'Africa e la Comunità economica europea* (Torino: Einaudi, 1967), as did Uwe Kitzinger in *The Challenge of the Common Market*, pp. 88–107. In the 1960s, too, Max Liniger-Goumaz synthesized what back then looked like an emerging field of 'Eurafrican studies' in the form of an analysis and a comprehensive bibliography of writings on Eurafrica from the Pan-European organization to the EEC. For the bibliography, see Max Liniger-Goumaz, *Eurafrique* (Geneva: Les Éditions du temps, 1970); and, for the survey, Max Liniger-Goumaz, *Eurafrique: Utopie ou réalité?* (Yaoundé: Editions CLE, 1972). These promising beginnings are signposts to research directions that still, fifty years later, remain largely unexplored.

how do we explain and analyse this complex of (1) Eurafrica's loss of political salience, resulting from African decolonization in the early 1960s; (2) Eurafrica's central structural elements nonetheless being carried over into the new association regime; and (3) Eurafrica's sinking into oblivion within research, in general, and EU studies, in particular? Could these processes even be jointly analysed, since they seem to operate at quite different levels? We think they could; indeed, we think this necessary in order to cut to the heart of the Eurafrican matter. In other words, by approaching these three problems as inter-related we will also be able to provide a historical conceptualization of Eurafrica as such.

Vanishing mediator: The historical logic of Eurafrica

In order to do this we need to set out from the Eurafrican complex itself and try to come to terms with the apparent paradox that we have just outlined: the fact that Eurafrica was premised on an opposition to independence while simultaneously, as we reach the postwar period, distancing itself from colonialism, which explains why Eurafrica could appeal to colonialists and anti-colonialists alike. We glimpse an answer as soon as we turn the question on its head: Was it perhaps this ability to encompass contradictory historical tendencies and satisfy opposing political interests that explains Eurafrica's successful realization?

In this book we have argued that Eurafrica was a political project that gained strength and momentum under historical circumstances that, starting with the 'Wilsonian moment' after World War I, gradually trapped Europe's imperial states in a double bind. All over their empires they had to reckon with increasingly militant political demands for national independence and sovereignty at the same time as they confronted the unavoidable prerequisite of integrating the resources of Europe and Africa into a viable strategic and economic area. Such circumstances made Eurafrica appear as a rational option, in the view of many European leaders. Or, as Enzo Grilli puts it: 'Association based on Euro-Africanism, was then extensively used to try to preserve the influence of the metropole, while allowing the colonies to acquire various degrees of autonomy.[18] However, Eurafrica was embraced not just because it served as a political and economic formation in which national independence was simply harmonized with regional economic and military integration, but rather because it was a formation that apparently made it possible to avoid the undesired aspects of both. Eurafrica envisioned the granting of a type of conditional autonomy or quasi-independence, specifically designed to serve as a bulwark against their negative corollaries in the form of protectionism, nationalist competition and anti-Western resentment; and it allowed for regional integration and consolidation of Europe's control of Africa, but without having to carry the blame for colonial exploitation and explicit white supremacy.

As we have seen, too, not only was the Eurafrican programme able to avoid these negative dimensions but also to purvey its solution as a new community, built on an equal partnership, mutual trust and interdependence, the different polities of which could now chart a course towards a brighter future. Historian Thomas Moser – in the only truly comprehensive treatment of the topic so far – sums up this aspect by stating that Eurafrica served as an 'integrating and guiding image' (*Integrationsleitbild*), which impacted considerably on 'the evolution of [European] integration as well as on decolonization in the transition from the late colonial to the post-colonial era'.[19] His interpretation echoes that of René Girault, who asserts that the decision of the Treaty of Rome to associate the colonial possessions 'constituted an important milestone in France's politics of decolonization'.[20] While there is some

---

[18] Enzo R. Grilli, *The European Community and the Developing Countries* (Cambridge: Cambridge University Press, 1993), p. 1.

[19] Thomas Moser, *Europäische Integration, Dekolonisation, Eurafrika: Eine historische Analyse über die Entstehungsbedingungen der Eurafrikanischen Gemeinschaft von der Weltwirtschaftskrise bis zum Jaunde-Vertrag, 1929–1963* (Baden-Baden: Nomos Verlagsgesellschaft, 2000), p. 516.

[20] René Girault, 'La France entre l'Europe et l'Afrique', in Enrico Serra (ed.), *Il Rilancio dell'Europa e i trattati di Roma/La Relance européenne et les traités de Rome: Actes du colloque de Rome, 25–28 mars 1987* (Brussels: Bruylant, 1989), p. 376.

truth in both these statements, Moser's final conclusion is less accurate: 'The Eurafrican community founded, in anticolonial spirit and for the first time in the history of their relationship, a partnership of equality between Europeans and Africans and thus gave an essential contribution to securing peace and regulating conflicts in a bi-polar world'.[21] Girault is just as tendentious as he asserts that France, 'by obliging its European partners to take care of the OCTs, [...] pushed Europe to think about aid to underdeveloped countries'.[22]

Our analysis of the EEC negotiations process lends no support to such conclusions. On the contrary, the 'spirit' of the EEC negotiations was imbued by old colonial paradigms and structures of reference. Also, what resulted was not a partnership of equality, but a licensed patronage in which the superior partner would continue overseeing and developing the inferior one. Moreover, Moser's and Girault's optimistic assessments fail to account for the dialectical character of the Eurafrican project, which secured a continuation for colonialism and at the same time went beyond it.[23]

In order to make sense of this, let us return to a point made in Chapter 2. There we saw that the Eurafrican idea originally rested on the myth of the dark continent and the evolutionist paradigm stressing the white man's civilizing mission, and on the sense that Europe was in decline and could attain such scale as was necessary for its sustainability only by internationalizing the colonial exploitation of Africa. These were the *ideological* components of the Eurafrican project as it emerged in the interwar period. By the time Eurafrica was realized through the association of the African colonies to the EEC, these

---

[21] Moser, *Europäische Integration, Dekolonisation, Eurafrika*, p. 517.

[22] Girault, 'La France entre l'Europe et l'Afrique', p. 377.

[23] Martin Rempe, by contrast, recognizes the Eurafrican association regime as a 'compromise', enabling France to align its African and European spheres of influence, and to eventually choose Europe as 'far more attractive'. As Rempe argues, Eurafrica contributed to the gradual decolonization of French interests, yet leaves the question open as to whether this also served to decolonize Africa. See Martin Rempe, 'Decolonization by Europeanization? The early EEC and the transformation of French-African relations', *KFG Working Paper Series*, No. 27, May 2011, Freie Universität, Berlin.

components were all transmuted. Now, Eurafrica was motivated by the importance of bringing social and economic development to the world's poor and by the strategic interests of the West faced with 'communist totalitarianism' and its alleged Pan-African or Pan-Arabic filiations. Yet, beneath these transformed ideological motivations, the underlying economic and geopolitical machinery remained steady. In the late 1950s, as in the early 1920s, Europe's economy needed Africa's markets and resources, and the two continents were seen as locked in a relationship of geopolitical complementarity. In the political and ideological register, then, Eurafrica was transformed from the founding days of the Pan-European Union to its realization in the form of EEC association. In the geopolitical and geo-economic register, by contrast, it demonstrates a remarkable constancy.

The historical importance of Eurafrica, and the reason for its successful establishment, would thus seem to lie in this capacity to effect an energy exchange, a transition of political investment, between two differing ideologies and *thereby* to ensure a continuation of old relations of dominance even under the new system. Or, to put this differently, Eurafrica changed the ways in which the world system and especially the relations between Europe and Africa were described and understood, and this in order to allow trade, traffic and power to remain unchanged. Therefore Eurafrica was far more than an 'integrating image', as Moser argues; it was an actually existing historical institution and community, but of the specific, transitory character that is best described as what Fredric Jameson has called a 'vanishing mediator': a historical catalyst that ensures a smooth passage from one historical period or paradigm of thought to its different successor.

Jameson develops his concept of the 'vanishing mediator' in an analysis of Max Weber's theory of the Protestant ethic. As a doctrine mediating between medieval religious structures and the secularized world of modernity, Protestantism initially presented itself as a superior and more authentic form of religious doctrine as opposed to Catholicism. Yet, through its rationalization of religious experience into an individual concern (of solitary reading and prayer demanding excruciating self-discipline), in relation to which the ceremonies and hierarchies of the Church started to appear like false ornamentation, the Protestant ethic prepared the way for a secularized society in which religion as such would become superfluous for individual self-fulfilment. In Jameson's reading of Weber's analysis, this then implies that the Protestant ethic had a specific historical 'purpose' to fulfil, after which it could be dismantled and forgotten.[24]

This seems to correspond to Eurafrica's function in the history of European integration and colonialism. In a first phase, Europe's colonial states, France in particular, understand that colonial sovereignty can be sustained in Africa only by collaborating with other European states – that is, by forming Eurafrica. This Eurafrican formation then fosters European integration and a partial Europeanization of colonialism. Once the responsibility for investments in Africa and the advantages of African trade is coordinated at an international level, the Eurafrican system can shed its colonial designation and draw on other sources for its legitimation, such as the United Nations and the emerging development discourse. When this is achieved, Eurafrica has fulfilled its function and can be dropped as a designation of the newly instituted community which is now indistinguishable from the world order as such, a postcolonial order in which relations between Africa and Europe are settled through international negotiations (the Yaoundé and Lomé Conventions), but in which the economic relations inherited from the colonial era are nonetheless kept intact. All this is achieved through the vanishing mediation of the Eurafrican formation, the function of which, as it appears in hindsight, is to preserve existent relations of dominance by way of a change of inscription. Having fulfilled this function, Eurafrica 'vanishes', thus creating the impression of a historical break or discontinuity – between colonial and postcolonial, pre- and post-European integration, white supremacy and 'partnership', 'colonial exploitation' and 'development', 'civilizing

---

[24] Fredric Jameson, 'The vanishing mediator; or, Max Weber as storyteller', in Jameson, *The Ideologies of Theory, Essays 1971–1986; Volume 2: The Syntax of History* (Minneapolis: University of Minnesota Press, 1988), pp. 3–34.

mission' and 'third-world aid', the rupture being nicely symbolized by the *annus mirabilis* of 1957, which saw both the Treaty of Rome's establishment of the Eurafrican community and the first colonial territory in Africa (Ghana) emerging from colonial subjugation to independent statehood. As a vanishing mediator, then, Eurafrica produced the preconditions for its own disappearance. Yet, the transition from a colonial world order dominated by Europe into the world regime of global capitalism would not have been possible without its mediation.

This interpretation of the Eurafrican project has several advantages. For one thing, it helps to explain the resilience of the Eurafrican project, which over a period of several decades served as a geopolitical representation that could harbour so many diverging economic, strategic and geopolitical interests and tendencies that it could finally count on approval from virtually all political groupings of the West, and also from a substantial part of the African elite, with the exception only of staunch anti-imperialists, communists and Pan-Africanists.

Second, and from the perspective of a global theory of twentieth-century European and African history, the neglected causality and vanishing mediator of Eurafrica is able to make sense both of *the political and discursive discontinuity* and *the infrastructural or economic continuity* between the late colonial period and an emerging neo-colonial globalization. We put stress on the global vantage point here, for it is only from such a perspective that we have been able to observe the intrinsic relations between processes that are usually understood as separate: European integration on the one hand, African decolonization on the other. Once the intrinsic link between these is identified, we become aware of the historical importance of Eurafrica as a historical catalyst that explains both the continuity of the underlying economic system and the political and ideological discontinuity that makes us ignore this very continuity. Thus, by evincing the relation between the foundation of the EU and Africa's decolonization we have in this book detected a historical causality common to both, and this shows that what history books picture as the end of an old system and the start of a new one was not a discontinuity but a gradual process that made the old system seamlessly pass over into a new one, without changing the fundamental parameters determining the relation of Africa and Europe. What appeared to be a discontinuity therefore turns out to be a continuity, and we can thus appreciate how this continuity necessitated the generation of the ideological mirage of a rupture: Eurafrica as a new dawn following the night of colonialism.

If this is true, we also understand how Eurafrica as a vanishing mediator helped to enable two 'myths' or historical frames that have dominated historical accounts of both the EU and postcolonial Africa: the idea of the EU as a pure origin and new start; and the idea of decolonization as a rupture providing African states with parity and agency in international relations. We also realize that, in combination, the two myths contribute to a third variety of myth and historical error, exemplified by Moser and Girault above, according to which the EEC is then credited with having made decolonization and African independence possible. Once these myths are established and worked out in so many institutional and intellectual contexts, they displace, erase and suppress historical causality itself, and replace it with an idea of political constitution, which is then commemorated and celebrated in a variety of cultural manifestations and, not least, transformed into an episteme serving as the starting point for so much research and intellectual labour, or what we today call EU studies. These myths, in other words, will serve as a foundation of the very paradigm within which the history of the EU and its relationship to both colonial and postcolonial Africa is elaborated.

In this history, as should be clear by now, the historicity of the Eurafrican project drops out of the picture, indeed must be made invisible, for otherwise neither the Treaty of Rome and the EEC, nor the 'moment' of African decolonization could be represented as new beginnings, but rather would emerge as moments in a continuous story of Europe's century-long dominance over Africa.

Eurafrica's disappearance from history

As indicated, then, the third advantage of the interpretation we offer is its ability to explain why Eurafrica has been consigned to oblivion in most research on the history of European integration and the history of colonialism. For, as we have stated, it is today virtually unknown that most of the visions, movements and concrete institutional arrangements working towards European integration in the inter- and postwar periods placed Africa's incorporation into the European enterprise as a central objective. But here we need to supplement this metahistorical framework of Eurafrica's function as a vanishing mediator by grasping some more concrete frames of historical explanation that have served to perpetuate Eurafrica's exclusion from the vast field of European integration studies as well as most other areas of historical inquiry. Some of these we already touched on in our introductory chapter, and they revolve around what we may call methodological continentalism, methodological nationalism and methodological Eurocentrism.

In the first case, the histories of Europe and Africa are conceived as insular continental entities. As Carl Ritter, one of the founders of human geography, stated: 'Each continent is like itself alone [...] each one was so planned and formed as to have its own special function in the progress of human culture.'[25] This framework, still part and parcel of mental maps daily fabricated to make sense of history and current affairs, prompts the idea that continental landmasses literally make sense – that is, they produce meaning by signifying apparently meaningful distinctions between human societies and events for the simple reason that such things can be spatially referred to different continental units. The pattern was set in Europe, long seen as the central continent, of course. Now, Europe is no separate landmass, but it awarded itself status as a continent because it could be argued

---

[25] Carl Ritter, *Comparative Geography* [1864], trans. William L. Cage (reprint, New York: American Book Company, 1973), p. 183. Quoted in Martin W. Lewis and Kären E. Wigen, *The Myth of Continents: A Critique of Metageography* (Berkeley and Los Angeles: The University of California Press, 1997), p. 30.

that it formed a coherent cultural region. As Martin Lewis and Kären Wigen point out, the definition of Europe as a continent in cultural terms implied that other continents could be similarly defined.[26] At stake in continentalism is thus a specific geographical, environmental and racial determinism. As we have seen, the Eurafrican programme was in one sense imprisoned in continentalism, because it saw Europe and Africa as opposed but complementary in economic, historical and racial terms. In another sense, it went beyond continentalism as it was conditioned by a geopolitical imagination that conceived of the world in terms not of continents but of world regions or panregions. Evidence of this is the way in which the proponents of Eurafrica regarded the Mediterranean Sea; Africa and Europe were not separated by it, but united by it. As François Mitterrand contended, the Mediterranean was the bright blue lake at the heart of Eurafrica;[27] and Herman Sörgel wanted to turn the lake into a giant hydroelectric dam, as we saw in Chapter 2. In this context, then, the suppression of Eurafrica from history has a spatial or geographical counterpart in the transformation of the Mediterranean from a uniting surface into a separating mote, a transformation that both inspires and is inspired by a 'myth of continents' that disregards connections between the histories of Africa and Europe. EU studies offers an excellent illustration of this, as it continues to inscribe the history of European integration as something that took place only on the European landmass.[28]

Moving on to the second case, of methodological nationalism, it is clear that this is another reason why Eurafrica has not entered the surveys of Europe's colonial history. Indeed, historians of colonialism still seem constrained by the national and linguistic barriers laid in

---

[26] Lewis and Wigen, *The Myth of Continents*, pp. 36–7.

[27] François Mitterrand, *Aux Frontières de l'Union Française* (Paris: René Julliard, 1953), pp. 153–5.

[28] For an instructive illustration of this tendency to define even imperial aspects of the history of the EU in continental terms, see Gary Marks, 'Europe and its empires: From Rome to the European Union'. *Journal of Common Market Studies*, Vol. 50, No. 1, 2012, pp. 1–20; and our response: Peo Hansen and Stefan Jonsson, 'Imperial origins of European integration and the case of Eurafrica: A reply to Gary Marks' "Europe and its empires"', *Journal of Common Market Studies*, Vol. 50, No. 6, 2012, pp. 1028–41.

place by the old colonial powers; and, at best, they compensate for this by engaging in traditional exercises of comparative history that never approach the intergovernmental and supranational levels and logics of European integration.[29] From this perspective, the detailed knowledge that we have of Europe's colonial history in no way constitutes a colonial history *of Europe*, but it is rather a set of compilations, comparisons and surveys of the various colonial projects, engagements and involvements of so many different European colonial powers. The primary unit of this historiography remains the nation state (or, better, the imperial/colonial state), which provides an organizing framework for the empirical data at hand. As long as colonialism is understood through such an epistemological frame, it apparently can have little significance for the European integration project. *As cultural memory and political history* colonialism will then exist as an object of knowledge in Europe only to the extent that this or that national culture or history can serve as its archival container or frame of reference.

Yet, having said this, we should also note that there is in fact a growing field of research that is examining the impact of colonialism and decolonization on historical as well as current notions of Europe and European identity, and which thus highlights that colonialism also needs to be approached as a shared (Western) European experience, which in many ways transgresses particular national outlooks. However, this research also suffers from an almost complete lack of engagement with the question of European integration.[30]

---

[29] A showcase of this tendency is a recent book entitled *L'Europe face à son passé colonial*, edited by Olivier Dard and Daniel Lefeuvre (Paris: Riveneuve editions, 2008), which despite its promising title actually does not say a word about Europe and its colonial past. Rather, the book contains the usual inventory of the colonial pasts of France, Portugal, Italy, Germany, etc. Illustrative also is James R. Lehning's *European Colonialism Since 1700* (Cambridge: Cambridge University Press, 2013), published in a prestigious new series of textbooks called 'New Approaches to European History', which does not even register that there was a *European* colonialism beyond that of Europe's various imperial states. Lehning mentions the EEC only once, as he asserts – incorrectly – that the EEC 'created an alternative engine of metropolitan prosperity in which it was difficult [for France] to fit the colonial empire' (p. 285).

[30] For an example, see Dipesh Chakrabarty, *Provincializing Europe* (Princeton: Princeton University Press, 2000).

Considering that critical explorations of notions of 'Europe' are the hallmark of postcolonial studies, this neglect constitutes a puzzle, particularly in view of the fact that no project since European colonialism has carried itself more proudly *in the name of Europe* than the historical European integration and the current European Union. As such, postcolonial studies have failed to address the organizational and institutional settings – such as the EU – where 'European' policy is actually being articulated and where the official historiography is being propagated.

That Europe *as Europe* – that is, as a politically, economically and legally sanctioned organization in its own right, and not merely as a nebulous historical, cultural or civilizational unit – has a colonial history thus remains a well-kept secret. This point is also substantiated by the ways in which the history of the European Union is conceived and disseminated by some of its most influential practitioners. Historian Norman Davies' view of the matter is typical, claiming, as he does in his magnum opus *Europe: A History*, that '[d]ecolonization was a necessary precondition for the emergence of a new European Community of equal, democratic partners.'[31] Likewise, William Hitchcock states that in Western Europe of the 1950s economic expansion and the dissolution of the European colonial empires were 'closely linked' phenomena: 'As Europe grew richer, its states increasingly bound together by economic and political ties, the colonies shrank in importance.'[32] Along the same lines, Clemens Wurm argues that '[t]he objective of European unity gained measurable importance as France, under pressure from colonial nationalism and the superpowers, was forced to abandon its colonial illusions.' Rather than discerning of France's European strategy as a means to retain, reform and develop its colonial empire, Wurm, like so many other scholars, thus frames the French position as one reducible to an either/or logic: 'Power through the Empire *or* through Europe was the

---

[31] Norman Davies, *Europe: A History* (Oxford: Oxford University Press, 1996), p. 1068.
[32] William I. Hitchcock, *The Struggle for Europe: The Turbulent History of a Divided Continent 1945–2002* (London: Profile Books, 2003), p. 162.

French Alternative.'[33] In the early 1960s, commenting on the Mollet government's objectives a few years earlier, U. W. Kitzinger, who was Secretary of the Council of Europe's Economic Committee, correctly asserted that it was precisely the other way around. France did not have to choose between Empire *or* Europe; through Eurafrican association it rather managed to retain both: 'For the new French government the [European] Economic Community was in fact a Eurafrican as much as a European scheme.'[34] 'Paris', as Cosgrove could confirm in 1969, 'was adamant that her colonial links should not be weakened by the creation of the Common Market.'[35]

Although acknowledging that colonialism had a bearing on European integration in the early postwar years, Walter Lipgens – the late doyen of the history of European integration – takes care to postulate such a colonial impact exclusively in negative terms. By definition, then, postwar colonial ambitions are said to have worked to slow and obstruct the process of European integration and so can be tacitly written off as having been void of any dynamic or facilitating potential for this same process. Instead of probing the issue, Lipgens deduces it counterfactually and rhetorically by leaving the reader with a 'fruitless' yet revealing speculation as to 'how much more smoothly European unification in its first decisive stage would have proceeded if the almost total loss of empire had occurred, and had been seen to occur, at the same time as all the other losses arising from the Second World War, instead of taking a further fifteen years to complete.'[36] Such a framing thus effectively eliminates the possibility of the converse relation, where 'empire' also created an incentive for European integration.

Andrew Moravcsik, finally, goes the whole hog in his widely cited *The Choice for Europe*, designating not just empire but geopolitical

---

[33] Clemens Wurm, 'Two paths to Europe: Great Britain and France from a comparative perspective', in Clemens Wurm (ed.), *Western Europe and Germany: The Beginnings of European Integration, 1945–1960* (Oxford: Berg, 1995), p. 179, our emphasis.

[34] U. W. Kitzinger, 'Europe: The Six and the Seven', *International Organization*, Vol. 14, No. 1, 1960, p. 31.

[35] Cosgrove, 'The Common Market and its colonial heritage', p. 76.

[36] Walter A. Lipgens, *A History of European Integration*, Vol. 1, 1945–7 (Oxford: Clarendon Press, 1982), pp. 12–13.

aims in general as basically void of any significant explanatory clout when accounting for the birth of the EEC in the 1950s. Referring specifically to the French agenda, Moravcsik claims that 'geopolitical concerns' only 'played modest roles', by far trailing 'economic' motivations; in fact, geopolitical objectives 'probably mitigated *against* the Treaty'.[37] In order to discard geopolitical explanations, Moravcsik is also forced to make numerous deceptive assertions as concerns the general historical context in which the founding of the EEC occurred. As we should be led to believe, for instance, 'Colonial considerations decline quickly in the 1950s and 1960s.' By the same token, 'The EC emerged after, not before, the resolution of major geopolitical issues.' Accordingly, Moravcsik goes on, both advocates and sceptics of the Treaty of Rome negotiations were guided by 'the realization that geopolitical issues were no longer at stake'.[38] Empirically speaking, as we have shown, this is clearly inaccurate. But then we need to add that Moravcsik's contention builds on an arbitrary conceptual distinction between explanations drawing from the economic or commercial realm of interests and objectives on the one hand, and explanations drawing from the geopolitical realm on the other. Needless to say, since economic and geopolitical objectives are often crafted in interdependence – although neither can be collapsed into the other – this distinction, or either/or perspective, is unsustainable for purposes of empirical historical analysis.

This notwithstanding, Moravcsik makes no secret about his awareness of the great import of France's demands of associating (or 'including', as Moravcsik terms it) the colonial territories with the EEC. At first sight this would seem to cast doubt on his relegation of geopolitical explanations. Not so, however, because in Moravcsik's view colonial association under the Treaty of Rome had next to nothing to do with geopolitics but belonged in the column for economic explanations: 'The two conditions imposed by the Socialist congress of 1956

---

[37] Andrew Moravcsik, *The Choice for Europe: Social Purpose and State Power from Messina to Maastricht* (Ithaca: Cornell University Press, 1998), p. 121, italics in original.
[38] Ibid., pp. 34, 135–6.

on the [EEC] negotiations were in large part economic: social harmonization and the inclusion of overseas territories.'[39]

To be sure, on one occasion Moravscik acknowledges that France's determination 'to maintain the economic viability of present and former French colonies' was 'predicted by both the political economy and geopolitical explanations'. And this is of course how it should be, indeed must be, since any economic activity in *colonies* is predicated on some type of geopolitical arrangement able to sustain such activity. To subtract geopolitical aspects from France's plans to have the EEC secure her colonies' 'economic viability' is, then, clearly a maths that does not add up. Yet Moravcsik feels perfectly confident in his pursuit of doing precisely this. What makes this even more peculiar is that from there he goes on to group 'decolonization' among France's 'geopolitical concerns' without any hint of what he must be perfectly aware of – namely, that France's EEC scheme (or Eurafrican scheme) to boost the colonial 'economic viability' by way of Algerian incorporation and colonial association had everything to do with keeping decolonization at bay. This method of erecting a conceptual firewall between economic and geopolitical explanations for the founding of the EEC thus proves a safe way of getting the matter wrong. For as we have seen, the birth of the EEC rather needs to be understood as resulting from a mutually conducive dynamic of economic, geopolitical as well as cultural factors, a dynamic that, needless to say, is very well captured in the Eurafrican scheme.

In consequence of such and other similar accounts, both European integration as a historical process and the EEC/EU as an organizational and institutional entity have been placed outside and beyond the history of colonialism.

Additionally, the disappearance of Eurafrica and the disavowal of the connection between European integration and colonialism also have to do with the fact that the Eurafrican project does not fit the dominant historiographical paradigm that understands the postwar relationship between Europe and Africa as an aspect of the general

[39] Ibid., p. 121.

Cold War situation and with the presumed historical rupture of 'decolonization' as a pivotal moment. Most accounts of EU history are informed by a strict adherence to a Cold War analytical framework as developed within, inter alia, International Relations scholarship. In this framework, Africa and the North–South dimension are neglected as factors impacting and shaping the historical trajectory of European integration, and the import of colonialism is at best treated in a cursory fashion. As should have become obvious from our account so far, Eurafrica cannot be reduced to a simple auxiliary to the Cold War and the efforts to contain the spread of Communism in Africa. To a significant extent, of course, it did form part of that too. But, and to apply Matthew Connelly's astute idea of 'taking off the Cold War lens', Eurafrica must also be construed as a strategy of containment in its own right, targeting various anti-colonial and anti-Western movements that were growing in the Southern hemisphere and which were not, by far, reducible to Moscow puppets – i.e. Pan-Africanism, Pan-Arabism and Pan-Islamism.[40] As late as 1958 *The New York Times* was still describing Africa as 'the greatest "uncommitted" region of the globe today', continuing to live 'a dim sort of half-life' at a distance from the main battlegrounds of the Cold War.[41] Indeed, the political actors, intellectuals and institutions shaping the content and direction of European integration also saw it as deeply entrenched in a North–South struggle, and thus as a response to an allegedly deepening conflict between Christian and Muslim civilizations, between universal values and jihad, and between the white European race to the one side and the 'hordes' of brown, black and yellow races to the other.[42]

This is not to deny that the path towards European integration and the paths towards independence taken by anti-colonial movements in

---

[40] See Matthew Connelly's pioneering 'Taking off the Cold War lens: Visions of North–South conflict during the Algerian War for Independence', *American Historical Review*, Vol. 105, No. 3, 2002, pp. 739–69; and also his *A Diplomatic Revolution: Algeria's Fight for Independence and the Origins of the Post-Cold War Era* (New York: Oxford University Press, 2000).

[41] 'Struggle for Africa' (editorial), *The New York Times*, 19 January 1958.

[42] Connelly, 'Taking off the Cold War lens'; *A Diplomatic Revolution*.

Africa and Asia were heavily conditioned by the Cold War. The very designation of the newly independent states as a 'third world' – supplementing the capitalist 'first world' and the socialist 'second world' – seems to have been perpetuated by the Cold War global order. As we have seen, however, in the 1950s this influence was overdetermined by a concerted European effort to secure supremacy over Africa and thus establish a 'third' geopolitical sphere, Eurafrica, that would remain out of reach of Soviet penetration and relatively independent of direct American influence. The underlying aim was to grant Europe a measure of geopolitical leverage and secure its economic sustainability, and at the same time defend Europe's interests against challenges posed by anti-colonial insurrections and wars of liberation – Vietnam, Algeria, Cameroon, to mention a few – and by the nonaligned movement of former colonies, those that convened at the Bandung meeting, or transformed the United Nations General Assembly into a platform for debating global injustices or endeavoured a united Pan-African front against Europe's colonial powers (see Figure 5.6). As *The New York Times* conveyed in June 1957:

> One of the outstanding French apostles of 'Eurafrica,' Pierre-Henri Teitgen, said in a speech at the Congress of Europe in Rome Monday that for Africa the alternatives were to choose 'the American bloc, the Soviet world, the Bandung coalition, the Asian-African group or free Europe.' He added that this choice would involve much more than merely an economic link, such as is provided in the common market treaty.[43]

Teitgen here listed the foreign policy challenges in relation to which the six European states that founded the EEC in 1957 sought to develop and modernize their imperial policy. The European integration process provided an opportunity for doing that, just as the geopolitical changes affecting the imperial order in the postwar context provided an opportunity for European integration. Taken together, these processes

---

[43] 'Ambiguity in France', *The New York Times*, 15 June 1957.

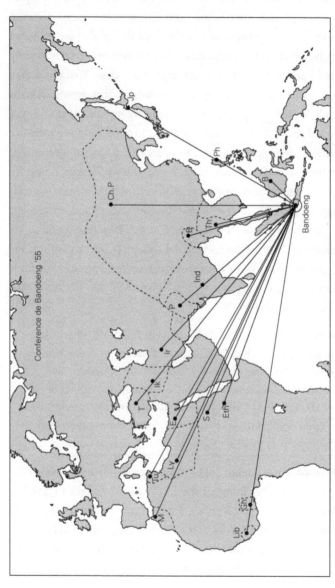

Figure 5.6 The Bandung movement, as feared by the French-Algerian organization 'Friends of the Sahara and Eurafrica'. The city of Bandung is connected to each capital of the states of the non-aligned movement. Source: *Eurafrique: Revue générale d'action africaine et méditerranéenne*, No. 14, April 1958. Bibliothèque nationale de France.

generated an internationalization of colonialism, what Ghana's first president Kwame Nkrumah denounced as 'collective colonialism' or what Europeans may have perceived as a 'reformed colonialism' or what French philosopher Alexandre Kojève, who was also an official at the Foreign Ministry, in 1957 oxymoronically called a 'giving colonialism'.[44] In justifying the association of the overseas territories as a way of improving the social and economic development of the colonies, in some ways the EEC did not differ from an older imperialism that had justified itself in much the same way. Yet, by bringing such a policy to an international level, the EEC's association of overseas countries and territories allowed Europe to posit its presence and interests in Africa as a new relationship of 'interdependence', which, just like 'Eurafrica', was a buzzword in the 1950s.

'European hunting ground': Decolonization held in check

This leads us to the fourth and major advantage of the interpretation we offer. It provides a superior explanation of the ways in which Africa and the relations between Europe and Africa evolved in the postcolonial era. For if the misrecognition that prevents us from relating the EU to colonial history is dispelled, and if the history of Eurafrica is put back into the picture, we understand why decolonization never constituted a significant rupture with the past – except in states where leaders and movements explicitly tried to break with the colonial rulers. The EEC's 'offer' of association with the Common Market here turned out to be an efficient antidote to Pan-Africanism, and this may even be said to have been its true historical purpose: to adjust Europe's foreign policy, modes of economic extraction and means of production to a nominally independent Africa, while ensuring that

---

44 Kwame Nkrumah, 'Address to the Nationalists' Conference, June 4, 1962' (Accra, 1962), p. 12. Alexandre Kojève, 'Colonialism from a European point of view', trans. Erik de Vries, *Interpretation*, Vol. 29, No. 1, 2001, pp. 91–130.

the continent's resources remained within Europe's reach. The success of this strategy is amply illustrated in Arnold Rivkin's (at the time Development Advisor to the World Bank) enthusiastic account in 1966 of the EEC's 'fruitful' Eurafrican association scheme. 'Guinea's attitude', Rivkin writes disparagingly, has 'been one of hostility to the association of other African states with the EEC. President Touré has viewed, not without reason, the existence of so attractive an alternative as the European Common Market as a serious obstacle to the achievement of his original Pan-African designs.'[45] In Rivkin's view, then, Guinea's and Ghana's stance on EEC association 'as a new neo-colonial application of the old "divide and rule" principle' cannot amount to anything but a mistaken obstinacy, totally at odds with these countries' own best interests.

As Nkrumah had it, the Treaty of Rome could 'be compared to the treaty that emanated from the Congress of Berlin' in 1885; 'the latter treaty established the undisputed sway of colonialism in Africa, the former marks the advent of neo-colonialism in Africa.'[46] Eurafrica, as conceived by the EEC, represented a new-fangled 'system of collective colonialism which will be stronger and more dangerous than the old evils we are striving to liquidate', Nkrumah stated.[47] More specifically, leaders such as Nkrumah and Touré saw the EEC's Eurafrican design not only as strategy to prevent national independence in Africa per se; more importantly perhaps, they also saw it as a deliberate attempt to frustrate the formation of any types of independently organized African integration and regionalization schemes – among numerous proposals we could mention the joint Ghana–Guinea proposals for an African Common Market.

---

[45] Arnold Rivkin, 'Africa and the European Common Market: A perspective', *Monograph Series in World Affairs*, Vol. 3, No. 4, (Denver: University of Denver, 1966), p. 40.

[46] Kwame Nkrumah, 'Address to the Ghana National Assembly', 30 May 1961; quoted in Guy Martin, *Africa in World Politics: A Pan-African Perspective* (Trenton and Asmara, Eritrea: Africa World Press, 2002), p. 9.

[47] Nkrumah, 'Address to the Nationalists' Conference', p. 12. Interestingly, Cosgrove also refers to 'collective colonialism', yet without any reference to Nkrumah: 'In some respects the association of African territories with the EEC can be said to have produced collective colonialism.' Cosgrove, 'The Common Market and its Colonial Heritage', p. 78.

Asked by *Der Spiegel* about Eurafrica and Guinea's relation to the European Common Market, Sekou Touré thus explained in 1959 that Guinea wanted to turn its economic relations in other directions. He dismissed Eurafrica as 'just a European idea for Africa', which in reality entailed 'an extension of Europe to Africa. The Europeans must get that out of their heads. That is spatial thinking, strategic thinking, be it military, political or economic.'[48] Likewise, Frantz Fanon denounced Eurafrica because 'it sanctioned the fragmentation of Africa into European areas of influence and only for the benefit of the European economies.'[49] He also regarded Eurafrica as a strategy to attain international support and European backing for France's increasingly desperate attempt to hold Algeria; '"Africa, hunting ground of France" tends to be substituted for a second formula, "Africa, hunting ground of Europe"', Fanon wrote.[50]

By contrast, Tunisian president Habib Bourguiba believed that the EEC's effort to create an integrated economic sphere encompassing Europe and Africa was a 'true opportunity' for both. Yet it could come about only under conditions of peace and independence for all involved. As long as France conducted a 'full-scale war' against an Algerian people engaged in a 'true struggle, a heroic struggle, an epic struggle for liberation', Eurafrica along with the plans for developing Sahara's oil and mineral resources would come to nothing. Bourguiba thus predicted that 'Eurafrica will die in Algeria.'[51]

If these voices represent one end of the spectrum of African opinions on Eurafrica at the crucial moment of decolonization, the other end was eloquently represented by the imposing figure of Félix Houphouët-Boigny, the first West African cabinet member under Guy

---

[48] 'Frankreichs Zeit in Afrika ist abgelaufen: Ein Spiegel-Gespräch mit dem Ministerpräsidenten von Guinea, Sekou Touré', *Der Spiegel*, 28 January 1959, pp. 40–7.

[49] Frantz Fanon, 'Appel aux Africains', in *Pour la révolution africaine: Écrits politiques* (Paris: Éditions La Découverte, 2006), p. 151; originally published in *El Moudjahid*, No. 29, 17 September 1958.

[50] Frantz Fanon, 'Une crise continuée', in *Pour la révolution africaine*, p. 126; originally published in *El Moudjahid*, No. 23, 5 May 1958.

[51] 'Wenn ein Volk seinen Verstand verliert. Ein Spiegel-Gespräch mit dem tunesischen Staatspräsidenten Burgiba', *Der Spiegel*, 18 September 1957, pp. 45–6.

Mollet and future president of Ivory Coast. As we saw in Chapter 4, he was a fervent supporter of Mollet's Eurafrican vision and instrumental in bringing about both the integration of the Sahara regions and the colonial association agreement in the Treaty of Rome. According to Houphouët-Boigny, African independence should be conducted in close partnership with the former colonial powers. As he argued, this was due in part to the political inexperience of the Africans, in part to the general world development towards closer international cooperation and interdependence, a situation in which, as he put it, 'even the largest, the most powerful [...] nations can no longer enjoy the deceptive luxury of isolation'.[52] Instead of African independence, then, Houphouët-Boigny, echoing Guy Mollet and others, called for Eurafrican interdependence.

It was such views that triggered Fanon to state that Houphouët-Boigny was 'objectively the most conscious obstacle to the evolution and liberation of Africa' and that the Africans would have 'much to gain by isolating him and hasten his fall'.[53] However, the majority of African leaders followed Houphouët-Boigny's example, if ever so hesitantly. They moved into the structures and networks laid in place by the now coordinated Europeans, often modelling themselves on the routines of the French and Belgian administrations, and allowed European landowners and companies to carry on as before. For African states stuck at the threshold of independence, Eurafrica was an arrangement that allowed the political elites of what subsequently became (nominally) independent states to posit themselves as partners in a world of 'interdependent' states and regional formations, while at the same time accommodating the economic demands and policies of their former colonial masters. This was to be conducted through arrangements – such as the 1963 Yaoundé Convention – from which both camps would benefit considerably, at the cost of the majority of Africans for whom change came slowly or not at all.

---

[52] 'African conciliator'. *The New York Times*, 8 August 1961.
[53] Fanon, 'Cette Afrique à venir', in *Pour la révolution africaine*, p. 203.

As Ali Mazrui discussed in 1963, the EEC association therefore raised uncertainties and objections on several levels among African leaders.[54] The situation was also summed up early on by Immanuel Wallerstein in two influential volumes: *Africa: The Politics of Independence* (1961); and *Africa: The Politics of Unity* (1967). Identifying the Treaty of Rome as the major factor affecting the economic structures of Africa in the early 1960s, Wallerstein was, at this point, unable to offer any conclusive assessment as to its beneficial or detrimental impact on African economic development per se.

What Wallerstein was clear about, however, were the *political* consequences of the association of the African colonies to the EEC, which, in his view, raised forbidding obstacles to all attempts at creating African integration and unity. Most of the African states in the former French Union simply found it more practical to consolidate links with the EEC than to realize the ideas presented by the movements for African unity, subsequently organized in the Organization of African Unity (OAU). These ideas included the establishment of an African Common Market and an African payments union, a coordinated industrial development and coordinated transport facilities and, finally, an African Development Bank. Of these, only the development bank had been realized by 1967.[55] Wallerstein also quoted the 1960 assessment by the United Nations Economic Commission for Africa (ECA):

> The preferential arrangements of the Rome Treaty will tend to preserve and even strengthen the traditional features of African trade, namely concentration on industrialized markets to the exclusion of any significant trade flows between the various monetary zones of the continent [...] There is therefore a danger that the Rome Treaty may tempt [the Associated States] to prefer the short-run advantage of

---

[54] Ali A. Mazrui, 'African attitudes to the European Economic Community', *International Affairs*, Vol. 39, No. 1, 1963, pp. 24–36.

[55] Immanuel Wallerstein, *Africa: The Politics of Independence and Unity* (new edn, Lincoln and London: University of Nebraska Press, 2005), part 2, pp. 129–51.

tariff concessions [in EEC markets] to the long-run gains of industrial development.[56]

In dry language, the ECA report here declared that Eurafrica had been a winning strategy, achieving precisely what it had set out to accomplish. This early assessment – that 'association with EEC can easily tend to perpetuate economic dependency'[57] – has since been corroborated by many. For instance, Obadiah Mailafia, in his comprehensive analysis of the economic development since African independence, concludes that the EEC's 'coercive association' offered 'a minimum of aid and trade concessions in exchange for continuation of European influence in the former colonies. EEC aid was oriented toward financing of infrastructures and was markedly biased against industrialization. It is therefore safe to conclude that association did not mark a major departure from the historical pattern of colonial development.'[58] Or, as Schofield Coryell put it at the time, in his evaluation of how the African territories had fared during the first five years of EEC association: 'They thus remain essentially what they were: agricultural appendages to Europe.'[59]

Wallerstein describes the process of decolonization in Africa as a political compromise between the colonial metropolitan governments and the nationalist leadership of Africa. The EEC states' decision to associate the colonial possessions in Africa was of course not a negotiated compromise in the strict sense, as it was made before independence, yet its realization hinged on unofficial consent of African elites, who discovered that Eurafrican association was an arrangement favouring them and their political goals. Wallerstein continues:

[56] 'The impact of Western European integration on African trade and development', UN Economic and Social Council Document E/CN.14/72, 7 December 1960. Quoted in Wallerstein, *Africa*, part 2, pp. 137–8.

[57] Ibid.

[58] Obadiah Mailafia, *Europe and Economic Reform in Africa: Structural Adjustment and Economic Diplomacy* (London: Routledge, 1997), p. 60.

[59] Schofield Coryell, 'French Africa and the Common Market', *Africa Today*, Vol. 9, November, 1962, p. 13.

[T]his compromise was made at the expense of lower strata of the society (that is, small farmers, landless agricultural labor, unskilled and semiskilled urban workers, the unemployed school-leavers). Not only was this compromise made at their expense. It was intended to be at their expense. The metropolitan powers were making concessions in order to separate the nationalist leadership from these strata and prevent a more coherent and conscious degree of radical political activity; most of the nationalist elite were either indifferent to the needs of these strata or explicitly frightened of the potential threat to their own positions.[60]

In our context, Eurafrica was the name of this compromise, through which Africa entered its postcolonial or neo-colonial era. If Wallerstein is right, this process wracked African peoples who now found themselves subordinated to an indigenous leadership often as ruthless and as alienated from their everyday concerns as the colonial administration once had been. We are familiar with the continuation of this history about the abuse of power and amassment of wealth by African elites driving their luxury Mercedes and Citroën limousines through the throngs of their suffering or starving populations. This is not the place to continue our account of this history, but we want to acknowledge that the history of *European* integration that we have told in this book has much to do with it. The Eurafrican project conceived in Europe between 1920 and 1960 was strongly complicit in seeing Africa off to an ill-fated beginning on its journey to independence.

Eurafrica's future: The new scramble for Africa

The past ten years have seen a renewed and rapidly increasing interest in Africa on the part of the European Union. In December 2007 a new 'Strategic Partnership' between the EU and Africa was established. As stated in the Lisbon Declaration: 'We have come together in awareness

---

[60] Wallerstein, *Africa*, part 2, p. 257.

of the lessons and experiences of the past, but also in the certainty that our common future requires an audacious approach, one that allows us to face with confidence the demands of our globalizing world.' 'On a global scale', the Declaration went on, 'we have today an increased understanding of our vital *interdependence* and are determined to work together in the global arena on the key political challenges of our time, such as energy and climate change, migration or gender issues.' Furthermore, the Lisbon Summit was hailed as offering 'a unique opportunity jointly to address the common contemporary challenges for our continents, in the year that we celebrate the 50th anniversary of the European integration and the 50th anniversary of the beginning of the independence of Africa'. This provided, the new Africa–EU partnership was presented as a 'partnership of equals', set to eliminate 'the traditional donor-recipient relationship' between the two continents.[61]

Speaking at the university in Dakar, Senegal, a few months prior to the signing of the Lisbon Declaration, French president Nicolas Sarkozy made an equally bold declaration: 'What France wants with Africa is co-development, shared development [...] What France wants with Africa is to prepare the advent of "Eurafrica", a great common destiny which awaits Europe and Africa.'[62]

The new 'partnership' between the EU and Africa goes well beyond the expansion of the long-standing EU–African trade and aid regime, as currently codified in the Cotonou Agreement (Yaoundé and Lomé's successor). Today, Africa is approached as an indispensable 'partner' in the EU's pursuit of a number of key objectives: geopolitical and security concerns (e.g. scarce strategic raw materials, terrorism, 'illegal immigration', trafficking, disease control, and food and energy security); economic concerns (e.g. raw materials and expanding outlets

---

61 Lisbon Declaration – EU Africa Summit, Lisbon, 8–9 December 2007, our emphasis, www.africa-eu-partnership.org/sites/default/files/documents/eas2007_lisbon_declaration_en.pdf

62 D. Flynn, 'Sarkozy proposes "Eurafrica" partnership on tour', Reuters, 26 July 2007, www.reuters.com/article/idUSL26102356?sp=true&view=sphere

for investment in Africa's emerging markets); and demographic and labour market concerns (e.g. labour immigration from Africa).

Considering it was relatively recent that *The Economist* blazoned abroad 'Hopeless Africa', this is a dramatic reversal of events.[63] Today, hardly a day passes without a news report highlighting the magnificent prospects for growth and investment in Africa, prospects that, of course, are augmented by the continent's seemingly endless wealth of natural resources. By the same token, hardly a day passes without a report of a major player making a new move in Africa. 'Call us crazy', said the chairman of the Russian investment bank Renaissance Capital, 'but when we look at Africa we believe this will be the fastest growing part of the world [...] over the next 20 years'.[64] All established and emerging global powers are today involved in an increasingly fierce battle over Africa's riches. Researchers and global media even suggest that we are witnessing a 'new scramble for Africa'.[65] To be sure, EU leaders are always fast to deny any such allegation. Distancing themselves from other major stakeholders – foremost China but also the USA, India, Russia, Brazil, the Gulf States, and Japan – they instead insist that the EU's African engagement is guided by 'interdependence' and committed to a mutually beneficial 'partnership of equals' that will promote development, economic growth, democratic governance, human rights, and peace and prosperity on the African continent.

The history of Eurafrica helps us understand this so-called new scramble for Africa, how it can happen and which stakes are involved. For in order to think theoretically about globality today, it is fundamental to know how the global was conceived in the past – that is, in historical times. Eurafrica was an intellectual endeavour and a political project that from the 1920s saw Europe's future survival – its continued

---

[63] 'Hopeless Africa', Leaders, *The Economist*, 11 May 2000.

[64] 'Russian bank nears brokerages deals in push to dominate Africa', *Financial Times*, 30 March 2010.

[65] Roger Southall and Henning Melber (eds), *A New Scramble for Africa? Imperialism, Investment and Development* (Scottsville: University of KwaZulu-Natal Press, 2009); 'China's New Scramble for Africa. Beijing's trade with the continent is good for both sides' (editorial), *Financial Times*, 26 August 2010.

existence *in* history as a power shaping global history – as totally bound up with Europe's successful merger with Africa. That is, Europe could rise out of the two world wars only in the shape of Eurafrica. Today, even as the Eurafrican project is largely forgotten, the content of current EU policy-making towards its African 'partner' demonstrates that it has continued influence under the surface; and the only way to comprehend the deep structures of current EU–African relations is to bring this history to life.

Bibliography

Archives Consulted

Bibliothèque nationale de France, Paris
Centre Virtuel de la Connaissance sur l'Europe, Luxembourg
Historical Archives of the European Union, Florence (HAEU)
    Consulted fonds:
    Albert-Marie Gordiani (AMG)
    BAC Fonds – EEC and ECSC Commissions (BAC)
    Council of Ministers of the EEC and EURATOM (CM2)
    Emile Noël (EN)
    European Movement (ME)
    French Foreign Ministry Collections (MAEF)
    General Secretariat of the Inter-Ministerial Committee for European
    Economic Cooperation questions (SGCICEE)
    International Paneuropean Union (PAN/EU)
    Special Council of Ministers of the ECSC – The Rome Treaties
    Negotiations 1955–1957
    Special Council of Ministers of the ECSC (CM1)
    Union of European Federalists (UEF)
Kenya National Archives, Nairobi
The Riksdag Library, Sweden

Printed Records of European Institutions and Organizations; State Governments and Parliaments; International Organizations

Journal Officiel de la République Française, 1955–1958.
Les recommandations de la conférence de Brazzaville, 6 February
    1944. Assemblée nationale, France. This document is available at
    www.assemblee-nationale.fr.

Die Kabinettsprotokolle der Bundesregierung, Vol. 9, 1956; Vol. 10, 1957. Munich: R. Oldenbourg Verlag, 1998, 2000.

Verhandlungen des deutschen Reichstags. Nationalversammlung, Stenographische Berichte, 1920–5. Available at www.reichstagsprotokolle.de

'Address given by Ernest Bevin to the House of Commons', 22 January 1948. This document is available at www.cvce.eu, Centre Virtuel de la Connaissance sur l'Europe.

La Banque Centrale du Congo Belge et du Ruanda-Urundi, 'Marché Commun Européen et Territoires d'Outre-Mer', *Bulletin de la Banque Centrale du Congo Belge et du Ruanda-Urundi*, Vol. 5, No. 9, 1956.

Council of Europe, *The Strasbourg Plan*, Strasbourg: Secretariat-General Council of Europe, 1952.

—Parliamentary Assembly, Opinion Committee on Economic Affairs and Development, 'Draft Treaty embodying the Statute of the European Community, adopted by the Ad Hoc Assembly', Doc 127, 7 May 1953.

—Parliamentary Assembly, 'Opinion (Appendix to the Rec. 45) of the Committee on Economic Questions [1] on certain economic aspects of the Draft Treaty embodying the Statute of the European Community', 11 May 1953.

European Movement, www.europeanmovement.eu/index.php?id=6790

European Union, 'Declaration of 9 May 1950', *Europa* (official website of the European Union), http://europa.eu/abc/symbols/9-may/decl_en.htm

OEEC (Organisation for European Economic Co-operation), *Investments in Overseas Territories in Africa, South of the Sahara*, Paris: OEEC, 1951.

—*Comments on the Strasbourg Plan*, Paris: OEEC, May 1954.

Speech by Mr Corniglion-Molinier, Debates in plenary session, The European Parliament, 11 May 1960, Draft Convention on the election of the European Parliament by direct universal suffrage, 30 April 1960, compiled by the European Parliament, *The case for elections to the European Parliament by direct universal suffrage* (DG for Parliamentary Documentation and Information, 1969), pp. 142–3.

Rapport des chefs de délégation aux Ministres des affaires etrangères (*The Brussels Report on the General Common Market*); Brussels, 21 April 1956.

The Brussels Report on the General Common Market (Luxembourg:

Information Service High Authority of The European Community for Coal and Steel, June 1956).

Lisbon Declaration – EU Africa Summit, Lisbon, 8–9 December 2007. This document is available at www.africa-eu-partnership.org

'The Impact of Western European Integration on African Trade and Development' (UN Economic and Social Council Document E/CN.14/72, 7 December 1960).

Treaties

Treaty establishing the European Coal and Steel Community. Signed 18 April 1951; entered into force 23 July 1952. This document is available at http://europa.eu/about-eu/basic-information/decision-making/treaties/index_en.htm.

European Defense Community Treaty. Signed in Paris, 27 May 1952. Unofficial translation. Archive of European Integration, University of Pittsburgh. (Traité instituant la Communauté européenne de défense [Paris, 27 mai 1952]. Mémorial du Grand-Duché de Luxembourg. Journal officiel du Grand-Duché de Luxembourg. Recueil de législation. 05.05.1954, n° 24. Luxembourg: Service Central de Législation.) This document is available in the Archive of European Integration, University of Pittsburg, at www.aei.pitt.edu.

Ad Hoc Assembly, *Draft Treaty Embodying the Statute of the European Community*, Paris: Secretariat of the Constitutional Committee, 1953.

Treaty establishing the European Economic Community, 25 March 1957. Signed 25 March 1957; entered into force 1 January 1958. This document is available at http://europa.eu/about-eu/basic-information/decision-making/treaties/index_en.htm; and for an English version in the Archive of European Integration, University of Pittsburgh, www.aei.pitt.edu www.aei.pitt.edu.

The North Atlantic Treaty. Signed 4 April 1949; entered into force 24 August 1949. This document is available at www.nato.int/cps/en/natolive/official_texts_17120.htm.

Periodica

Cahiers économiques et de liaison des Comités Eurafrique, 1959–1962.

Les Cahiers de Jeune Europe, 1957–1958.

The Economist, 1950–1958.

Eurafrique. Revue générale d'action africaine et méditerranéenne, 1951–1964.

Marchés coloniaux du monde, 1948–1956; replaced by *Marchés tropicaux du monde*, 1956–1958; replaced by *Marchés tropicaux et méditerranéens*, 1958–1960.

Le Monde, 1955–1957.

The New York Times, 1920–1960.

Paneuropa, 1924–1938.

Der Spiegel, 1950–1960.

Union française et parlement, 1949–1958; replaced by *Revue de la Communauté France Eurafrique*, 1959–1960.

Le XXe Siècle fédéraliste, 1957–1959.

Books, Articles and Chapters

Abiri, E. and Thörn, H. (eds), *Horizons: Perspectives on a Global Africa*, Gothenburg: Museion, Gothenburg University, 2005.

d'Abzac-Epezy, C. and Vial, P., 'In search of a European consciousness: French military elites and the idea of europe, 1947–54', in A. Deighton (ed.), *Building Postwar Europe: National Decision-Makers and European Institutions, 1948–63*, Houndmills: Palgrave Macmillan, 1995.

Adamthwaite, A., *Grandeur and Misery: France's Bid for Power in Europe 1914–1940*, London: Arnold, 1995.

— 'Britain, France, the United States and Euro-Africa, 1945–1949', in M-T. Bitsch and G. Bossuat (eds), *L'Europe unie et l'Afrique: De l'idée d'Eurafrique à la convention de Lomé I*, Brussels: Bruylant, 2005.

Adebajo, A. and Whiteman, K. (eds), *The EU and Africa: From Eurafrique to Afro-Europa*, London: Hurst and Company, 2012.

Adler-Nissen, R. and Pram Gad, U. (eds), *European Integration and Postcolonial Sovereignty Games: The EU Overseas Countries and Territories*, London: Routledge, 2012.

Ageron, C.-R., 'L'idée d'Eurafrique et le débat colonial franco-allemand de l'entre-deux-guerres', *Revue d'histoire moderne et contemporaine* 22 (1975), pp. 446–75.

Ageron, C.-R. and Michel, M. (eds), *L'Afrique noire française: L'heure des indépendences*, Paris: CNRS Éditions, 2010.

Aimaq, J., *For Europe or Empire? French Colonial Ambitions and the European Army Plan*, Lund: Lund University Press, 1996.

Albertini, R. von, *Decolonization: The Administration and Future of the Colonies, 1919–1960*, Garden City: Doubleday, 1971.

Amin, S., *L'eurocentrisme: Critique d'une ideologie*, Paris: Anthropos, 1988.

Andemicael, B. (ed.), *Regionalism and the United Nations*, New York: United Nations Institute for Training and Research, 1979.

Anderson, P., 'Under the sign of the interim', in P. Gowan and P. Anderson (eds), *The Question of Europe*, London: Verso, 1997.

Andreis, M., *L'Africa e la Comunità economica europea*, Torino: Einaudi, 1967.

Antonsich, M., '*Geopolitica*: The "geographical and imperial consciousness" of fascist Italy', *Geopolitics* 14 (2009), pp. 256–77.

Armand, L., 'Pourquoi un ensemble industriel au Sahara', article in two parts, *Union française et parlement* 4, No. 39 (June 1953), pp. 12–13; and 5, No. 40 (July–August 1953), pp. 7–8.

—*Le Sahara, l'Afrique et l'Europe*, Conférence prononcé le vendredi 25 février 1955, Lyon: Société d'économie politique et d'économie sociale, 1955.

Aron, R., 'Reflections of the foreign policy of France', *International Affairs* 21 (1945), pp. 437–47.

—*France Steadfast and Changing: The Fourth to the Fifth Republic*, Cambridge: Harvard University Press, 1960. (Originally published as *Immuable et changeante. De la IVe à la Ve République*, Paris: Calman-Lévy, 1959.)

Balogh, T., 'Africa and the Common Market', *Journal of Common Market Studies* 1 (1962), pp. 79–112.

Bayly, C. and Harper, T., *Forgotten Wars: The End of Britain's Asian Empire*, London: Allen Lane, 2007.

Ben-Ghiat, R., 'Modernity is just over there: Colonialism and Italian national identity', *Interventions* 8 (2006), pp. 380–92.

Bernal, M., *Black Athena: The Afroasiatic Roots of Classical Civilization*, Vol.

1: The Fabrication of Ancient Greece, 1785–1985, New Brunswick: Rutgers University Press, 1987.

Bertrand, R., 'The European Common Market proposal', *International Organization* 10 (1956), pp. 559–74.

Biber, A., 'Die Bekämpfung der technologischen Arbeitslosigkeit durch Kolonisation', *Paneuropa* 11 (1935), pp. 232–3.

Bitsch, M.-T. and Bossuat, G. (eds), *L'Europe unie et l'Afrique: De l'idée d'Eurafrique à la convention de Lomé I*, Brussels: Bruylant, 2005.

Bjøl, E., *La France devant l'Europe: La politique européenne de la IVe République*, Copenhagen: Munkgsgaard, 1966.

Blaut, J. M., *The Colonizer's Model of the World, Vol. 1: Geographical Diffusionism and Eurocentric History; Vol. 2: Eight Eurocentric Historians*, New York: Guilford Press, 1993 and 2000.

Bonin, H., Hodeir, C. and Klein, J. F. (eds), *L'esprit économique imperial (1830–1970): Groupes de pression et réseaux du patronat colonial en France et dans l'empire*, Paris: Publications de la SFHOM, 2008.

Bossuat, G. (ed.), *D'Alger à Rome (1943–1957): Choix de documents*, Louvain-la-Neuve: Ciaco, 1989.

—*L'Europe des Français, 1943–1959: La IVe République aux sources de l'Europe communautaire*, Paris: Publications de la Sorbonne, 1996.

Brady, S. J., *Eisenhower and Adenauer: Alliance Maintenance Under Pressure, 1953–1960*, Lanham: Lexington Books, 2010.

Brantlinger, P., 'Victorians and Africans: The genealogy of the myth of the dark continent', in H. L. Gates, Jr. (ed.), *'Race,' Writing, and Difference*, Chicago: The University of Chicago Press, 1985.

Brasted, H. V., Bridge, C. and Kent, J., 'Cold war, informal empire and the tranfer of power: Some "paradoxes" of British decolonisation resolved?', in M. Dockrill (ed.), *Europe Within the Global System 1938–1960: Great Britain, France, Italy and Germany: From Great Powers to Regional Powers*, Bochum: Universitätsverlag Dr N. Brockmeyer, 1995.

Brogi, A., *Questions of Self-Esteem: The United States and the Cold War Choices in France and Italy, 1944–1958*, Westport: Praeger, 2002.

Bromberger, M. and Bromberger, S., *Jean Monnet and the United States of Europe*, New York: Coward-McCann, 1969.

Brown, J. M. and Louis, Wm. R. (eds), *The Oxford History of the British Empire, Volume IV: The Twentieth Century*, Oxford: Oxford University Press, 1999.

Bruneteau, B. (ed.), *Histoire de l'idée européenne au premier XXe siècle à travers les textes*, Paris: Armand Colin, 2006.

Bullock, A., *Ernest Bevin: Foreign Secretary, 1945–1951*, London: Heinemann, 1983.

Butler, L. J., *Britain and Empire: Adjusting to a Post-Imperial World*, London: I. B. Tauris, 2002.

Caillaux, J., *D'Agadir à la grande pénitance*, Paris: Flammarion, 1933.

Camps, M., *Britain and the European Community 1955–1963*, Princeton: Princeton University Press, 1964.

Castells, M., *The Information Age: Economy, Society and Culture*, 3 Vols, Oxford: Blackwell, 1998.

Cesari, L., 'The declining value of Indochina: France and the economics of empire, 1950–1955', in M. A. Lawrence and F. Logevall (eds), *The First Vietnam War: Colonial Conflict and Cold War Crisis*, Cambridge: Harvard University Press, 2007.

Chakrabarty, D., *Provincializing Europe*, Princeton: Princeton University Press, 2000.

Chatty, M., Doctoral Dissertation, Örebro: Örebro University, forthcoming.

Chipman, J., *French Power in Africa*, Oxford: Basil Blackwell, 1989.

Cioc, M., *Pax Atomica: The Nuclear Defense Debate in West Germany During the Adenauer Era*, New York: Columbia University Press, 1988.

Collins, M., 'Decolonization and the "Federal Moment"', *Diplomacy & Statecraft* 24 (2013), pp. 21–40.

Connelly, M., 'Taking off the Cold War lens: Visions of North–South conflict during the Algerian War for Independence', *American Historical Review* 105 (2000), pp. 739–69.

—*A Diplomatic Revolution: Algeria's Fight for Independence and the Origins of the Post-Cold War Era*, New York: Oxford University Press, 2002.

Coryell, S., 'French Africa and the Common Market', *Africa Today* 9 (November 1962), pp. 12–13.

Cosgrove, C. A., 'The Common Market and its colonial heritage', *Journal of Contemporary History* 4 (1969), pp. 73–87.

Coudenhove-Kalergi, R., *Paneuropa*, 1923, 2nd edn, Vienna and Leipzig: Paneuropa-Verlag, 1926.

—'Alarm', *Paneuropa* 3, No. 4 (1927), pp. 1–5.

—'Krieg oder Frieden?', *Paneuropa* 3, No. 1 (1927), pp. 1–6.

—'Die europäische Nationalbewegung', *Paneuropa* 4, No. 1 (1928), pp. 1–12.

—'Afrika', *Paneuropa* 5, No. 2 (1929), pp. 3–18.

—'Entwurf für einen Paneuropäischen Pakt', *Paneuropa* 6, No. 5 (1930), pp. 149–65.

—'Reparationen und Kolonien', *Paneuropa* 8, No. 1 (1932), pp. 7–11.

—*Eine Idee erobert Europa: Meine Lebenserinnerungen*, Vienna: Verlag Kurt Desch, 1958.

Dard, O. and Lefeuvre, D. (eds), *L'Europe face à son passé colonial*, Paris: Riveneuve editions, 2008.

Davidson, B., *Africa in History: Themes and Outlines*, London: Phoenix, 1991.

Davies, N., *Europe: A History*, Oxford: Oxford University Press, 1996.

Defferre, G., 'Lettre à Guy Mollet', 17 May 1956, in G. Bossuat (ed.), *D'Alger à Rome (1943–1957): Choix de documents*, Louvain-la-Neuve: Ciaco, 1989.

Deighton, A. (ed.), *Building Postwar Europe: National Decision-Makers and European Institutions, 1948–63*, Houndmills: Palgrave Macmillan, 1995.

—'Ernest Bevin and the idea of *Euro-Africa* from the interwar to the postwar period', in M-T. Bitsch and G. Bossuat (eds), *L'Europe unie et l'Afrique: De l'idée d'Eurafrique à la convention de Lomé I*, Brussels: Bruylant, 2005.

—'Entente neo-coloniale? Ernest Bevin and the proposals for an Anglo-French third world power', *Diplomacy and Statecraft* 17 (2006), pp. 835–52.

de Lattre, J.-M., *La mise en valeur de l'ensemble eurafricain français et la participation des capitaux étrangers: Sociétés à participation étrangère; Compagnies à charte*, Paris: Libraire générale de droit et de jurisprudence, 1954.

—'Les grands ensembles africains', *Politique étrangère* 20 (1955), pp. 541–74.

—'Les grands ensembles eurafricains', *Le Monde*, 2 December 1956.

—'Sahara, clé de voûte de l'ensemble eurafricain français', *Politique étrangère* 22 (1957), pp. 364–6.

Deltombe, T., Domergue, M. and Tatsitsa, J., *Kamerun! Une guerre cachée aux origines de la Francafrique, 1948–1971*, Paris: La Découverte, 2011.

de Monsabert, General., 'North Africa in Atlantic Strategy', *Foreign Affairs* 31 (1953), pp. 418–26.

Deschamps, É., 'Quelle Afrique pour une Europe unie? l'Idée d'Eurafrique à l'aube des années trentes', in M. Dumoulin (ed.), *Penser l'Europe à l'aube des années trentes: Quelques contributions belges*, Université de Louvain, Recueil de travaux d'histoire et philologie, Brussels: Éditions Nauwelaerts, 1995.

—'Robert Schuman, un apôtre oublié de l'Eurafrique?', in S. Schirman (ed.), *Quelles architectures pour quelle Europe: Des projets d'une Europe unie à l'Union européenne (1945–1992)*, Brussels: Peter Lang, 2011.

Dessinges, P. M., 'Le Conseil de l'Europe et l'Afrique', *L'Observateur*, 9 October 1952.

Destrée, J., 'L'Afrique, colonie européenne', in *Pour en finir avec la guerre*, Brussels: Eglantine, 1931.

Deutsch, O., 'Paneuropäisches Wirtschaftsprogram', *Paneuropa* 3, No. 1 (1927), pp. 7–17.

Diebold Jr, W., *The Schuman Plan: A Study in Economic Cooperation, 1950–1959*, New York: Council on Foreign Relations, Frederick A. Praeger, 1959.

Dilks, D., 'Britain and Europe, 1948–1950: The Prime Minister, the Foreign Secretary and the Cabinet', in R. Poidevin (ed.), *Origins of the European Integration (March 1948–May 1950)*, Bruxelles: Bruylant et al., 1986.

Dix, A., *Was geht uns Afrika an? Das heutige Afrika in Weltwirtschaft, Weltverkehr, Weltpolitik*, Berlin: Stilke, 1931.

—*Weltkrise und Kolonialpolitik: Die Zukunft zweier Erdteile*, Berlin: Neff, 1932.

Dockrill, M. (ed.), *Europe Within the Global System 1938–1960: Great Britain, France, Italy and Germany: From Great Powers to Regional Powers*, Bochum: Universitätsverlag Dr N. Brockmeyer, 1995.

Dockrill, M. and Young, J. W. (eds), *British Foreign Policy, 1945–56*, Houndmills: Macmillan, 1989.

Dodds, K. and Atkinson, D. (eds), *Geopolitical Traditions: A Century of Geopolitical Thought*, London: Routledge, 2009.

Duchêne, F., *Jean Monnet: The First Statesman of Interdependence*, New York: W. W. Norton and Company, 1994.

Duke, S., *The Elusive Quest for European Security: From EDC to CFSP*, Houndmills: Macmillan, 2000.

Durand-Réville, L., in *La nouvelle revue française d'outre-mer*, No. 12, December 1956. This document is available at www.cvce.eu, Centre Virtuel de la Connaissance sur l'Europe.

Dutter, G., 'Doing business with the Nazis: French economic relations with Germany under the Popular Front', *Journal of Modern History* 63 (1991), pp. 296–326.

Etinger, J., *Bonn greift nach Afrika*, Berlin: Dietz Verlag, 1961.

European Movement, *Europe Unites: The Hague Congress and After*, London: Hollis and Carter, 1949.

Evans, M., *Algeria: France's Undeclared War*, Oxford: Oxford University Press, 2012.

Fanon, F., '*Pour la révolution africaine: Écrits politiques*, Paris: Éditions La Découverte, 2006.

Farran, J., 'La marmite de l'Europe', *Paris Match*, 9 February 1957.

Fleury, A., 'Paneurope et l'Afrique', in M-T. Bitsch and G. Bossuat (eds), *L'Europe unie et l'Afrique: De l'idée d'Eurafrique à la convention de Lomé I*, Brussels: Bruylant, 2005.

Furniss, Jr., E. S., 'France, NATO, and European Security', *International Organization* 10 (1956), pp. 544–58.

Fursdon, E., *The European Defence Community: A History*, London: Macmillan, 1980.

Gall, A., *Das Atlantropa-Projekt: Die Geschichte einer gescheiterten Vision; Herman Sörgel und die Absenkung des Mittelmeers*, Frankfurt am Main: Campus Verlag, 1998.

Gallagher, J., *The Decline, Revival and Fall of the British Empire*, Cambridge: Cambridge University Press, 1982.

Galtung, J., *The European Community: A Superpower in the Making*, Oslo: Universitetsforlaget and London: George Allen & Unwin, 1973.

Garavini, G., *After Empires: European Integration, Decolonization, and the Challenge from the Global South, 1957–1986*, Oxford: Oxford University Press, 2012.

Gates, Jr., H. L. (ed.), '*Race,' Writing, and Difference*, Chicago: The University of Chicago Press, 1985.

Gedat, G.-A., *Was wird aus diesem Afrika: Erlebter Kampf um einen Erdteil*, Stuttgart: Steinkopf, 1938.

—*Europas Zukunft liegt in Afrika*, Stuttgart: Steinkopf, 1954.

Gilbert, M., 'Narrating the Process: Questioning the Progressive Story of European Integration', *Journal of Common Market Studies* 46 (2008), pp. 641–62.

Girardet, R., *L'idée coloniale en France de 1871–1962*, 2nd edn, Paris: Hachette, 2009.

Girault, R., 'La France entre l'Europe et l'Afrique', in E. Serra (ed.), *Il Rilanco dell'Europa e i trattati di Roma/La Relance européenne et les traités de Rome: Actes du colloque de Rome, 25–28 mars 1987*, Brussels: Bruylant, 1989.

—'Les indépendances des pays d'Afrique noire dans les relations internationales', in C-R. Ageron and M. Michel (eds), *L'Afrique noire française: L'heure des indépendences*, Paris: CNRS Éditions, 2010.

Goedings, S. A. W., *Labor Migration in an Integrating Europe: National Migration Policies and the Free Movement of Workers, 1950–1968*, The Hague: Sdu Uitgevers, 2005.

Gold, P., *Europe or Africa: A Contemporary Study of the Spanish North African Enclaves of Ceuta and Melilla*, Liverpool: Liverpool University Press, 2000.

Gowan, P. and Anderson, P. (eds), *The Question of Europe*, London: Verso, 1997.

Granieri, R. J., *The Ambivalent Alliance: Konrad Adenauer, the CDU/CSU, and the West, 1949–1966*, New York: Berghahn Books, 2003.

Grilli, E. R., *The European Community and the Developing Countries*, Cambridge: Cambridge University Press, 1993.

Grimm, H., *Volk ohne Raum*, 2 vols, Munich: Langen-Müller, 1926.

Grosser, A., 'France and Germany in the Atlantic Community', *International Organization* 17 (1963), pp. 550–73.

Grünewald, M., 'Afrika und das Emigrantenproblem', *Paneuropa* 11, Nos 6–8 (1935), pp. 230–32.

Guernier, E. L., *L'Afrique: Champ d'expansion de l'Europe*, Paris: Armand Colin, 1933.

— 'Afrika als Kolonisationsland', *Paneuropa* 11, No. 1 (1935), pp. 7–11.

— *France-Outre Mer*, 29 January (1958).

Guillen, P., 'Europe as a cure of French impotence? The Guy Mollet government and the negotiation of the Treaties of Rome', in Ennio Di Nolfo (ed.), *Power in Europe? II: Great Britain, France, Germany and Italy and the Origins of the EEC 1952–1957*, Berlin: Walter de Gruyter, 1992.

Haas, E. B., *The Uniting of Europe: Political, Social, and Economic Forces 1950–1957*, Notre Dame: University of Notre Dame Press, 1958.

Hansen, P., *Europeans Only? Essays on Identity Politics and the European Union*, Umeå: Umeå University, 2000.

—'European integration, European identity and the colonial connection', *European Journal of Social Theory* 5 (2002), pp. 489–98.

Hansen, P. and Jonsson, S., 'Demographic colonialism: EU–African migration management and the legacy of Eurafrica', *Globalizations* 8 (2011), pp. 261–76.

—'Imperial origins of European integration and the case of Eurafrica: A reply to Gary Marks' "Europe and Its Empires", *Journal of Common Market Studies* 50 (2012), pp. 1028–41.

Harryvan, A. G. and van der Harst, J., 'A bumpy road to Lomé: The Netherlands, Association, and the Yaounde Treaties, 1956–1969', in M-T. Bitsch and G. Bossuat (eds), *L'Europe unie et l'Afrique: De l'idée d'Eurafrique à la convention de Lomé I*, Brussels: Bruylant, 2005.

Heffernan, M., 'Fin de siècle, fin du monde: On the origins of European geopolitics', in K. Dodds and D. Atkinson (eds), *Geopolitical Traditions: A Century of Geopolitical Thought*, London and New York: Routledge, 2009.

Herwig, H. H., 'Geopolitik: Haushofer, Hitler and Lebensraum', in C. S. Gray and G. Sloan (eds), *Geopolitics, Geography and Strategy*, London: Frank Cass, 1999.

Heywood, R. W., 'West European Community and the Eurafrica Concept in the 1950s', *Journal of European Integration* 4 (1981), pp. 199–210.

Hick, A., 'The European Union of Federalists (EUF)', in W. Lipgens (ed.), *Documents on the History of European Integration*, Vol. 4, Berlin: Walter de Gruyter, 1991.

—'The "European Movement"', in W. Lipgens (ed.), *Documents on the History of European Integration*, Vol. 4, Berlin: Walter de Gruyter, 1991.

Himpele, F., 'Läuft Afrika der EWG davon?', *Die Welt*, 2 June 1960. This document is available at www.cvce.eu, Centre Virtuel de la Connaissance sur l'Europe.

Hitchcock, W. I., *France Restored: Cold War Diplomacy and the Quest for Leadership in Europe, 1944–1954*, Chapel Hill: The University of North Carolina Press, 1998.

—*The Struggle for Europe: The Turbulent History of a Divided Continent 1945–2002*, London: Profile Books, 2003.

Hitler, A., *Mein Kampf*, Boston: Houghton and Mifflin, 1943.

Hodeir, C. and Pierre, M., *L'Exposition coloniale de 1931*, Brussels: André Versaille, 2011.

Hugo, V., 'Discours sur l'Afrique du 18 mai 1879', *Actes et paroles. Depuis l'exil*, Vol. 2, Paris: Nelson, without date.

Imlay, T. C., 'International socialism and decolonization during the 1950s: Competing rights and the postcolonial order', *The American Historical Review* 118 (2013), pp. 1105–32.

International Organization, 'Trusteeship and Non-Self-Governing Territories', 12 (1958), pp. 100–2, 107.

Irving, R. E. M., *Christian Democracy in France*, London: George Allen & Unwin, 1973.

Jackson, J., *France: The Dark Years 1940–1944*, Oxford: Oxford University Press, 2001.

Jameson, F., 'The vanishing mediator; or, Max Weber as storyteller', in *The Ideologies of Theory, Essays 1971–1986, Vol. 2: The Syntax of History*, Minneapolis: University of Minnesota Press, 1988.

Jennings, E. T., *Vichy in the Tropics: Péain's National Revolution in Madagascar, Guadeloupe, and Indochina, 1940–44*, Stanford: Stanford University Press, 2001.

Kaplan, L., *The United States and NATO: The Formative Years*, Lexington: The University Press of Kentucky, 1984.

Kelleher, C. M., *Germany and the Politics of Nuclear Weapons*, New York: Columbia University Press, 1975.

Kent, J., 'Bevin's imperialism and the idea of Euro-Africa, 1945–49', in M. Dockrill and J. W. Young (eds), *British Foreign Policy, 1945–56*, Houndmills: Macmillan, 1989.

— *The Internationalization of Colonialism: Britain, France, and Black Africa, 1939–1956*, Oxford: Clarendon Press, 1992.

Kim, S.-R., 'France's agony between "*Vocation Européenne et Mondiale*": The Union Française as an obstacle in the French policy of supranational European integration, 1952–1954', *Journal of European Integration History* 8 (2002), pp. 61–84.

Kitzinger, U. W., 'Europe: The Six and the Seven', *International Organization* 14 (1960), pp. 20–36.

— *The Challenge of the Common Market*, Oxford: Basil Blackwell, 1962.

Kjellén, R., *Samtidens stormakter*, Vol. 1, Stockholm: Hugo Gebers förlag, 1914. (Translated into German as *Die Großmächte der Gegenwart*, Leipzig: Teubner, 1914.)

Köhler, H., *Adenauer: Eine politische Biographie*, Frankfurt am Main: Propyläen Verlag, 1994.

Kojève, A., 'Colonialism from a European point of view', trans. Erik de Vries, *Interpretation* 29 (2001), pp. 91–130.

Koller, C., '*Von Wilden aller Rassen niedergemetzelt*': *Die Diskussion um die Verwendung von Kolonialtruppen in Europa zwischen Rassismus, Kolonial- und Militärpolitik, 1914–1930*, Stuttgart: Franz Steiner Verlag, 2001.

Kottos, L., 'A "European Commonwealth": Britain, the European League for

Economic Co-operation, and European debates on empire, 1947–1957', *Journal of Contemporary European Studies* 20 (2012), pp. 497–515.

Kraft, L., 'Pan-Africanism: Political, economic, strategic or scientific?', *International Affairs* 24 (1948), pp. 218–28.

Kühne, W., 'The EU security role in Chad and the Central African Republic', in A. Adebajo and K. Whiteman (eds), *The EU and Africa: From Eurafrique to Afro-Europa*, London: Hurst and Company, 2012.

Kyle, K., *Suez: Britain's End of Empire in the Middle East*, London: I. B. Tauris, 2002, 2nd rev. edn.

Labonne, E., *Politique économique de l'Union Française – Industrialisation et armement*, Deux conférences à l'Ecole nationale d'administration, Paris: Atelier d'Impressions S.L.N, 1948.

—*Politique économique de l'Union Française – Industrialisation et équipement stratégique*, Étude – Programme, Paris: [unidentified publisher], 1949.

—*Politique industrielle et stratégique de l'Union Française, Les Z.O.I.A. Zones d'organisation industrielle et stratégique africaines*, Paris: Révue Militaire d'Information, 1955.

Lacroix-Riz, A., 'Les relations patronales franco-allemandes à propos de l'empire colonial dans les années 1930', in H. Bonin, C. Hodeir and J. F. Klein (eds), *L'esprit économique imperial (1830–1970): Groupes de pression et réseaux du patronat colonial en France et dans l'empire*, Paris: Publications de la SFHOM, 2008.

Laurent, P.-H., 'The Diplomacy of the Rome Treaty, 1956–57', *Journal of Contemporary History* 7 (1972), pp. 209–20.

Laurentie, H., 'L'empire au secours de la métropole', in P. Liquière (ed.), *Restaurer, reformer, agir: la France en 1945*, Paris: La documentation française, 1995.

Lawrence, M. A., 'Forging the "Great Combination": Britain and the Indochina problem, 1945–1950', in M. A. Lawrence and F. Logevall (eds), *The First Vietnam War: Colonial Conflict and Cold War Crisis*, Cambridge: Harvard University Press, 2007.

Lawrence, M. A. and Logevall, F. (eds), *The First Vietnam War: Colonial Conflict and Cold War Crisis*, Cambridge: Harvard University Press, 2007.

Legoll, P., *Charles de Gaulle et Konrad Adenauer. La cordiale entente*, Paris: Harmattan, 2004.

Lehning, J. R., *European Colonialism Since 1700*, Cambridge: Cambridge University Press, 2013.

Lemaignen, R., *L'Europe au berceau: Souvenirs d'un technocrate*, Paris: Plon, 1964.

Le Naour, J.-Y., *La honte noire: L'Allemagne et les troupes coloniales françaises, 1914–1945*, Paris: Hachette, 2003.

Lentz, W., 'Eurafrika—Fata Morgana oder Ernst?', *Die politische Meinung: Monatshefte für Fragen der Zeit* 2 (1957), pp. 33–38.

Lewis, M. W. and Wigen, K. E., *The Myth of Continents: A Critique of Metageography*, Berkeley and Los Angeles: The University of California Press, 1997.

Liniger-Goumaz, M., *Eurafrique*, Geneva: Les Éditions du temps, 1970.

—*Eurafrique: Utopie ou réalité?*, Yaoundé: Editions CLE, 1972.

Lipgens, W., *A History of European Integration*, Vol. 1: 1945–1947: The Formation of the European Unity Movement, Oxford: Clarendon Press, 1982.

—(ed.), *Documents on the History of European Integration*, Vol. 4, Berlin: Walter de Gruyter, 1991.

Liquière, P. (ed.), *Restaurer, reformer, agir: la France en 1945*, Paris: La documentation française, 1995.

Logevall, F., *Embers of War: The Fall of an Empire and the Making of America's Vietnam*, New York: Random House, 2012.

Louis, Wm. R., 'Colonial appeasement, 1936–1938', *Revue belge de philologie et d'historie* 49 (1971), pp. 1175–91.

—*The British Empire in the Middle East 1945–1951: Arab Nationalism, The United States, and Postwar Imperialism*, Oxford: Oxford University Press, 1984.

—*Ends of British Imperialism: The Scramble for Empire, Suez and Decolonization*, London: I. B. Tauris, 2006.

Louis, Wm. R. and Owen, R. (eds), *Suez 1956: The Crisis and its Consequences*, Oxford: Clarendon Press, 1989.

Luethy, H., *France Against Herself*, New York: Frederick A. Praeger, 1955.

Lundestad, G., *'Empire' by Integration: The United States and European Integration, 1945–1997*, Oxford: Oxford University Press, 1998.

Lusane, C., *Hitler's Black Victims: The Historical Experiences of European Blacks, Africans and African Americans During the Nazi Era*, New York: Routledge, 2003.

Lynch, F. M. B., *France and the International Economy: From Vichy to the Treaty of Rome*, London: Routledge, 1997.

Maclellan, N. and Chesneaux, J., *After Moruroa: France in the South Pacific*, Melbourne: Ocean Press, 1998.

Mailafia, O., *Europe and Economic Reform in Africa: Structural Adjustment and Economic Diplomacy*, London: Routledge, 1997.

Manela, E., *The Wilsonian Moment: Self-Determination and the International Origins of Anticolonial Nationalism*, Oxford: Oxford University Press, 2007.

Mann, H., 'Anfänge Europas', in *Sieben Jahre Chronik der Gedanken und Vorgänge: Essays*, ed. P-P. Schneider, Frankfurt am Main: Fischer Taschebuch Verlag, 1994.

Marjolin, R., *Architect of European Unity: Memoirs 1911–1986*, London: Weidenfeld and Nicolson, 1989.

Marks, G., 'Europe and its Empires: From Rome to the European Union', *Journal of Common Market Studies* 50 (2012), pp. 1–20.

Marks, S., *The Ebbing of European Ascendancy: An International History of the World 1914–1945*, London: Bloomsbury Academic, 2002.

Marshall, D. B., *The French Colonial Myth and Constitution-Making in the Fourth Republic*, New Haven: Yale University Press, 1973.

Martel, G., 'Decolonisation after Suez: Retreat or rationalisation?', *Australian Journal of Politics and History* 46 (2000), pp. 403–17.

Martin, G., *Africa in World Politics: A Pan-African Perspective*, Trenton and Asmara: Africa World Press, 2002.

May, A. (ed.), *Britain, the Commonwealth and Europe: The Commonwealth and Britain's Applications to Join the European Communities*, Houndmills: Macmillan, 2001.

Mayer, R., 'Un ensemble fédéral occidental: Note de René Mayer', in G. Bossuat (ed.), *D'Alger à Rome: Choix des documents*, Louvain-la-Neuve: Ciaco, 1989.

Mayne, R., *The Recovery of Europe: From Devastation to Unity*, London: Weidenfeld and Nicolson, 1970.

Mazower, M., *No Enchanted Palace: The End of Empire and the Ideological Origins of the United Nations*, Princeton: Princeton University Press, 2009.

Mazrui, A. A., 'African attitudes to the European Economic Community', *International Affairs* 39 (1963), pp. 24–36.

—*The African Condition: A Political Diagnosis*, London: Heinemann, 1980.

—*Africa and Other Civilizations: Conquest and Counter-Conquest*, The Collected Essays of Ali A. Mazrui, Trenton: World Africa Press, 2002.

Mbembe, A., *Sortir de la grande nuit: Essai sur l'Afrique décolonisée*, Paris: Éditions La Découverte, 2010.

McKay, V., *Africa in World Politics*, New York: Harper & Row, 1963.

Metzger, C., *L'empire colonial français dans la stratégie du Troisième Reich (1936–1945)*, Brussels: Peter Lang, 2002.

—'L'Allemagne et l'Eurafrique', in M-T. Bitsch and G. Bossuat (eds), *L'Europe unie et l'Afrique: De l'idée d'Eurafrique à la convention de Lomé I*, Brussels: Bruylant, 2005.

Meynier, O. [Anonymous], 'L'Eurafrique est crée, L'Eurafrique vit …', *Eurafrique: Revue d'action africaine et méditerranéenne*, No. 9 (January 1957), pp. 15–16.

—'L'Eurafrique – Tache urgente', *Eurafrique: Revue d'action africaine et méditerranéenne*, No. 11 (July 1957), pp. 2–3.

Migani, G., *La France et l'Afrique sub-saharienne, 1957–1963: Histoire d'une décolonisation entre idéaux eurafricains et politique de puissance*, Brussels: Peter Lang, 2008.

Miller, C., *Theories of Africans: Francophone Literature and Anthropology in Africa*, Chicago: The University of Chicago Press, 1990.

Milward, A. S., *The European Rescue of the Nation-State*, London: Routledge, 2000.

Mitterrand, F., *Aux Frontières de l'Union Française*, Paris: René Julliard, 1953.

Mollet, G., 'The Euratom Treaty: The Common European Market', *Vital Speeches of the Day* 23 (March 1957), pp. 349–52.

—*Bilan et perspectives socialistes*, Paris: Plon, 1958.

Monnet, J., *Memoirs*, trans. Richard Mayne, Garden City, NY: Doubleday, 1978.

Montarsolo, Y., 'Albert Sarraut et l'idée d'Eurafrique', in M-T. Bitsch and G. Bossuat (eds), *L'Europe unie et l'Afrique: De l'idée d'Eurafrique à la convention de Lomé I*, Brussels: Bruylant, 2005.

—*L'Eurafrique – contrepoint de l'idée d'Europe: Le cas français de la fin de la deuxième guerre mondiale aux négociations des Traités de Rome*, Aix-en-Provence: Publications de l'Université de Provence, 2010.

Moravcsik, A., *The Choice for Europe: Social Purpose and State Power from Messina to Maastricht*, Ithaca: Cornell University Press, 1998.

Morel, E. D., *Africa and the Peace of Europe*, London: National Labour Press, 1917.

—*The Horror on the Rhine*, Pamphlet No. 44a, 7th edn, London: Union of Democratic Control, 1921.

—*The Black Man's Burden: The White Man in Africa from the Fifteenth Century to World War I*, New York: Monthly Review Press, 1969 (reprint).

Morton, P., *Hybrid Modernities: Architecture and Representation at the 1931 Colonial Exposition, Paris*, Cambridge: The MIT Press, 2000.

Moser, T., *Europäische Integration, Dekolonisation, Eurafrika: Eine historische Analyse über die Entstehungsbedingungen der Eurafrikanischen Gemeinschaft von der Weltwirtschaftskrise bis zum Jaunde-Vertrag, 1929–1963*, Baden-Baden: Nomos Verlagsgesellschaft, 2000.

Moussa, P., *Les chances économiques de la communauté franco-africaine*, Paris: Armand Collin, 1957.

—*Les roues de la fortune. Souvenirs d'un financier*, Paris: Fayard, 1989.

Mudimbe, V. Y., *The Invention of Africa: Gnosis, Philosophy, and the Order of Knowledge*, Bloomington: Indiana University Press, 1988.

—*The Idea of Africa*, Bloomington: Indiana University Press, 1994.

Muller, K., '"Concentric circles" at the periphery of the European Union', *Australian Journal of Politics and History* 46 (2000), pp. 322–35.

—'Iconographie de l'Eurafrique', in M-T. Bitsch and G. Bossuat (eds), *L'Europe unie et l'Afrique: De l'idée d'Eurafrique à la convention de Lomé I*, Brussels: Bruylant, 2005.

Murphy, D. T., *The Heroic Earth: Geopolitical Thought in Weimar Germany, 1918–1933*, Kent: The Kent State University Press, 1997.

Musil, R. 'Helpless Europe: A digressive journey', in *Precision and Soul: Essays and Addresses*, eds and trans. B. Pike and D. S. Luft, Chicago: The University of Chicago Press, 1990.

Nelson, K. L., 'The "Black Horror on the Rhine": Race as a factor in post-World War I diplomacy', *The Journal of Modern History* 42 (1970), pp. 606–27.

Neumann, I. B., 'European identity, EU expansion, and the integration/exclusion nexus', *Alternatives* 23 (1998), pp. 397–416.

Nkrumah, K., 'Address to the Nationalists' Conference, June 4, 1962', Accra: Unidentified Publisher, 1962.

Nord, P., *L'Eurafrique, notre dernière chance*, Paris: Arthème Fayard, 1955.

Nordblad, J., 'The un-European idea: Vichy and Eurafrica in the historiography of Europeanism', *The European Legacy* 19 (2014), forthcoming.

Nugent, P., *Africa Since Independence: A Comparative History*, Houndmills: Palgrave, 2004.

O'Loughlin, J. and van der Wusten, H., 'Political geography of panregions', *The Geographical Review* 80 (1990), pp. 1–20.

Orsini di Camerota, P. A., *Eurafrica: L'Africa per l'Europa, l'Europa per l'Africa*, Rome: Paolo Cremonese, 1934.

—*I problemi economici dell'Africa e l'Europa*, Rome: Edizioni Cinque Lune, 1961.

Ortega y Gasset, J., *The Revolt of the Masses*, New York: Norton, 1957, new ed.

Palayret, J.-M., 'Les mouvements proeuropéens et la question de l'Eurafrique, du Congrès de La Haye à la Convention de Yaoundé (1948–1963)', in M-T. Bitsch and G. Bossuat (eds), *L'Europe unie et l'Afrique: De l'idée d'Eurafrique à la convention de Lomé I*, Brussels: Bruylant, 2005.

Parker, G., *Western Geopolitical Thought in the Twentieth Century*, London: Croom Helm, 1985.

Parsons, C., *A Certain Idea of Europe*, Ithaca: Cornell University Press, 2003.

Paxton, R. O., *Vichy France: Old Guard and New Order 1940–1944*, New York: Columbia University Press, 1972, 2001.

Pineau, C., *1956/Suez*, Paris: Éditions Robert Laffont, 1976.

Pitman, P. M., '"A General Named Eisenhower": Atlantic crisis and the origins of the European Economic Community', in M. Trachtenberg (ed.), *Between Empire and Alliance: America and Europe During the Cold War*, Lanham: Rowman & Littlefield, 2003.

Poidevin, R. (ed.), *Origins of the European Integration (March 1948–May 1950)*, Bruxelles: Bruylant et al., 1986.

Reid, E., *Time of Fear and Hope: The Making of the North Atlantic Treaty 1947–1949*, Toronto: McClelland and Stewart, 1977.

Rempe, M., 'Decolonization by Europeanization? The early EEC and the transformation of French-African relations', *KFG Working Paper Series*, No. 27, May 2011, Kolleg-Forschergruppe (KFG) 'The Transformative Power of Europe', Freie Universität, Berlin.

Ritter, C., *Comparative Geography*, trans. William L. Cage, reprint, New York: American Book Company, 1973 (1864).

Rivkin, A., 'Africa and the European Common Market: A perspective', *Monograph Series in World Affairs*, Denver: University of Denver, 1966.

Robertson, A. H., *European Institutions*, The London Institute of World Affairs, London: Stevens & Sons, 1959.

—'The Council of Europe and the United Nations', in B. Andemicael (ed.), *Regionalism and the United Nations*, New York: United Nations Institute for Training and Research, 1979.

Rodney, W., *How Europe Underdeveloped Africa*, rev. edn, Cape Town: Pambazuka Press, 2012.

Rosato, S., *Europe United: Power Politics and the Making of the European Community*, Ithaca: Cornell University Press, 2011.

Ruane, K., *The Rise and Fall of the European Defence Community: Anglo-American Relations and the Crisis of European Defence, 1950–55*, Houndmills: Macmillan, 2000.

Russell, D., '"The Jolly Old Empire": Labour, the Commonwealth and Europe, 1945–51', in A. May (ed.), *Britain, the Commonwealth and Europe: The Commonwealth and Britain's Applications to Join the European Communities*, Houndmills: Macmillan, 2001.

Sarraut, A., *Grandeur et servitudes coloniales* (1931), Paris: L'Harmattan, 2011, new edn.

Saville, J., *The Politics of Continuity: British Foreign Policy and the Labour Government, 1945–46*, London: Verso, 1993.

Schmale, W., 'Before self-reflexivity: Imperialism and colonialism in the early discourses of European integration', in M. Spiering and M. Wintle (eds), *European Identity and the Second World War*, Houndmills: Palgrave Macmillan, 2011.

Schmokel, W. W., *Dream of Empire: German Colonialism, 1919–1945*, New Haven: Yale University Press, 1964.

Schnee, H., *Afrika für Europa: die koloniale Schuldlüge*, Berlin: Kolonialverlag Sachers and Kuschel, 1924.

Schuman, R., 'Unité européenne et Eurafrique: Politique révolutionnaire – Aperçu d'ensemble', *Union française et parlement*, January (1957).

—*Pour l'Europe*, Paris: Nagel Editions, 1963.

—*For Europe*, Avignon: Institut Robert Schuman pour l'Europe, 2000.

Schwartz, H.-P., *Konrad Adenauer: A German Politician and Statesman in a Period of War, Revolution and Reconstruction, Vol. 1: From the German Empire to the Federal Republic, 1876–1952; Vol. 2: The Statesman, 1952–1967*, Oxford: Berghahn Books, 1995, 1997.

Sèbe, B., 'In the shadow of the Algerian War: The United States and the Common Organisation of Saharan Regions (OCRS), 1957–62', *The Journal of Imperial and Commonwealth History* 38 (2010), pp. 303–22.

Senghor, L., *Liberté II: Nation et voie africaine du socialisme*, Paris: Le Seuil, 1952.

Sergi, G., *The Mediterranean Race: A Study of the Origin of European Peoples*, London: Walter Scott, 1901.

Serra, E. (ed.), *Il Rilancio dell'Europa e i trattati di Roma/La Relance européenne et les traités de Rome: Actes du colloque de Rome, 25-28 mars 1987*, Brussels: Bruylant, 1989.

Shepard, T., *The Invention of Decolonization: The Algerian War and the Remaking of France*, Ithaca: Cornell University Press, 2006.

Shipway, M., *The Road to War: France and Vietnam, 1944-1947*, New York: Berghahn Books, 1996/2003.

—*Decolonization and its Impact: A Comparative Approach to the End of the Colonial Empires*, Malden: Blackwell, 2008.

Shore, C., *Building Europe: The Cultural Politics of European Integration*, London: Routledge, 2000.

Smith, T., 'The French colonial consensus and people's war, 1946-58', *Journal of Contemporary History* 9 (1974), pp. 217-47.

Soper, T., 'The EEC and aid to Africa', *International Affairs* 41 (1965), pp. 463-77.

Sörgel, H., *Atlantropa*, Munich: Piloty and Loehle; Zürich: Fretz and Wasmuth, 1932.

Southall, R. and Melber, H. (eds), *A New Scramble for Africa? Imperialism, Investment and Development*, Scottsville: University of KwaZulu-Natal Press, 2009.

Spaak, P.-H., 'Discours sur l'OTAN et le Marché commun', *Mars et Mercure*, No. 3 (1957).

—'The West in disarray', *Foreign Affairs* 35 (1957), pp. 184-90.

—*The Continuing Battle: Memoirs of a European 1936-1966*, London: Weidenfeld and Nicolson, English translation, 1971 [1969].

Spero [pseudonym], 'Notland für Juden in Afrika', *Paneuropa* 11, No. 3 (1935), pp. 78-80.

Spiering, M. and Wintle, M. (eds), *European Identity and the Second World War*, Houndmills: Palgrave Macmillan, 2011.

Stockwell, A. J., 'Imperialism and nationalism in South-East Asia', in J. M. Brown and Wm. R. Louis (eds), *The Oxford History of the British Empire, Volume IV: The Twentieth Century*, Oxford: Oxford University Press, 1999.

Stoddard, L., *The Rising Tide of Colour Against White World-Supremacy*, 1922, reprint, Honolulu: University Press of the Pacific, 2003.

—*The Clashing Tides of Colour*, New York and London: Charles Scribner's Sons, 1935.

Stresemann, G., *Vermächtnis: der Nachlass in drei Bänden*, Vol. 2 (ed.) Henry Bernhard, Berlin: Ullstein, 1932.

Theweleit, K., *Männerphantasien, Vol. 1: Frauen, Fluten, Körper, Geschichte*, 2nd edn, Munich and Zürich: Piper Verlag, 2000.

Thomas, M., *The French Empire at War 1940–45*, Manchester: Manchester University Press, 1998.

—*The French North African Crisis: Colonial Breakdown and Anglo–French Relations, 1945–62*, Houndmills: Macmillan, 2000.

—'The British government and the end of French Algeria, 1958–62', *Journal of Strategic Studies* 25 (2002), pp. 172–98.

—'Defending a lost cause? France and the United States vision of imperial rule in French North Africa, 1945–1956', *Diplomatic History* 26 (2002), pp. 215–47.

—'French imperial reconstruction and the development of the Indochina War, 1945–1950', in M. A. Lawrence and F. Logevall (eds), *The First Vietnam War: Colonial Conflict and Cold War Crisis*, Cambridge: Harvard University Press, 2007.

Trachtenberg, M., *A Constructed Peace: The Making of the European Settlement, 1945–1963*, Princeton: Princeton University Press, 1999.

—(ed.), *Between Empire and Alliance: America and Europe during the Cold War*, Lanham: Rowman & Littlefield, 2003.

Tyre, S., 'The Gaullist, the French Army and Algeria before 1958: Common cause or marriage of convenience?', *Journal of Strategic Studies* 25 (2002), pp. 97–117.

Unger, G., *Gaston Defferre*, Paris: Fayard, 2011.

United Nations, 'Question Concerning Non-Self-Governing Territories and the International Trusteeship System', *Yearbook of the United Nations*, Ch. 1, 1958.

Uri, P., *Penser pour l'action: Un fondateur de l'Europe*, Paris: O. Jacob, 1991.

Vahsen, U., *Eurafrikanische Entwicklungskooperation: Die Assoziierungspolitik der EWG gegenüber dem subsaharischen Afrika in den 1960er Jahren*, Stuttgart: Franz Steiner Verlag, 2010.

Vaisse, M., 'France and the Suez Crisis', in Wm. R. Louis and R. Owen (eds), *Suez 1956: The Crisis and its Consequences*, Oxford: Clarendon Press, 1989.

Valois, G., *L'Afrique, chantier de l'Europe*, Cahiers bleues, No. 111, Paris: Librairie Valois, 1931.

—*Note sur L'Afrique, chantier de l'Europe*, Brussels: Institut d'économie européenne, 1931.

van Laak, D., *Imperiale Infrastruktur: Deutsche Planungen für eine Erschließung Afrikas, 1880 bis 1960*, Paderborn: Ferdinand Schöningh, 2004.

—*Über alles in der Welt: Deutscher Imperialismus im 19. und 20. Jahrhundert*, Munich: Verlag C. H. Beck, 2005.

Varsori, A., 'Italy in the international system: From great power illusion to the reality of a middle rank power: 1945–57', in M. Dockrill (ed.), *Europe Within the Global System 1938–1960: Great Britain, France, Italy and Germany: From Great Powers to Regional Powers*, Bochum: Universitätsverlag Dr N. Brockmeyer, 1995.

Viard, R., *L'Eurafrique: Pour une nouvelle économie européenne*, Paris: Férnand Sorlot, 1942.

Wall, I. M., *The United States and the Making of Postwar France*, Cambridge: Cambridge University Press, 1991.

—*France, the United States, and the Algerian War*, Berkeley: University of California Press, 2001.

Wallerstein, I., *Africa: The Politics of Independence and Unity*, Lincoln and London: University of Nebraska Press, 2005 (new edn).

Wigger, I., '"Black shame" – The campaign against "racial degeneration" and female degradation in interwar Europe', *Race & Class* 51 (2010), pp. 33–46.

Williams, F., *Ernest Bevin: Portrait of a Great Englishman*, London: Hutchinson, 1952.

Wiredu, K., *Philosophy and an African Culture*, Cambridge: Cambridge University Press, 1980.

Woytinski, W., *Die Vereinigten Staaten von Europa*, Berlin: J. H. W. Dietz Verlagsbuchhandlung, 1926.

Wurm, C., 'Two paths to Europe: Great Britain and France from a comparative perspective', in C. Wurm (ed.), *Western Europe and Germany: The Beginnings of European Integration, 1945–1960*, Oxford: Berg, 1995.

—(ed.), *Western Europe and Germany: The Beginnings of European Integration, 1945–1960*, Oxford: Berg, 1995.

Yates, D. A., 'France, the EU, and Africa', in A. Adebajo and K. Whiteman (eds), *The EU and Africa: From Eurafrique to Afro-Europa*, London: Hurst and Company, 2012.

Young, J. W., *Britain, France and the Unity of Europe 1945–1951*, Leicester: Leicester University Press, 1984.

—*Cold War Europe 1945–1991: A Political History*, 2nd edn, London: Arnold, 1996.

—*Britain and European Unity, 1945–1999*, Houndmills: Macmillan, 2nd edn, 2000.

Young, M. B., *The Vietnam Wars 1945–1990*, New York: Harper Perennial, 1991.

Young, R. C., *White Mythologies: Writing History and the* West, New York: Routledge, 1990.

Zache, H., *Das deutsche Kolonialbuch*, Berlin and Leipzig: Wilhelm Andermann Verlag, 1926. (Reprinted as *Die deutschen Kolonien in Wort und Bild*, Wiesbaden: Marix Verlag, 2004.)

Zeleza, P. T., 'Africa: the changing meanings of "African" culture and identity', in E. Abiri and H. Thörn (eds), *Horizons: Perspectives on a Global Africa*, Gothenburg: Museion, Gothenburg University, 2005.

—*Rethinking Africa's Globalization*, Vol. 1: The Intellectual Challenges, Trenton: World Africa Press, 2003.

Zimmermann, H., *Money and Security: Troops, Monetary Policy, and West-Germany's Relations with the United States and Britain, 1950–1971*, Cambridge: Cambridge University Press, 2002.

Zintgraf, A., 'Die Besiedlungsfähigkeit Afrikas', *Paneuropa* 5, No. 10 (1929), pp. 24–36.

Zischka, A., *Afrika: Europas Gemeinschaftsaufgabe Nr. 1*, Oldenburg: Gerhard Stalling Verlag, 1951.

Index